THE MAGICAL STRANGER

A Son's Journey into His Father's Life

STEPHEN RODRICK

HARPER
www.harpercollins.com

 For information, address HarperCollins Publishers, 10 East 53rd Street, New York, NY 10022.

HarperCollins books may be purchased for educational, business, or sales promotional use. For information, please e-mail the Special Markets Department at SPsales@harpercollins.com.

FIRST EDITION

Designed by William Ruoto

Frontispiece courtesy of the author

Library of Congress Cataloging-in-Publication Data

Rodrick, Stephen.

The magical stranger : a son's journey into his father's life / Stephen Rodrick.—1st ed.

p. cm

ISBN 978-0-06-200476-5

1. Rodrick, Peter T., 1943–1979. 2. Rodrick, Stephen, 1966–. 3. United States. Navy—Officers—Biography. 4. Air pilots, Military—United States—Biography. 5. Fathers and sons—United States—Biography. I. Title.

V63.R74R6 4 2013

359.0092—dc23 [B] 2012043637

13 14 15 16 17 OV/RRD 10 9 8 7 6 5 4 3 2 1

on the sea

rupted by a news bulletin reporting the crash of a Navy T-2 a few hundred yards short of NAS Meridian's runway.

The T-2 was Dad's plane. She turned off the television and tried not to go to pieces. A car pulled into the driveway, either Dad or the base chaplain. The door opened and there was my father, a bandage on his forehead, his flight suit ripped and blackened from ejecting.

That was five moves and four cruises ago. Barbara Rodrick has raised three children on her own while her husband has spent 1,100 days of the last six years at sea, making hundreds of landings on the *Oriskany*, the *Forrestal*, the *Nimitz*, and now the *Kitty Hawk*.

There are more lonely days ahead. Today, he leaves for a six-month deployment in the Pacific, his third cruise flying an EA-6B Prowler, a radar-jamming plane nicknamed the Flying Pig for its maneuverability issues. He swears to her that this is the last one; next will be the Pentagon or some other shore duty. He promises he will be there for her. She believes him. He does not tell her he's applying for the space shuttle program.

Her two girls are low-maintenance. I am not. I arrive a month premature, with my dad's brains but not much else. My chart reads "slight discoordination of his right side." That's an understatement. At school, I talk and talk, gulp air, and talk more. Fill-in-the-oval tests put me in advanced classes. Actual grades remove me from advanced classes. Listening eludes me, as do the intersecting laces of my shoes. I see pediatric psychiatrists, take Ritalin, and participate in complicated behavior-modification programs involving baseball cards.

There are many parent-teacher conferences. I sit outside

the door on a folding chair while my mother cries and apologizes for me. It's weird; do they think I can't hear them?

IT'S TIME FOR DAD TO GO. Terry, as stoic as I'm melodramatic, throws Dad's duffel bag into our Buick station wagon. Dad pauses for a moment in the garage and stares at his white MG. It's already up on blocks and covered with a tarp. A neighbor snaps a family photo on the front yard. Slivers of light flit through the evergreens. Everyone loads into the car for the fifteen-minute drive to Whidbey Island Naval Air Station.

Except me. I have papers to deliver. This isn't a small thing. I went 0-for-1978 in baseball, so I didn't play this year. Delivering papers is the only structure in my ADD/Dad-always-gone life. Mom thinks it's a good idea that I stay with my regular routine even on departure days. I don't argue. Car doors slam while I stuff rubber-banded papers into my carrier bag. Dad backs the wagon out of the drive and pulls away. I give a last wave. He doesn't see me.

I finish my route and stop at an old water tower. It sits at the top of a hill separating two phases of subdivisions carved out of the trees. I toss my Sears ten-speed down the hill and watch the spokes spin. I've been through this before. A sports and politics junkie living in a house full of females, I will retreat to my room. I'll lie in bed, stare at NFL pennants and toss an orange Nerf football off the ceiling, constructing an intricate fantasy world of triumphant campaigns and touchdown passes. And I'll be alone. At school, "underachiever" and "hyperactive" will be written on my report cards. There will be lectures about wasting God's gifts. Mom will cry. Every few weeks, a postcard will arrive from Hong Kong, Singapore, or some other Shangri-La, exhorting me to do better.

But there's hope for me this time. Hope for everybody, really. Dad's dream comes true on the Fourth of July. Peter Rodrick will become commanding officer of his own squadron, VAQ-135, the Black Ravens. He will be just thirty-six, one of the youngest skippers in the Navy. He's on the fast track, maybe all the way to admiral.

But that's grown-up talk. All I know is that on December 10 I fly from Seattle to Honolulu and ride back to San Diego with Dad aboard the *Kitty Hawk.* The voyage will take six days, longer than I've ever spent alone with him.

Finally, there will be time. I can come clean about faking sick so I could watch the Red Sox–Yankees one-game playoff last October. The Sox are Dad's team. He'll understand. Finally, I can learn what my father does. I know he flies jets off carriers, but how? Finally, I can ask him why things seem so hard all the time.

Time passes slowly. I'm already trying to follow him. I deliver papers every day, just like Dad did as a kid. But he saved his earnings and bought his mother her first dishwasher. I squander mine on the five-ice-cream-sandwich lunch. The sugar bath does not improve my concentration skills.

I'm also an altar boy, just like him. But his serving skills were in high demand, praised by the monsignor. Me? One Sunday, I stagger backward from the Bible's weight during the final blessing. The congregation titters—is he going to drop the thing?—until the priest announces, "I'm going to let the lad sit down before he hurts himself."

In July, my sisters and I are farmed out to my aunt and

uncle in Michigan so Mom can fly to the Philippines for Dad's change-of-command ceremony. My parents are tan and happy in the pictures she brings back. When they part, Mom breaks down, crying, inconsolable, consumed with fear she will never see him again. Everyone tells her she's crazy.

I don't help matters. I smuggle a hundred firecrackers back to Oak Harbor in my suitcase. Mom finds out. She screams through tears.

"I don't think your father has any idea the kind of son he has!"

That's quite possible. She says she'd cancel my Hawaii trip, except she needs a break from me. Instead, I'm grounded for the rest of the summer. The other wives come over almost every night. I watch Cathy Brown cry in Mom's arms. She is pregnant and scared. The other wives smoke cigarettes, drink Riunite, and talk about their absent husbands. Are they safe? Are they faithful? Is this what they signed up for when they sat under oak trees and watched their men march off demerits at the academy?

I listen from the stairs, then sneak into my little sister's room and watch her sleep. I've been told not to, but I can't stop myself. I remove my shoes, walk in quietly, and roll Chrissie onto her back; I'm petrified she's going to suffocate to death.

Gray settles back over the island. The illusion of summer is gone. At last, it is fall. We are down to numbers I can understand: twenty-three days, twenty-two days . . . The *Kitty Hawk* drops anchor in the Philippines, just two weeks away from Pearl Harbor. I brag about my trip to trapped customers when I collect for the paper. They smile, back away, and close their screen doors. And yet I'm still talking! I care about nothing else.

But on November 4, sixty-six Americans are taken hostage in the U.S. embassy in Iran. I fold my papers and stare at pictures of blindfolded Americans. I don't connect the dots. Then, in the middle of a November night, Dad calls from the officers' club in Subic Bay. Mom says he wants to talk to me. I rub the sleep out of my eyes and cradle the phone. He says he's sorry. The boat is being turned around, off to the Persian Gulf as a show of strength. I don't know what that means. I just know there will be no trip to Hawaii.

So I sulk. A week passes. Thanksgiving dinner is eaten at the officers' club. The mothers are pale and hollow-eyed, the kids ecstatic; there is an endless ice-cream sundae bar. Dad's letters arrive from somewhere. They used to be marked on the back with the number of days until his return. Now he just circles the seal on the envelope with a question mark and an unhappy face.

Soon, it's the morning of November 28. Mom sleeps in; Chrissie has been up with the croup. Terry and I eat two bowls of Frosted Flakes. As usual, we don't talk. Dad's not here, but Mom still has the house set at his prescribed 63 degrees. I sit on a heating vent and read a skiing magazine.

By 11:00 a.m., I'm trying, unsuccessfully, to skate backward at the Roller Barn for eighth-grade gym class. I can tell you the electoral college breakdown of the Carter-Ford presidential election and the status of Kenny Stabler's wobbly knees, but when it comes to the things that confer acceptance upon boys—hitting a baseball, building a catapult for Webelos, roller-skating backward—I'm hopeless. I need someone to show me how, someone to tell me that it really doesn't matter anyway. But that man is always 8,000 miles away.

So I fall on my ass. The cool kids snicker. My gym teacher calls me over. I'm relieved at first because it stops the laughing. But the teacher's permanently upbeat face has gone flat. She points to a man standing by the snack bar. He wears a black uniform and carries a white hat in his hand. It is Lieutenant Commander Laddie Coburn, Dad's best friend. I slowly skate over and sit down on a bench. He hesitates, sits down next to me, and puts a hand on my knee.

"Your father has been in an accident."

He says there's hope; the helos are still looking. I do not believe him. I am now thirteen and I've grown up around the Navy. If they haven't found him by now, they aren't going to.

He drives me home, and the world rushes toward me hotter and faster than ever before. I choke back vomit. We arrive at the house on North Conifer Drive. This time, the chaplain's car is in the driveway. My sisters walk hand in hand in the front yard. Inside, the wives have already gathered. They smoke Virginia Slims and laugh without conviction. A fresh casserole sits untouched on the table. Mom looks different; she became old the moment the doorbell rang.

I play the radio in my room. 710 KIRO mentions a missing Prowler between traffic reports. Terry wanders in. She says something. I do not hear.

Later that day, it is confirmed that Commander Peter Rodrick and three crew members, Lieutenant Commander William Coffey, Lieutenant James Brown Jr., and Lieutenant Junior Grade John Chorey, are dead. There are no bodies to recover. The men leave four widows and seven children under the age of fifteen.

I still deliver my papers. Almost done. An old crone who

never tips steps into her weedy yard. She wraps me in a hug. She heard about Dad on the news. Her tears drop onto my last remaining newspaper. The blot grows and expands, obliterating words.

It's dark now. I put my bike back in the garage, next to Dad's shrouded MG. I slip past the grown-ups—now so anxious to talk!—up the stairs and into my parents' bedroom. I breathe in deeply. Nothing. I frantically look in the medicine cabinet and then under the sink, but the bottle, and the smell, is gone.

AN HOUR BEFORE MY FATHER'S MEMORIAL service, a family friend slips me a tablet, probably Valium, leaving me with a detached, third-person feel for the rest of the day. At the chapel, four caps sit on the altar. Three of the wives are quiet, but Cathy Brown, now the widow of Lieutenant James Brown Jr., loudly bleeds grief, holding a tiny daughter who will never know her father. There are no coffins, but much talk of a loving God. More than four hundred people sing "Eternal Father," the Navy anthem to "those in peril on the sea."

Afterward, my family sits mute in our station wagon. Laddie Coburn leans through an open window and tries to console Mom.

"C'mon, Barb, you can start a whole new life."

Her response is a whisper.

"No."

Chapter Two

Mom kept her word. It's 2009 and she makes coffee for one, pouring Folgers into a thirty-year-old coffee mug. The cup is chipped and discolored with long-ago lipstick traces. The Black Ravens squadron logo is faint and the name "Pete" fades a little more with every wash. She is sixty-seven now and lives outside Flint, Michigan, where she moved our family after Dad's accident. An arthritic knee slows her down, but she still possesses the quick laugh and wide brown eyes that made my father fall in love with her fifty years ago. There's the toothy smile and the southern fake swear words. "Judas Priest" swapped for Jesus Christ.

I'm not the greatest son, but I know what matters to her. Earlier that year, I sent an email to the general mailbox of VAQ-135, my dad's old squadron. I was looking for new coffee mugs. The squadron's commanding officer, Commander Brent "Doogie" Breining, wrote me back. He thanked my family for our sacrifice—this happens a lot—and noted that his change-of-command ceremony would occur on July 2, 2009, two days short of the thirtieth anniversary of my father taking command of the Black Ravens. Would I like to come out to Whidbey Island for the ceremony? There would be a formal dinner—a dining-out—the night before where I could meet the guys in the squadron, fliers like my father. And who knows? They'd invite some Black Raven alumni; maybe one of them might even have known Dad. The next day, there'd be a formal ceremony where Commander James Hunter "Tupper" Ware would formally relieve Doogie. Afterward, I could get a tour of the base and even sit in the cockpit of an EA-6B Prowler, Dad's old plane still in service thirty years later.

I'm a writer; I inhabit other people's lives for a living. The Navy left me without a father but with some useful skills. I am adept at playing the new kid, making my way in strange worlds, never knowing where the bathrooms are located. This is what I do. Still, Breining's invitation frightened me. Some historians trace the start of the war on terror to November 4, 1979, the day the hostages were taken in Tehran. That would make Dad's crash the first American collateral damage. Thirty years later, fathers still fly EA-6B Prowlers off carriers. Their sons still skate at the Roller Barn. The war goes on and on. All that changes are the "Welcome Home" signs. But my family surrendered long ago. We fled that world, refugees never speaking of our destroyed homeland.

A colleague nicknamed me—half mocking—the magical stranger because I get people to tell me things. But to me, the magical stranger has always been my father. He was brilliant and unknowable, holy but absent, a born leader who gave me little direction. Peter Rodrick was one of only 4,000 men in the world qualified to land jets on a carrier after dark. And he was an apparition, gone two hundred days of the year from when I was six until he died. Even when he was home, he was away, working sixteen-hour days, writing up flight plans, and diagramming aerial tactics. He was such a ghost that I didn't fully accept he was gone for years. It just felt like he was on an extended cruise.

Evidence of the actual man was harder to come by. Most of it was locked away in cruise boxes and crates in Mom's basement: a framed picture from the *Brockton Enterprise* of a boy with a pole on the first day of fishing season; a long black leather sleeve holding a sword, and a small metal box containing envelopes with single dollar bills sent to him on his birthday by his father, the envelopes still coming for years after he died.

I had made some tentative steps at connecting with Dad, but they always ended in sadness. I visited his marker at Arlington National Cemetery twice when I was in Washington as a college kid. I would climb the hill up to his section and sit down on the hard ground. I'd pick out the dirt that lodged between letters reading IN MEMORY OF PETER THOMAS RODRICK CDR US NAVY JAN 6 1943–NOV 28 1979. I'd cry and flip a middle finger at tour guides droning on about Audie Murphy to tourists in passing trolleys. I never told my family.

An early attempt to write about the past burned me. In 2002, I turned thirty-six, Dad's age when he died. My wife and I lived in suburban Boston, an hour from Dad's hometown of Brockton. We were talking about starting a family, and she wanted to raise our children in a blissful suburban security neither one of us had as kids. I wanted to live in LA or New York. But there were larger issues. She was convinced that I wouldn't be a proper father until I had made peace with my own dad.

I readily agreed. I pitched a magazine story on Navy pilots and eventually spent three weeks on the USS *Kitty Hawk*, Dad's last ship. I sat in the chapel where Dad prayed every morning. I left on a transport plane from the same catapult he used on his final flight. I finally understood a flake of his life. But the end result was the opposite of what I had hoped. My wife asked for a divorce a few weeks after I returned, believing Dad's transient life and early death had ingrained in me a restlessness and sadness that would not be eased by babies and backyard cookouts. I assumed she was right, shouldering the blame for our joint failure.

The story didn't exactly open up a dialogue within my immediate family. We went to an Outback Steakhouse shortly after its publication, but the conversation was slow. Finally, Mom spoke.

"I liked the story very much."

My older sister scowled.

"I can't believe you described me as stoic."

We then ordered a Bloomin' Onion. That was the end of the conversation.

So I put Dad back into a cardboard box full of photos I kept in a room I rarely used. Newly single, I split my time between Brooklyn and Los Angeles, moving back and forth between LAX and JFK eight to ten times a year as if someone or something was chasing me. Dad was dropped from my itinerary until Commander Breining's invitation. I vacillated for weeks, staring at the ornate lettering of the official invitation. In the end, my new girlfriend Alix's curiosity about my past pushed me to buy two airline tickets just a week prior to the ceremony.

I immediately began to regret it. We flew from New York to Seattle on a July afternoon. An hour after landing, we pulled onto the Mukilteo ferry, an idyllic twenty-minute voyage from suburban Seattle to the southern tip of Whidbey Island. It was a trip I'd made dozens of times as a child. The afternoon was a "blue-sky day," a Navy term for endless visibility, just like the day of Dad's accident. Alix dozed while I squinted through the glare and thought of Dad losing perspective between sea and sky—one of the many theories for his crash.

I spotted a woman struggling with two small children in the car ahead of us. Her Subaru station wagon had a Fly Navy bumper sticker and was packed with toys and luggage. I guessed she was returning home after visiting relatives while the children's father floated on a different ocean.

The woman looked to be about Mom's age when she became a widow. Barbara Rodrick was thirty-seven and still beautiful when Dad's plane crashed sixty-three miles southeast of Diego Garcia in the Indian Ocean. She has been on zero dates since the mishap, as the Navy likes to call plane crashes. I felt this was heroic when I was younger, her terminal fidelity a fitting coda to my father's own bravery. As an adult, I began to think it was beyond sad.

We approached the island. The ferry's loudspeakers instructed drivers to return to their cars. Up ahead, the woman expertly wrangled her hyperactive son into his car seat as he kicked and thrashed.

The boy jarred something in my memory. When I was five, Dad was studying for a master's degree in aeronautical engineering at the Naval Postgraduate School in Monterey, California. One day, my sister and I were riding in the back of our blue Chevrolet station wagon as Mom ran errands. This was in the time before mandatory seat belts, much less car seats. I tried to crank down the window with my tiny fingers but pulled the wrong handle. The door opened and I tumbled onto the asphalt.

Somehow, Mom didn't notice. My sister and I were Irish twins, born eleven months apart. We fought constantly. Now, watching her tormenter tumble out the door, Terry saw her opportunity. She kept quiet.

Luckily, I landed on the curb side of the road. The passing cars looked like motorized dinosaurs from the ground. A block or two away, Mom looked in the rear window and screamed at Terry.

"Where's your brother?"

"He fell out back at the light."

Mom turned the station wagon around, squealing rubber. She pulled up in front of me and jumped out of the car. Her hands were shaking but her bouffant hairdo was still perfect. She dusted me off, looked around to see if anyone she knew was watching, and whispered in my ear.

"Do not mention this to your father."

Back on the ferry, I watched the woman double-check her kids' restraints. She gave her little boy a sippy cup, combed his hair, and smoothly moved into the driver's seat. She was completely in command. I couldn't look away. It was a scene from a play I had never seen.

Chapter Three

A FEW MILES AWAY, A MAN I had not yet met prepared to take Dad's last job.

Commander James Hunter Ware III carefully laid out a white uniform on the bed in his Anacortes, Washington, home. He took out a ruler and made sure his medals were perfectly aligned, a trick he learned at the Naval Academy. On paper, he was the American man as hero. There was the buzz cut, the flight jacket, and a cowboy's squint. His garage housed his Harley, a beat-up Ford pickup truck, a still for his nasty homemade hard cider, and license plates from five states. He was an Eagle Scout, an Annapolis grad, and a former test pilot. For a decade, he had flown in harm's way—most recently jamming Taliban communications in the skies above Afghanistan—and then landed his EA-6B Prowler in the dark on the deck of a carrier. There were ribbons on his uniform to prove it.

Tonight, Ware dressed for VAQ-135's dining-out, a formal dinner marking the squadron's change of command. Tomorrow, he would become skipper of a squadron heading to sea, the Navy's glamour job.

There was so much he wanted to do. He'd been in enough squadrons where number chasing was the only goal: percentage of sorties completed, percentage of sailors promoted, percentage of wives participating in Toys for Tots, blah, blah, blah. The Navy was no longer about sailors, thought Hunter;

it was about stats and checking boxes. As far as he knew, a stat wasn't what would get a Prowler aboard a carrier in a driving rainstorm. It was the 167 men and women of VAQ-135, and they'd have to do it with the four oldest EA-6B Prowlers in the fleet.

Ware knew it sounded new agey, but his command was going to stress "sailors taking care of sailors." That didn't mean screwups and misconduct would be ignored—Ware had no tolerance for shitty sailors and excuses—but it did mean looking out for one another, taking personal responsibility, and not passing the buck—long a VAQ-135 staple. Ware guessed if he could pull that off, not nearly as easy as it sounded, getting jets in the air and getting jets home safe wouldn't be a problem. Promotions and sortie completion quotas would follow, and pretty soon he'd have his dream: the top electronic attack squadron in the U.S. Navy. If all that happened, his own future—he had dreams of commanding his own ship—would be his to write.

Ware could change lives with a signature, but at home he was still a figurehead king. Downstairs, he could hear his daughters—twelve-year-old Brenna and ten-year-old Caitlin—chattering with his wife, Beth, and his mother, Cindy, about dance classes, Harry Potter, and sleepovers. He caught snippets of dialogue as he drifted in and out of earshot. He knew his daughters better than most Navy dads, but sometimes he felt like a stranger in his own home, trying to understand a language not his own.

Ware spent a lot of time laughing about how little power he held over his own life. (It beat crying.) A Pentagon fleet monkey decided when he came and went. Another fleet monkey ruled on his screwups. Entire days were spent trying to protect himself and his sailors from the flying bullshit being pushed by men living in the D.C. echo chamber—men who hadn't been to sea for years, men who had forgotten what it was like to spend eight months away, missing babies being born.

In reality, Ware didn't even hold the deed to his own name. He was named James after his father and grandfather, but raised as Hunter, shortened to Hunt by his mom and Beth. But that was only within the confines of his Anacortes home, a twenty-minute drive from the back gate of Naval Air Station Whidbey Island. In the Navy, Ware was known by his call sign, "Tupper," a not-clever play on his last name. Ware grew up dreaming of Maverick and Ice, so he didn't much like being known by the trademarked name of a brand of plastic containers. Still, he knew it could be much worse: The Black Ravens' ready room featured a Crapper and a Turd. In the real Navy, call signs were ego-killing nicknames designed to strip away rank and privilege, making everyone equal in the cockpit—a good thing when skies turned black. Tupper knew call signs would be gone soon, or at least the R-rated ones—victims of a politically correct Navy hell-bent on not offending anyone. Sure, it would suck to tell your son that your call sign was slang for shit, but where was the line? He didn't know. He was serving in a Navy that was waging two wars while afraid of its own shadow.

Sometimes, he had to remind himself why he got into the flying business. It was simple: he had no choice. He knew it sounded corny, but when he saw *Top Gun* at sixteen, that was it. Suddenly, every conversation was about Annapolis, flying jets off carriers, and the need for speed. (He wrecked three cars in high school.) Spare quarters were spent down at the arcade playing After Burner, a Navy pilot video game. There was no Plan B. The Air Force Academy sent a representative to his house and promised Tupper a slot if he wanted it. Tupper shook his hand and looked him in the eye.

"Thanks, but I'm not interested. I want to fly jets off carriers."

But now even flying jets off carriers had lost some of its allure: too many rules and regs to follow. Couldn't fly the Prowler below 500 feet, couldn't make a hard break toward the carrier at more than 350 knots. Sometimes, Tupper muttered to himself: "What the hell is this? The goddamned Air Force?"

And the paperwork! Forms for this, forms for that. Fit reps to write, everyone gets an award come end of cruise. Jesus Christ! Sometimes he felt like Dilbert with gold wings.

But he pushed all of that out of his mind. Tomorrow was what mattered. "Concentrate on the important things," he told himself. "This is what you've been waiting for."

Beth came into the room.

"Hunt, we've got to go in ten minutes."

BETH WAS THE ONE WHO HAD sacrificed the most.

They met at Penn State after he had been rejected by Annapolis—his first Navy kick in the crotch—and she stuck with him when he got into the Naval Academy on his second try. Their relationship was ruled by absence from the start. At the academy, Tupper would go over the wall and jump into Beth's car and they'd head off to D.C. for a day. But then there was flight school in Pensacola, Florida, and Meridian, Mississippi. On the rare free weekend, he'd call Beth in Pennsylvania and they'd find a spot on the map halfway between them.

Tupper hemmed and hawed about whether to end it. Navy life wasn't easy for a young wife. Beth was the first college graduate from a working-class Pittsburgh family; there were things she wanted to do. Tupper thought maybe it would be better if he went at it alone for a while.

He turned it over in his head for months. But he was miserable without her. He called her one day and told her he was going to fly his A-4 Skyhawk into State College and visit Penn State for a ROTC event. Could she meet him there?

She agreed. His plan was a complete lie. He made the 1,000-mile drive from Meridian to State College in his Mitsubishi Eclipse and arrived a day before her. He bluffed his way into Snyder Hall, his old dorm, and went up to room 406. He knocked on the door. Two guys answered and stared at the buzz-cut Hunter in his green flight jacket. He asked them if he could buy a few hours in his old room in exchange for some Fly Navy coffee mugs, a case of beer, and some squadron patches. The boys agreed.

Beth arrived the next day. Hunter took her up to see his old room. He pushed open the door and she lost her breath. The kids had blown up one hundred balloons and tied them to the ceiling. They fell on Tupper and Beth when they opened the door. Hunter pulled out an engagement ring. Beth said yes. They both wept.

They picked a wedding date six months down the road and reserved a mansion in Coraopolis, just outside of Pittsburgh. Tupper plugged through the rest of flight school. He passed his final flight tests. He was scheduled to receive his wings of gold on May 28, 1995, at NAS Meridian, not far from where my father's T-2 crashed. There was just one problem: May 28 was his wedding day.

Tupper told his commanding officer that he wouldn't be there. He was told that wasn't acceptable. Ensign Ware and a Navy captain played chicken for a day. Eventually, the Navy conceded. Tupper and Beth were married as scheduled. The following week, Beth pinned on his wings in the CO's office back in Meridian.

Tupper had put Beth before the Navy. That wouldn't happen again for a very long time.

TUPPER WATCHED AS BETH BRUSHED OUT her brunette hair. He would take command in less than eighteen hours, but he didn't feel triumphant. Instead he felt sorrow—sorrow for what he was about to put Beth and the kids through. Sorrow for what he had missed. He'd already been gone most of the spring and summer on workups, getting ready for a six-month deployment that began in three weeks. It would fall on Beth to take care of the girls and, as skipper's wife, watch over the families left behind, just like it had fallen on my mother thirty years ago. She had cut back her hours as a dietitian working with disadvantaged young mothers because someone had to be there for the girls, someone had to give them a sense of stability, and it certainly wasn't going to be their father.

It was just another in a long list of sacrifices she had made for her husband. They had been together for over twenty years and between workups, cruises, and overseas detachments,

Tupper calculated he had been gone for five of them. The girls had grown used to it in their own way. Beth found Caitlin the perfect pet: a dwarf hamster with the life expectancy of two years, exactly the length of a Navy tour of duty. But that was when they were younger. Now Beth was worn out and the girls were old enough to know what they were missing. So was Tupper. Recently, Beth started asking tough questions.

"How much more? Hunt, I can't do this forever. I'm tired. The girls are tired."

"Just a little bit longer."

He thought of everything he had put her through. Back in 2000, he'd been tapped for test pilot school in Patuxent River, Maryland, a sign his career was on the fast track. Tupper told Beth he'd be home for dinner most nights, a welcome relief for her after he'd been at sea for most of their babies' lives. But there was always a new jet to master, a new manual to plow through, a flight plan that needed revising. He made it home for dinner once a week at best.

Beth didn't take it well. He'd come home in the evening, and she'd be splayed on the couch, the kids screaming in their playpens still needing to be fed. He thought she was depressed. It went on for six months, his vibrant bride reduced to a crumpled wreck on the sofa.

Finally, a Pax River flight surgeon suggested Beth have her thyroid checked out. Tests were run and the diagnosis was a hyperactive thyroid. Meds were prescribed, but it was a slow climb out of her hole and Tupper wasn't there for her. Then came 9/11, and he was stuck at test pilot school for another year. Troops and jets poured into Afghanistan and Iraq and he wasn't part of it. To fill the time, he decided to get a master's degree in engineering from Johns Hopkins at night. He saw his family even less. There is a saying in the Navy: "There are horses that ride and horses that don't, and if you ride, be prepared to get ridden to death." Tupper galloped into his future, and no one warned him about the cost.

Tupper and Beth worked out a way to make parting less painful. A few months before each cruise, they began a home project that they had no chance of completing before his deployment. (This year it was redoing the backyard.) They would inevitably come up short and snipe at each other just before he left. Somehow, bruising their love made things easier. Tupper knew that civilians found their elaborate routine beyond crazy, but inside the Navy, their friends just nodded. Whatever it takes.

It was time to go. Tupper went down the stairs and talked to his girls: Brenna, the prim ballerina, and Caitlin, who loved to wrestle weeds out in the yard with her dad. Recently, Tupper had watched a video of a younger version of himself recording Brenna's favorite bedtime stories so she wouldn't forget him while he was away on his first cruise. There were tears in his eyes as he read, just as there were tears as he watched it a decade later. Still, he went away. And not just that once, but over and over again. He had just turned forty. He was starting to add up all the damage that had been done. Had it been worth it? He didn't know.

Beth came down the stairs, still as beautiful to him as the day they met. She gave the girls some final instructions, and then the couple jumped into Beth's BMW SUV. Tupper carefully backed the car out of their cul-de-sac and asked his wife one question.

"Ready?"

THE WARES SKIRTED THE QUAINT HOTELS and art galleries of seaside Anacortes and then drove past the less-photogenic Shell refineries on Washington State Route 20. For a while, they rode in silence. Tupper didn't like to admit it, but he was a brooder, prone to dark silences that could keep him quiet except for mandatory radio calls on a six-hour combat flight. The melancholia had been there since he was a kid. He cried when his parents put an old chair out by the curb, convinced the chair had feelings. He told his mother that it wasn't right to abandon it. Cindy Ware had to lie and tell him another family of chairs needed the chair even more. Around the same time, Jim took him fishing for the first time. His boy had just reeled in his first catch when his dad noticed he had tears in his eyes.

"Dad, can a fish scream?"

But as they turned off toward the Hope Island Inn by the Sea, Tupper's default melancholy vanished, replaced by something else: unfettered relief. He knew the emotion well. It was the feeling that you've cheated death, whether a real one or just a career killer. He'd known the feeling as a pilot a handful of times around the carrier, mostly back when he was a rookie pilot, a nugget, having trouble getting aboard. You name it—almost ramp strikes, coming in too fast, overshooting the carrier's four arresting wires—Tupper had problems with it early in his career.

The United States is the only country in the world that

has pilots land on carriers in the dark—other countries having decided it is far too dangerous—and it is an ass-tightening experience under the best of circumstances. Most of the Navy now flew variations of the F/A-18 Hornet, a modern jet that projected all your information—airspeed, altitude, rate of descent—right in front of you with a head-up display. The HUD meant you could keep looking straight ahead, searching out the speck that is a carrier on a dark night, without having to scan back inside the cockpit to look at your instruments. The plane even had an autopilot setting where if you lined the Hornet up behind the carrier it would land itself like a Mercedes parking itself on a Manhattan street.

But Tupper didn't fly a Hornet. Like my father, he had been assigned to the EA-6B Prowler. The Prowler had no HUD display; its basic airframe was designed a half century ago for the long-discontinued A-6 Intruder attack bomber. There's a refueling hook on the nose of a Prowler, so Tupper had to peek out and to the left of his cockpit window when lining his jet up on final approach while simultaneously watching the meatball, an infrared spotlight flashed from the carrier's deck. If he was on course, the lights flashed green. Too low and the light went red, telling him to pull up before he plowed into the back of the carrier.

Tupper would then drop his tailhook and try to catch one of the four wires—actually thick cables—stretched across the carrier's deck that would bring him from 150 miles per hour to zero in a second. An old Prowler joke was that the only thing scarier than landing the Prowler on a carrier at night was to be one of the three other guys along just for the ride. The up-front navigator at least could see what was ahead and offer some muttered advice. The two electronic countermeasure officers in the back just hung on—listening to the beep of the radar altimeter warning of low altitude—cursing and praying into their masks.

On deck, relief came for Tupper only after he caught the wire, preferably the two or three. (One meant you came in too low and risked smashing into the back of the boat; four meant you were too fast and nearly overshot the carrier.) He'd power down the Prowler's twin Pratt & Whitney engines. Only then did the stress release from his body, a furious adrenaline drain that sometimes caused his back and arms to spasm, making parking the jet on the edge of the carrier's deck a dicey final move. Tupper consoled himself after a bad landing with a shrug and a "Well, at least I didn't kill someone. I survived."

And that's the best Tupper could say about his time as XO—executive officer—of VAQ-135 under Doogie Breining. Tupper had survived and Breining had not killed anyone. Beyond that, Doogie's tour had been a shit show.

Dining-out follows a strict protocol and order borrowed from the early British Royal Navy. This was particularly appropriate tonight since Breining was about as popular with his men as Captain Bligh had been with the sailors on the *Bounty.* He was a smart man—his call sign came from the NBC show starring Neil Patrick Harris as an adolescent doctor—but socially awkward, something Tupper and Beth picked up on while dining with the Breinings after joining the squadron a year earlier. Attempts to make small talk were met with smaller talk and then long, uncomfortable silences.

Ware and Breining were contemporaries, but Tupper

couldn't remember ever seeing Doogie out for a beer at the officers' club or socializing with other aviators at the Brown Lantern, a Navy watering hole in Anacortes. In the work-hard, fly-hard, set-your-hair-on-fire world of naval aviation, being a loner was a professional flaw. You didn't need to be a boozer, although that helped, but you needed a sense of humor, which Doogie Breining didn't have.

Breining's social awkwardness had not gone unnoticed, but he was well connected. He did a tour at Special Operations Command at MacDill Air Force Base, where he held a mouthful of a job, flying hour program chief. He did a bang-up job managing flight hours and sorties for the base's pilots. An impressed general wrote a rave recommendation, and he screened for command.

Tupper didn't play the angles like Doogie. He prided himself on his tunnel vision when it came to flying. *"Concentrate on what's in front of you. Can't worry about yesterday's pass or tomorrow's flight."* It was a useful tool as a carrier pilot but a crushing liability as an officer trying to negotiate a career. He screened for command in 2008, and his personnel officer asked if he'd have a problem serving as Doogie Breining's executive officer, his second-in-command. This was a common courtesy afforded commanders in a small community like Whidbey. Except for a forward-deployed squadron in Japan and a Marine detachment in Cherry Point, North Carolina, the entire active Prowler community was based on Whidbey. Hoping to head off pairing officers who despise each other or fought over a woman a decade ago, officers were given an unofficial right of first refusal when being assigned to a squadron as a commander. Breining's reputation was an open secret, but somehow Tupper was clueless. If he'd heard the stories, he'd forgotten them. He told his personnel officer he was fine with the pairing. Pals told him he'd made a grave mistake. They were right.

As Doogie's XO, Ware was Breining's Biden, charged with supporting the front office no matter what, but he did it with increasing dread. He bit his lip as Breining screamed at officers over minor mistakes. And he watched as the power of being CO went to Doogie's head. Coming back to the *Nimitz* after a port call, Breining didn't want to submit his bag to a routine search, claiming a commander's prerogative not to be searched. It was Breining's right, but senior officers rarely invoked it. It caused a scene as sailors gawked from down the gangplank, wondering what was causing the holdup. Tupper defused the situation with the *Nimitz*'s MPs, but he seethed inside.

Down the chain of command, the squadron's junior officers cringed as Doogie sent routine paperwork back with WTF and SEE ME scrawled across the front. One lieutenant commander had the misfortune of having an office near the CO, and his hands would begin to shake whenever Doogie yelled his name. A star junior pilot told Tupper he was thinking of quitting flying to get away from Doogie. Tupper talked him out of it; three years later the pilot was chosen for the Blue Angels.

On it went. Then there was the holiday fiasco. The entire base was off on a federal holiday, but Breining made his squadron report that morning so they could catch up on the paper he wanted pushed. There was just one officer missing: Doogie. Word was he was skiing with his family. His junior officers struck back in a way only testosterone-filled twenty-seven-year-old men can: they swiped Doogie's rarely used beer mug from the officers' club, pissed in it, and returned it to its place of honor without a wash.

All of this left Tupper feeling like a passenger in a car driven by a drunk who refused to give up the wheel or use his brakes. He knew that VAQ-135 had become a mess he would eventually have to clean up, but there wasn't a lot he could do about it. It was a dilemma that stretched back to Bligh and Fletcher Christian. Unless there was a grave dereliction of duty, the XO simply did not contradict the commanding officer.

Tupper at least still had the solace of flying. But even that got messed up. A few months earlier, the Black Ravens were returning from a six-month cruise on the *Nimitz* in the Persian Gulf. With Doogie's management style—small screw-ups got junior officers routinely grounded—the cruise had seemed never ending. Even the port calls were lame. Finally, after 182 days, the *Nimitz* was just off the coast of San Diego, flying range from Whidbey. It was time to go home.

One of the highlights of a skipper's command is the fly-off, when he leads his planes in tight formation—wings nearly touching—over his home airfield before landing and reuniting with the families. In the Pacific Northwest, cloud cover can make this a dangerous move. The men did a preflight brief on the *Nimitz*, as they did for every flight. It was agreed that the squadron's four jets would rendezvous above Smith Island, just a few miles from Whidbey. If the skies were clear, they would fly their four jets into Whidbey in formation. If not, they'd go in separately at five-minute intervals. Doogie was the flight's mission commander, the officer responsible for the briefing and for executing the flight plan, but, in theory, once in the air it wouldn't be Doogie's call. He was a navigator—the pilots would decide.

By the time the planes arrived over Smith, the skies were overcast, with multiple layers of thick clouds. Now was the moment for Tupper or another pilot to speak up. But no one dared cross Doogie. The Black Ravens headed to Whidbey in formation, the clouds so thick Tupper couldn't see the other jets just a few feet away. He was the second jet of a four-plane formation, boxed in by Prowlers on both sides. He had nowhere to go if something went wrong. A slight jerk of the stick or some turbulence and wings could touch. People might die, ten minutes from home. In his head, Tupper kept repeating the same thought.

"This is a mistake. This is a mistake."

The Prowlers broke through the cloud cover a mile short of Whidbey. The Black Ravens flew by in formation, put on a show for the home folks, and then landed safely. They taxied to a stop, popped open their canopies, and climbed down. Five minutes later, Tupper ordered everyone except Doogie into the squadron ready room. He screamed at his aviators.

"That was seriously fucked. Unsat. I don't care if it was the goddamned CO's fly-in. That was unsafe. We will not do that on my watch."

Later, Doogie saw that Tupper was pissed. He asked him what was the matter. Tupper considered letting him have it, but he didn't.

"We didn't fly the flight that we briefed, sir. We didn't fly the brief."

But that was all in the past. Doogie would be gone in

the morning. Finally, Tupper would be able to place his own stamp on the squadron. He only had sixteen months and there was so much he wanted to change. Tupper and Beth made their way into the restaurant. Someone remarked they had not seen Tupper smile that much since he arrived in the squadron eighteen months ago. Everyone knew the reason.

The future was now in Tupper's hands. There was just tonight's dinner to get through. Alcohol would help.

Chapter Four

I MADE MY WAY TO THE same dinner by a different route. Off the ferry, Alix and I drove past lush farmland converted into weekend estates for Microsoft millionaires. Signs pointed the way to artists' colonies. But Whidbey Island is thirty-five miles long. By the time you reach Oak Harbor, pickups with blue base stickers replace VW Bugs and "Co-Exist" decals. We quickly drove through town, and I gawked at box stores that now filled once-open fields. The Roller Barn was still there, outsized and bright red. My old neighborhood was just a mile away, but there was no time.

We checked into a motel and changed into our formal wear—Alix in a black dress, me in a too-tight borrowed tuxedo—and headed down to the lobby. A matronly front-desk clerk interrupted us and asked where we were headed.

"It's a Navy thing, right?"

I said yes. Before I could provide any more information she launched into a monologue about her Navy life. Her husband was recently retired, but now her daughter was overseas, serving on a cruiser. Times were tough, but she loved—loved!—the Navy. I'd forgotten the cut-to-the-chase nature of military conversations. No wasting time with pleasantries while waiting for secrets to spill out over time. Someone could be shipped overseas tomorrow. You got down to whatever crosses you were bearing quickly.

"So why are you two here?"

I helped myself to some lobby popcorn and gave the clerk a sketch of my backstory, including Dad's accident. Her smile vanished. After thirty years, I still didn't know when to disclose my dad's death. When a new acquaintance asked me about my parents, I usually joked, "And now we have hit the sad portion of the conversation" before coughing up the particulars. Rationally, I knew the best time to talk about my dad's death was never; it wasn't a stranger's business. But another part of me relished dropping the tragedy on anyone who seemed on the verge of breaking into Lee Greenwood's "God Bless the U.S.A."

The exchange made me dread tonight's dinner even more. We arrived early and pulled into the gravel parking lot. I turned off the engine but didn't budge. I told Alix the whole trip was a really bad idea. She insisted we actually get out of the car before fleeing.

"We'll stay just a little while and then we can leave."

There was a nerve-calming walk around the parking lot and then we headed inside. The inn was a regular Navy hangout with the added benefit of not being on actual base property. The sun bounced off the sea and through the windows. We were early and the dining room was empty except for a gray-haired man and his wife. Breining had invited former squadron skippers in the area to the dinner. Only one couple took him up on the offer. They clung to each other tenderly as they stared out at the water. I took a breath and tapped the man on his shoulder. He turned around slowly, and I reached out my hand.

"You're Zeke Zardeskas, right?"

Surprised, the old man sized me up. My hair was too long

to be active Navy, and I was a tad young to be an old CO returning to the scene of long-gone triumphs.

"Yes, I am. How did you know? Have we met?"

"We have, a long time ago. My name is Stephen Rodrick, Pete Rodrick's son."

His wife gasped.

"Oh my God."

The couple looked like they had seen a ghost. They had in a way. Zachary "Zeke" Zardeskas had been Dad's XO. It wasn't as bad as Doogie and Tupper, but the two were not close. They tolerated each other, but their wives didn't get along at all. Mom thought Diana was a drama queen. She said Diana panicked at minor problems and passed on rumors of the squadron's comings and goings to the other wives, creating confusion and fear.

But it was the Zardeskases' actions after my father's accident that left a permanent mark on my mother. Zeke had taken the command pin off Dad's spare uniform before shipping his effects home. This was both understandable—it could take weeks for a command pin to be shipped from the States to an aircraft carrier—and loathsome—if you needed a pin to show authority, you'd already lost—and it broke Mom's heart. Back home, Diana suffered a meltdown after the accident. She wasn't exactly a calming influence for Mom; my aunt ordered her out of our house after the memorial service because of her wailing.

Now Zeke and Diana stood in front of me, senior citizens. We caught up quickly. He had made captain, served in Washington, and then returned to the area for retirement. They talked of their kids. I could feel jealousy about the life my family never had creeping up my throat. But I just smiled. I didn't have time to process everything because the room soon filled with close-cropped young men in dress whites, all with shiny wives or girlfriends on their arms. (And they were almost all young men. About 10 percent of Navy aviators are now female, but VAQ-135 only had one at the time.)

The officers looked at Alix and me with a distant curiosity. They nodded politely and then steered their dates onto the restaurant's terrace for pictures. Clad in white uniforms and aviator glasses, they looked impossibly young. I wondered if they knew how quickly their moment would pass.

Breining and his wife, Nicole, didn't join in the photos. I thanked him for inviting us, and we made awkward, stilted conversation. He was a compact man—his wife was almost a full head taller—and smiling seemed like an act of will for him. Making small talk is a basic job skill for me, and I can usually find common ground with anyone. It shouldn't have been difficult with Doogie: he was a flier like my father, holding the same rank and job, but it still felt like we were speaking past each other with a seven-second delay.

Mercifully, we were seated a few minutes later. The head table was made up of Alix and me, the Breinings, the Zardeskases, and Commander Vincent Johnson—the squadron's new executive officer—and his wife, Marci. Two seats remained empty.

Then, an older officer, his cap in the crook of his arm, emerged from a scrum of other officers. He held a chair for his wife and then reached his hand across the table.

"I'm Tupper and this is Beth. I'd like to apologize in

advance for whatever damage tonight does to your view of the United States Navy."

Everyone laughed, except for Doogie.

A FEW MINUTES LATER, A SHORT, squat young officer wheeled in a cart holding a boom box. His call sign was Oompa because of his stature and he was the Vice, aka the master of ceremonies. He shouted into the room.

"Officer's call!"

Everyone stood at attention. Oompa pushed play and "Anchors Aweigh" sifted out of the tinny speakers. Then someone shouted, "Parade the beef." A tray of steaks was carted around the tables. There was a series of toasts. Most were lighthearted but formal. Breining said, "To the Commander in Chief" and everyone shouted back "To the Commander in Chief." "To the wives!" "To the wives!" And so on. But then, for a moment, things turned solemn.

"To missing comrades," said Commander Breining. He looked at me for a moment.

Every movement at a dining-out—going to the bathroom, taking off a jacket—requires formal permission. Do anything without prior approval and you are guilty of an infraction. Your punishment is drinking out of the grog bowl, a mixture of whiskey, gin, wine, and Tabasco sauce. Soon, Doc, the squadron's female flight doctor, declared a desire to urinate.

"Mr. Vice, I request that table four be allowed to use the facilities."

Oompa answered.

"Doc, your request is denied. Drink from the bowl of grog."

Doc did as she was told, but then she started rifling rolls at the Vice. In a few seconds, rolls were bouncing off my head, much to Doogie's consternation. I fired one back. Tupper gave me a thumbs-up. Dinner staggered on for another two hours. Eventually, the tables were allowed to use the bathroom. Doc clutched my arm and smiled at me crazily.

"Who are you and why are you here?"

I didn't know what to say. A few hours later, Doc passed out in the gravel driveway of another officer's home while looking for her car keys. By then, I was back in my motel room staring at the ceiling, still trying to answer her question.

NAMES AND FACES LONG PAST SWIRLED through my head that night. One of them was Timmy Newman. Timmy was my best friend when I was five. He was a curly-haired boy whose dad was also a pilot. We met in Monterey the year I fell out of the car. There were play dates with Hot Rods and whispers across blue mats during kindergarten naptime. Our friendship was typically Navy, intense and sporadic. After kindergarten, his dad was sent off somewhere and my father to NAS Alameda outside of San Francisco. Timmy just disappeared one day. That's how it went.

Three years later, I found myself in Mrs. Hunt's third-grade class at Clover Valley Elementary, a quarter mile from NAS Whidbey's gates. We had just arrived in town. It was the first day of school, and, as usual, I knew no one. I sat down at my desk and stared at a dog-eared Matt Christopher book that I carried with me everywhere. A finger tapped me on my shoulder. I spun around. There was Timmy Newman in a white turtleneck.

His dad was flying Prowlers too! For little boys, our reunification was a profound miracle, too fantastic to contemplate. We became inseparable, chattering over cheese pizza, CCD, and Cub Scouts. Nothing could part us.

Then, one damp January morning, Timmy came to school late. His father's Prowler received a weak catapult launch off the *Constellation* in the Mediterranean. Not having enough power to maintain altitude, Commander Roger Newman and his crew ejected from their plane. Tim's dad survived, but a crewmember drowned. Timmy told me about it while we played four square at recess.

We were eight.

We remained best friends over the next five years, riding bikes and belting each other with his dad's old boxing gloves. Then came Dad's accident. A month or two after the crash, Tim and I joined some other kids on a school trip to Mount Baker for a day of skiing. The bus wound its way over the Deception Pass Bridge and Tim reluctantly handed me a copy of the local paper. There was a small headline about Dad's crash.

The story reported that after an investigation the Navy ruled nothing was mechanically wrong with Dad's Prowler and the probable cause of the crash was pilot error. There were no real details. I read it twice and then handed it back to Tim. I stared out the bus window, not wanting him to see the tears in my eyes. He waited a moment and then spoke quietly. I could barely hear him above the screaming of our classmates.

"I didn't know if I should show you this."

"No, I'm glad you did."

That was a lie. We moved from Whidbey Island a few months later. I never saw Tim Newman again.

SINCE THEN, I'VE LIVED WITH THE fact that Dad was responsible for his own death and that of his crew. What exactly he did wrong was never fully explained. I remember grownups whispering about flying low without a radar altimeter. But none of it mattered. The mishap was ruled pilot error. Dad was the pilot. Simple as that.

It was a wound that never healed. My father, everyone said, was a straight arrow, a grinder who worked eighteen hours a day. He'd won mathematics prizes and been promoted ahead of his peers. On the carrier, he briefed, he flew, he debriefed, and then he went to Mass. That was it. He was not a cowboy. Yet the Navy maintained it was his mistake that created a riptide of tragedy that destroyed four families.

I didn't talk about this with anyone. (I didn't know if anyone else in my family had read the story.) In my world, no one spoke about Dad except in hushed, reverent platitudes. I possessed dangerous information that could destroy that. It was my dark secret. I kept quiet and avoided Whidbey Island for three decades. How could I not? What if I ran into someone who remembered him? I carried his sin. And that's what I thought it was: a sin. Dad's Catholicism had soaked me good. No action that killed four men could be a mere mistake.

A FEW MILES AWAY, TUPPER TRIED to get some sleep as well. He'd come home to his dad freaking out. Two drunken men had started banging on the door about an hour before Tupper and Beth made it home. His dad wondered if he should call the cops. Tupper laughed and told him not to worry. He had an idea who it was. He checked in on his girls and loosened the collar on his uniform. Then he checked his voice mail.

There were multiple calls from his buddy Roast, a friend from his younger Prowler days in VAQ-134, the Lancers. Tupper and Roast had led the Gutter Rats, a motley assortment of junior officers who flew hard and partied harder. They'd flown over Iraq together and spent hundreds of hours with their thumbs up their asses while the squadron was deployed at Prince Sultan Air Base in Saudi Arabia for Operation Enduring Freedom. Roast was a great pilot who tired of the bullshit. He got out, took a straight job, and flew part-time for the National Guard out of Omaha.

"Hey Tupper, I've flown cross country for a Gutter Rat reunion. You fucking pussy, where the fuck are you? You better let us in before one of us takes a shit in your driveway."

Tupper laughed. There was no sign of Roast or Flounder, another Gutter Rat. They must have circled back into town for more provisions.

A few minutes later there was pounding on his porch. Tupper cursed with a smile and opened the front door. There were Roast and Flounder, gang-tackling each other. Tupper invited them in, and they tiptoed as quietly as drunk men can tiptoe onto the back porch. A bottle of whiskey appeared. Cigars were lit. For a few hours, Tupper was back in an old scene.

MAYBE IT WAS A NATURAL REBELLION against fatherhood, the stress of the cockpit, and finally being freed of the shackles of the academy and flight school, but once Tupper became a Navy pilot he decided he wasn't going to take shit from anyone. He built a reputation as the guy who always pushed the joke a little too far. The tradition actually started in his final days at the academy when—with graduation assured—he posed for a photograph on the roof of Bancroft Hall, the academy's dormitory, as "the Secret Ninja," wearing only a black mask and black socks. That made him a minor legend, but other actions had the opposite effect. He went to a Prowler tactics school and started bullshitting with a much older Marine instructor. But when the Marine ripped on Tupper and Tupper came back with the classic "That's not what your daughter said last night," the Marine had to be held back from popping Tupper in the mouth.

Not that he was alone. As a junior officer he was often flying circles over Iraq enforcing no-fly zones. Port calls were rare, so you had to take advantage when you could. Back then, Tupper, Roast, and his buddies were all binge drinkers, if you wanted to put a label on it. One night, Tupper and the rest of the squadron were partying in a Singapore hotel suite. Tupper found the conversation so scintillating that he didn't want to leave to urinate, so he grabbed a hotel glass and relieved himself. He put it back on the table and watched with horror as his skipper came dangerously close to downing his piss. He almost got a new call sign: D-Hop, for "drinks his own piss." Tupper was glad it didn't take.

He was getting a reputation as a cowboy in the cockpit. Toward the end of a 1999 cruise, Tupper brought his Prowler into the *Constellation* on a tuck-under break where he flipped the Prowler on its back and rotated 270 degrees on his approach. This was dangerous and forbidden, but Tupper couldn't resist. The men thought it was badass. The skipper was pissed. Tupper didn't care.

In a way, Tupper was just following his superiors. Back in Anacortes after a hard night of drinking, one of his early skippers asked him to throw him through a store window. The cops intervened before Tupper could execute a direct order.

Things changed as he got older. He made lieutenant commander in 2003 and was assigned to the Scorpions of VAQ-132 for his department head tour, a stint that would decide if he'd make command. It was time to put childish things away, or at least store them on a higher shelf. Tupper made one of his trademark wiseass remarks early in his tenure, and the squadron's XO took him aside. The commander showed Tupper the paper trail on his career up to that point. It read something like this:

> Incredibly competent, will do anything and move mountains, leader, rock star, going places, and he has a tendency to light his hair on fire. There's risk there.

Tupper read the words and told his boss he heard him loud and clear. He stopped drinking with the junior officers and did his best to keep his mouth shut.

But tonight was an ode to the old days. They smoked and drank and bullshitted for hours. Tupper protested that it was getting late, but he loved it. He had joined the Navy for this, the sheer unpredictability of it all, a midnight flight over Kandahar or the possibility that even in early middle age in sleepy Anacortes a night might go to dawn. Sure, he'd rather not have to talk Roast out of shitting in his front yard when he left, but that was just the cost of doing business.

He had already stocked his garage fridge with cases of beer in preparation for the day his Black Ravens green-lighted him, another Navy tradition: a junior officer calls the skipper and just whispers "Green Light," a sign that the entire squadron is about to raid the skipper's house demanding pizza and beer.

Roast and friends cleared out around four, just as morning twilight began creeping up in Anacortes. Tupper filled the dishwasher and wiped down the counters—he had an OCD streak a mile wide—and grabbed three hours of sleep.

He woke before seven and showered and shaved quietly, trying not to wake Beth and the girls. He noticed his dress uniform was missing its command pin, so he ducked out of the house with his father and drove to Whidbey Naval Air Station and waited for the Navy Exchange to open.

Together alone, Tupper and his father often couldn't find the words even though they were close. While Jim and Cindy Ware waited on the birth of their first son, Jim's brother Bev was killed in Vietnam and awarded the Silver Star posthumously. Jim Ware would be the first to tell you he never fully recovered from that day. He adored his first son. There would be two more, even if he was so exhausting—Hunt was found scaling a fence trying to escape on his first day at day care—that they put off having another child until he was five.

When he was fourteen, Hunter and Jim joined some other Boy Scouts and dads for a weekend sailing trip up the Chesapeake on two sailboats. The weather turned ugly soon after the group left the Sassafras River and headed into the mouth of Chesapeake Bay. Thunder sounded and rain fell sideways. The dad-in-charge panicked. He shouted contradictory instructions as visibility deteriorated. The boats rammed each other. Jim Ware's son vanished below deck. Hunter turned on the boat's navigational system, an antiquated gizmo that told you your position based on sonar buoys in the water. He had never seen the system before, but he mastered it in fifteen minutes. His father shouted down to his son.

"Which way should we go? What do we do?"

Hunt told him to relax. He started issuing commands to Jim on the bridge: steer the boat to the left; steer it a little to the right. Hunter had both boats snugly anchored in a quiet cove within an hour.

Tupper and his old man picked up the pin and settled into his new office with Styrofoam cups of coffee and stale doughnuts. They didn't say much. But at that moment—before the band began practicing—the silence was welcome. His dad flashed him a proud smile. That was all Tupper needed.

LATER THAT MORNING, HANGAR 8 FILLED with over two hundred people. Two gleaming Prowlers separated rows of folding chairs. Kids in blue blazers chased each other around as Alix and I took our seats.

I thought of Dad and my only memory of him in this same hangar. I was twelve, and there was some paperwork he wanted to pick up after Sunday Mass on base. We walked into the hangar, and Dad spotted a young enlisted man on guard duty. His nightstick was twirling down around his waist. Dad strode directly toward him, looking as imposing as a man in a turtleneck, leather sports jacket, and flared plaid pants can look. He moved the baton back up the sailor's shoulder.

"This is how it is to be worn. Got it?"

The sailor, a kid really, whispered a response.

"Yes, sir."

I was embarrassed and proud. Now I looked through the crowd at the sons and wondered what would happen to them without their fathers. Would they remember them? Would their example carry them through? Or would they crumple under the weight of what was expected and be lost?

The band began to play. The base commander welcomed everyone and a chaplain gave his blessing. Doogie spoke, mercifully briefly. Then he and Tupper met in the middle of the stage and saluted. Tupper read his orders, relieving Breining of command. Everyone clapped.

Tupper strode to the microphone. He took off his hat, fished his speech out of the hatband, and put the hat back on, all in one motion.

"That's an old Navy trick."

Beth and the girls sat in the front row. Tupper thanked his family and paid his respects to Doogie. Then he paused and looked out at the men and women of VAQ-135 standing in formation.

"We have sacrificed much in the nation's defense, and we will sacrifice much more in the years ahead. Some of us will lose loved ones, some will lose relationships, and some will miss the birth of our children."

He looked down at Beth holding hands with the girls.

"Others, such as myself, will return home to children very different than the ones we left. We accept these trials with open hearts and also with the determination that these sacrifices not be made in vain."

The ceremony ended. There were a few minutes before the reception at the officers' club, so Alix and I walked across the street to a mothballed EA-6B Prowler. In front of the plane were bronze statues of two small children, frozen in play as if captured in a light moment at the park. But their eyes gazed on golden plaques at the base of the Prowler. Each one contained the names of the twenty-eight men who had been killed flying the Prowler. I found Dad's name and something dawned on me: the kids' faces were frozen in the moment before they were told that their father was dead.

I wiped tears away and we headed over to the officers' club where I remembered dining with Dad once or twice on special occasions. The club's walls were covered with beer mugs and wooden cruise plaques celebrating the exploits of squadrons with nicknames like Scorpions and Flying Lizards on deployments to the Mediterranean, the Persian Gulf, Iraq, and Afghanistan. I stared at the names, recognizing one or two of Dad's friends. An old man tapped me on the shoulder. It was Zeke Zardeskas.

"If you want to talk about it, I'll tell you what I know."

I told him I'd think about it. It was time to go. I looked for Doogie to say good-bye. Whatever his faults, it was his kindness that brought me here and I wanted to thank him. I found him alone, relieved of command; none of his men feeling bound to talk with him. I thanked him for inviting me and asked if he'd seen Tupper. I then saw Doogie Breining genuinely smile for the first time.

"Tupper's been delayed. He'll be here in a few minutes."

Commander James Hunter Ware III had been skipper for an hour and he had lost his keys.

◇◇

Chapter Five

I LEARNED ON MY WHIDBEY TRIP that the Black Ravens' cruise was going to be the last one with Prowlers. They would begin transitioning to the EA-18G Growler, an electronic warfare version of the Hornet, when they got home.

I'd thought of writing about Dad and his flying days through the prism of modern pilots, but I always passed, the pain of examination too great to bear. But now the Prowler was on its last cruise. It was now or never. I called Mom not long after Ware took command of the Black Ravens and told her I wanted to write about Dad and the squadron. She had a question.

"Hon, is it going to be fiction or nonfiction?"

I took a breath and counted to ten.

"Mom, it's nonfiction. Have I ever written fiction in my life?"

"Okay, dear, I just was wondering."

I hung up a few minutes later. The more I thought about it, the more relevant her question became. My vision of my father was incomplete, a sort of fiction. Framed images of a serious man in a black uniform with an American flag behind him hung on the walls of my childhood home. On the mantelpiece were models of his planes, and inside a glass case there was a folded American flag presented on behalf of a grateful nation. What it all meant I didn't know.

THIS IS WHAT I REMEMBER.

A little boy knows some things. Mom and Dad come from different places. It's not about class or money; those are things I don't understand. It's geography, a word I can't quite pronounce but whose answers lie in a big blue book kept on a high shelf. He is from the North, she is from the South, and we live in the West.

I see it best on vacations. Dad is one of six kids, raised in Brockton, Massachusetts, home of somebody named Rocky Marciano. In December 1972, we drive there from somewhere in a storm arriving just in time for the wedding of Dad's baby sister, Marie. We go straight to the church and I fall asleep in a pew.

Then we go to his home. We live in a suburban tract home with air-conditioning and two bathrooms. My grandparents' home is old and smelly. The carpet is faded green, the ceilings are slanted, and an old cat slinks around the place. There is only one shower in the two-story home on Herrod Avenue, so we bathe in shifts that seem to last the whole day long.

Grandpa Rodrick is just sixty, but he seems to be the oldest man in the world. He just got laid off from his job in shipping at a shoe factory but still slicks his hair back with Brylcreem and eats franks and beans for breakfast every morning. The house has a family room just like ours, but there isn't much family about it. Right at 7:00 p.m., Grandpa retires to his La-Z-Boy and scowls at the *Boston Globe* while the Bruins skate around on Channel 38.

The kids are all adults now, but they still tiptoe around the old man. He tolerates me as long as I stay quiet. I plow through *Time* magazine's Year in Review from the 1930s and 1940s stacked on a bookshelf. Every once in a while, I asked a question. Who was Tojo? Where was Ethiopia and why did Italy invade? Sometimes, he answers, sometimes he just mutters.

"Jiminy Christmas, you knucklehead. Why do you need to know that?"

Grandma Rodrick is the exact opposite. On her wrist is a jangle of bracelets holding charms with pictures of her rapidly multiplying grandchildren. She still works for Kelly Girl, a temp agency, filling in at offices three or four days a week. I sit in the backseat with her and Mom on the way home from Mass. She sings "Take Me Out to the Ballgame" and nuzzles my face with her whiskery chin, smelling of Avon. Sometimes, she talks about grown-up things when she thinks I'm asleep. I hear about a miscarriage and a day driving around Brockton when she thought of ditching Grandpa.

Where Dad fits in his family is clear. He is the hero. Dad's family isn't exactly poor, but they are far from rich. Their pilot son gives color to their black-and-white world. The neighborhood is equally invested; I run errands with his sister, Lyn, and the grocer and the baker ask after Pete.

His black Irish features make him seem fierce, but he has a crinkly smile that makes you know he doesn't think he's better than you. His brothers and sisters approach him with serious looks and grown-up questions.

Dad's just about to turn thirty.

HIS FAMILY VIEWS MOM JUST AS I do: she is the prettiest creature, with light in her eyes. There's usually a touch of lipstick on gapped teeth inside a mouth that is always working a piece of Juicy Fruit gum. She's from Virginia Beach, Virginia, less than 600 miles from Brockton, but she might as well be from Mars.

Her dad is the cartoon opposite of Dad's dad. Bill Gentry is a joker; wisecracks slip from his mouth almost as quickly as marriage proposals. He's on his fourth or fifth rodeo. It is hard to get my parents to cough up details, but I'm smart and nosy and get it from here and there.

Sometimes, he takes me on his rounds in his sky blue boat of a car plopping me on a stranger's couch in front of a *Leave It to Beaver* rerun. A nice lady gives me a sandwich and pats my head. They disappear into another room, and Grandpa emerges precisely one Lumpy Rutherford episode later with a grin and sweat on his forehead.

He is cashless on the drive home. Grandpa Gentry pulls up to an automated tollbooth and fake-tosses coins into the collection box. He acts shocked and angry when the gate won't open. I can't stop laughing. The gate opens.

He golfs all the time and keeps soft-porn novels in easily accessible drawers. I read them behind paperback covers of *Johnny Tremain*. His humor is rough and crass, full of mugging and jiving, which seems strange since he calls blacks "the colored" and prides himself for no longer using the n-word. The older I get, the sadder he looks. Mom laughs at his jokes but worries behind his back. The message is clear: don't be like him.

Mom has one sister and no brothers, so her father is her only male reference point. Well, except for Mel. Sarah, Mom's mom, got sick of Grandpa Gentry's silly ways and set her sights on a more grown-up guy. That would be Marine Master Gunnery Sergeant Melvin Gunter. He fought in three wars, has two Purple Hearts, and drinks Budweiser like I drink cherry Kool-Aid. Mel and Sarah moved to his Alabama hills after he retired in 1973. We visit every spring. They raise pigs and peaches, tomatoes and cows, on sixty acres. Their home is near the end of a road that pitches and winds like crazy. Mel's momma lives up the road and shucks corn and green beans barefoot. She smiles without teeth and tells me about a no-good welfare cheat collecting from two counties.

"He's just trash."

Northerners are not welcome around here. Not even us, really. A man in overalls stops by one morning and tells Mel that he saw our Massachusetts license plates and wants to make sure he was okay. He then jokes about slashing our tires. Or maybe he isn't joking.

Every morning, Mel works in his peach orchards in a white T-shirt and army surplus pants. Down comes his ax; up goes a Budweiser tall boy. It is 7:30 a.m. After breakfast, we go fishing in his catfish pond. One afternoon, we catch a giant one, maybe three pounds, throw it in the now empty beer cooler, and drive his blue tractor back to the house. He gives me a wink and gets a hammer and nail. He pounds the catfish to the wall and skins it. I puke in the driveway.

He is asleep in his lounger by 2:00 p.m. I lift a Marlboro out of his hand and snuff it out in an ashtray. I sneak into his living room and stare at snapshots of dead Korean boys preserved behind cellophane in a dusty photo album. He wakes up and thumps me on the head.

"You're not old enough to see these things."

My glimpses into a man's world vanish as quickly as they happen. Mostly, I'm around women all day and night long. Mom's mom flies wherever we are and visits for weeks at a time. The good news is she makes me chicken and dumplings and a chocolate cake with golden filling for my birthday. The bad news is she's the most scared grown-up I've ever met. She doesn't drive and hasn't been to the movies for twenty years. That seems like a long time. Grandma only likes to talk about two things: how dangerous Dad's job is and how men are jerks. She seems only to be happy when she's talking about being unhappy. She wants everyone to be as scared as she is. Then, Grandma tells Mom that Dad is doing men's work and there's nothing she can do about it. She works Mom into a panic and then seals the exits.

How a boy and a girl from different sides of the Mason-Dixon line come together is a story I can't hear enough. Here's how it goes. Dad starts at the Naval Academy in 1960. The following year, he goes down to Virginia with the academy's brigade to watch Navy play Duke in a football game called the Oyster Bowl. There is a dance after the game filled with crew-cut boys and nice girls from Norfolk and Virginia Beach. My parents meet toward the end of the night. When she gets ready to leave, Dad—pushed forward by his friends—asks for her number. She gives it with a sugary smile.

Then he doesn't call for a month! I never find out why. He probably is just busy. He invites her to Annapolis for another dance. He is quiet. She is not. They like that about each other. They start going steady. Every weekend, she and a few girls carpool up to Annapolis. The girls stay in houses with housemothers who watch what goes on. Dad doesn't like this, so he borrows a car so they can go watch the submarine races. One weekend, she sits under an oak tree and watches Dad march off demerits for eating a cookie in math class. That's when Dad knows she is the one.

Dad proposes down on the Cape, not far from Kennedy's Camelot in Hyannis, on a summer weekend in 1963. Mom's ring is a little smaller than Jackie's. There's just one catch: Mom is a Baptist. She gets pamphlets in the mail from her almost father-in-law about mixed marriages. This confuses her. She thought mixed marriages were between black and white folks. Mom takes classes for six months and gets baptized just before Dad graduates from the Naval Academy in June 1964. It's a hot day and Dad gets a watch for being good at math.

He has leadership classes to take, so they put off marriage until after Christmas. Then, it finally happens. Dad's family flies down to Norfolk; it's the first flight for his brothers and sisters. Our Lady of Victory Chapel at Norfolk Naval Base is filled with naval officers, nanas in white gloves and Southern girls with bird-nest hats. My mother wears a white bridal gown of Alençon lace styled with long sleeves and a floor-length bell skirt. (Or at least that's what the *Brockton Daily Enterprise* says in a clip I dug out of Mom's closet.) Dad is in his dress uniform. The priest pronounces them man and wife. They leave church under an arch of swords provided by Dad's classmates. They jump into Dad's Corvette after the reception. Dad fishtails the car in the Virginia slush and they head south. Flight school starts in Pensacola in eight days.

Mom spends her first year as a Navy wife in a shotgun shack with a puke bucket by the bed. She is pregnant with Terry six weeks after the wedding. Mom's best friend, Brenda, married a Navy flier too, and she lives down the road. Every morning, Dad drops her off at Brenda's on his way to work. She slips into Brenda's bed, snuggles up until she has to puke again.

They move a few months later to Quonset Point Naval Air Station in Rhode Island, where Dad learns how to fly the E-2, a turboprop sub chaser. Terry arrives late on Halloween. There are no breaks. Mom becomes pregnant with me right after she recovers from childbirth. I arrive the following September, a month early and barely five pounds. Mom is twenty-four and has two children under the age of one.

It is September 30, 1966. We are an American family. Our story will never be this simple again.

Chapter Six

Tupper and Beth watched *Kindergarten Cop* with their girls on his last night home. He picked at a piece of German chocolate cake Beth had baked especially for him and watched his girls curl up with their poodle, Gretl. He blinked back tears and thought to himself, "I've taken command and it's breaking my heart."

He couldn't show the girls; that would be too much for them. That's what his journal would be for. Beth had given him some leatherbound books for his birthday because she knew that writing his thoughts down calmed him.

The girls were getting too old for Tupper to tuck them in, but they made an exception that night. After the girls went to sleep, he and Beth went over the bills a last time and talked dreamily of some land they owned a mile away high on a bluff overlooking Burrows Bay. Someday they hoped to build their dream house there, maybe even next year. He bottled up the last of his hard cider until midnight and then tried to get some sleep.

It didn't take. Tupper woke the next morning long before the 5:00 a.m. alarm clock. He packed his bag in the dark, muscle memory taking over. He looked out the window at the evergreens swaying in the gloom. He thought of when he first moved here with Beth in 1996. They had to look up Whidbey Island on a map and they thought at first it was small and remote, but thrilled at the adventure.

They now loved it as much as they loved the girls. He hated to leave.

Tupper headed downstairs and labeled all the wine bottles with green, yellow, and red stickers for Beth. Tupper had become a bit of a wine snob since the family did a tour of duty in Germany beginning in 2005 and he'd acquired about a hundred bottles. He'd returned from his last cruise to find that Beth and some friends had uncorked a $100 bottle of 1997 Castelgiocondo Brunello di Montalcino at the end of a girls' night out. That wouldn't happen again with his sticker system.

He then took a long, hot shower, slowly turning off the nozzle, knowing it would be the last one for months. Beth and the girls got up, and the family headed over to Penguins, a local coffee place. Tupper indulged himself with an orange-cranberry scone hot out of the oven. The family then piled into their SUV and made the ride up to NAS Whidbey Island under a blue sky.

On base, Beth and the girls held it together as Tupper spun through the gate that separated the parking lot and the Black Ravens' hangar. But then he looked back a last time and saw Caitlin looking away, tears running down her cheeks. He wouldn't be able to get the image out of his mind for weeks.

TUPPER HAD PLENTY OF WORK TO make him forget how much he missed his family. Taking over from Doogie was proving even harder than Tupper knew it would be. Half the squadron kept their heads down, hoping their new master wouldn't kick them as hard as the last guy, while the other half dropped their packs; a Navy term for fed-up sailors going through the motions, doing the minimum just to get by.

Tupper spoke often to his sailors about this being a new day for the Black Ravens, but they were skeptical; Tupper had been Doogie's second-in-command, and there was no evidence he'd do things any differently.

That was only half of the problem. Everyone knew this was the Black Ravens' last cruise with the ancient Prowlers. With VAQ-135 beginning transition to the EA-18G in a little more than a year, Tupper was like a general manager of a baseball team relocating to an excited new city with one more lame-duck season to play in a decrepit stadium before a handful of pissed-off fans. He had to keep sailors motivated to repair and mother Prowlers that would be scrapped for parts and metal next year.

There was a personal preservation angle as well. There would be seven squadron skippers on the *Nimitz* and only two of them would be recommended for further command. The rest would see their once-promising careers shunted to middle-management posts. But it wasn't a level playing field. He'd be competing against the COs of Hornet and Super Hornet squadrons. A head-to-head comparison of the Prowler and Hornet was not pretty. Hornets can fly at 1,200 miles per hour—nearly twice the speed of sound. Prowlers top out at 650 mph, slightly faster than a 737 flying between Indianapolis and Detroit. The Hornet carries Sidewinder missiles capable of obliterating enemy aircraft twenty miles away. The unarmed Prowler sends out electromagnetic waves to make enemy radars go snowy. The Hornet can drop three tons of bombs ranging from bunker busters to tactical nuclear weapons. The Prowler has the ability to absolutely wreck a terrorist's cell phone network.

There were going to be three Hornet squadrons on board the *Nimitz*, so squadrons could swap parts easily if something broke. The Black Ravens were the *Nimitz*'s only Prowlers and most were built during the Reagan administration, before some of their pilots were born. Break something on a decaying Prowler and you'd be on the phone with a fat man at NAS Jacksonville's parts depot who may or may not surrender the part. Then you'd wait days for the part to be flown out to the boat on the goddamned COD—Carrier Onboard Delivery, the carrier's transport squadron whose reputation for efficiency was slightly lower than a cut-rate East European airline. Your best option was cannibalizing parts from the Hangar Queen, aka the Prowler that never flies except on to the boat at the beginning of cruise and off at the end.

That was the hand Tupper was dealt. No use crying over it. There were 145 sailors and 22 officers under his command. They ranged in age from seventeen to fifty, men and women, black, white, and Latino. Some of them were pimple-faced seaman apprentices from broken homes and some were middle-aged chiefs who knew more about the Prowler than Tupper ever would.

The chiefs made up the squadron's middle management known in the Navy as the Goat Locker. If a skipper's Goat Locker was top-notch, his planes launched on time and his sortie completion rate was near 98 percent. That made the skipper's boss at Carrier Air Group happy. CAG was the captain who oversaw all the squadrons on a carrier, and if a skipper wanted to scramble up another rung on the Navy ladder he needed CAG's blessing. A crappy Goat Locker meant downed jets, backed-up paperwork, and CAG screaming through the telephone. If that happened to Tupper, the only thing he'd be commanding next was Caitlin's soccer team.

Tupper's Goat Locker was a mess, a by-product of Doogie's command and good people getting out because they couldn't handle being deployed eight months out of the year, every year. Those who remained were calling in sick and dragging their feet on paperwork and generally setting a bad example for sailors.

The fact that Dan Whittle, VAQ-135's master chief—the head of his Goat Locker—was missing in action did not help. Whittle had served nearly a quarter century in the Navy and was the veteran of multiple Prowler cruises. He was loved by his men, but he was never around. The Navy had given him limited duty to deal with family issues for the past six months, and he'd been a ghost around VAQ-135. He was back now—or so Tupper thought.

On his first morning as skipper, Tupper called Lieutenant Kevin Marshall, one of the squadron's nonflying administrative officers. He quickly went down his sailors, double-checking that they were all good to ship out for cruise in two weeks.

The conversation went quickly until Tupper got to Whittle.

"Is Master Chief Whittle ready to go?"

There was a long pause.

"Well, sir."

"Kevin, get in here."

Marshall walked down the long hall to Tupper's office.

"Kevin, we're less than two weeks away from cruise, and you're telling me my master chief can't deploy?"

Marshall explained where they were. Whittle was dealing with two kinds of trouble. One of his children had been seriously ill last year and he'd taken time off to deal with her problems. Tupper knew about that, but there was something else.

Two wars had stretched the Army to its limits, so the Pentagon had taken to borrowing Navy personnel to fill noncombat slots in Iraq and Afghanistan. In the Navy they were officially called IAs for Individual Augmentee but were known among the men as "goddamned IAs." Whittle had just returned from a Black Ravens cruise when the Navy sent him to Afghanistan in 2008 to train non-commissioned Afghan officers. But at night the officers tended to fade back into the countryside and their Taliban roots. That left Whittle and thirteen sailors supervising military convoys on the roads in and out of Camp Leatherneck in southern Afghanistan. Whittle and his men lived in constant fear of car bombs and other improvised explosive devices. Their fears were realized on September 20, 2008, when one of the trucks bound for Kandahar hit an IED, killing Army captain Bruno de Solenni and two Afghan soldiers. It fell to Whittle to ID and body-bag the three victims. He was never the same.

Tupper had a decision to make. Ship out with a burned-out master chief or ship out without a master chief. He thought about it for a day and then called the chief in his office. He'd already made his decision.

"Chief, are you ready to ship out?"

"Yes, sir."

"No, you're not. I'm leaving you at home."

Whittle began to cry, tears of shame and relief. Tupper

handed him a box of Kleenex. The two men talked for a few minutes. Whittle suggested maybe he could meet the Ravens in Singapore, a month into the cruise. Tupper knew that wouldn't happen. His sailor couldn't stop apologizing.

"I'm so sorry, sir. I'm letting you down."

"Shipmate, you're not letting anybody down. You have your own war to fight. But I can't take you with us."

Tupper and the Black Ravens had not even left Whidbey yet, and he was already a man down.

Chapter Seven

I don't remember much about my baby days, but I'm told that Dad helps out more than most men. He does the dishes, changes diapers, and lets Mom head out with the girls. But he isn't home alone all day with two screaming babies. He's at work flying or at game two of the 1967 World Series with his brother-in-law, or he's renting a small plane, letting his baby brother Paul take the controls as they circle above the Prudential Building in Boston.

We move to Meridian, Mississippi, in 1968. That's where Dad learns to fly jets and that's where he crashes his first plane. Two years later, it's on to Monterey so Dad can get his master's in aeronautical engineering at the Naval Postgraduate School. That's when I begin to remember things. One evening, Mom can't find me in our small yard in base housing. She grows frantic. I hear her before I can see her.

"STEPHEN THOMAS RODRICK."

I'm not really lost. I am playing catch with someone else's father. She is pissed.

"You can't wait for your father? Fine, you don't get to play with him either."

I whine that this doesn't seem fair. Dad Substitute cringes and pats me on the head.

"Good luck, buddy."

Mom is always there—she makes the sandwiches, she gives me my bath, she reads me *Cat in the Hat*—but Dad's cameos are more dramatic. It is the last day of kindergarten in Monterey. I'm sitting outside of my classroom wearing Garanimals, a blue shirt and plaid pants that I hate. Inside, Mom and my teacher make small talk. They are killing time, waiting for someone. And there he is, Dad. He is late and runs down the hallway in black shoes and khakis, right past me, and closes the door behind him.

I am five and small, but can already name the starting nine for the Oakland A's. I also cry a lot: when my sister punches me, when I can't make my hands do what I want them to do, most any time, really. The teacher wants to hold me back because of my size and emotional issues. Dad will not hear of it.

"He will be bored. It's a mistake. Don't do it."

End of discussion. That memory is blurry, an underexposed Polaroid probably explained to me later. More in focus are two sweaty men in dusty green uniforms. Dad is buying them sandwiches. They are from the Mayflower Moving Company. Dad's been transferred to NAS Alameda, so we're moving from Monterey to Pleasanton, California, thirty miles outside of San Francisco. It's a hot day in August. After the men finish eating, Dad peels off some bills from his black wallet. He shakes their hands and we head home.

Our new garage is filled with boxes and crates. Our garage is always filled with boxes and crates. Some of them with Florida and Rhode Island addresses predate me. Even when we are settled, we are not. Green and gray stickers from moving companies remain on the side of Dad's desk until Mom gives it away forty years later. Dad says everything is always ready to be packed up and shipped because there could be a disagreement with the Russians. I don't understand; the

Russians seem like pretty decent folks in the Soyuz scrapbooks Dad gives me on my birthday.

Dad is stuck flying A-3s out of NAS Alameda. I don't understand much, but I know this makes him mad. Vietnam is winding down and he never got in the fight. Late at night, Mom and Dad talk of classmates shot down and in prison camps or dead.

"Pete, you've got two small kids. Thank God you're not there."

I'm pretty sure Dad doesn't thank God. His buddies are flying Skyhawks and Intruders. He's flying something named a Skywarrior, but everyone calls it "the Whale." I think this is an odd name for a plane. One day, Dad gives me a mimeographed piece of paper with the history and photo of the plane. He reads it to me. The A-3 was created big and heavy in the mid-1950s so it could launch from an aircraft carrier and deliver nuclear bombs a thousand miles away. But the Whale's mission was made obsolete by intercontinental ballistic missiles that could deliver twice the nuclear payload twice as quick. The A-3 was turned into a tanker, circling carriers and refueling planes as they went off to bomb Vietnam and Cambodia.

In the early 1970s, the A-3 is converted into a radar-jamming plane hoping to stop the surface-to-air missiles killing Dad's friends in the skies over Vietnam. But Dad misses that too. His first A-3 cruise begins in the summer of 1973, just as naval air operations over Vietnam are ending.

I don't understand all that. I've got sports. Dad is a casual Celtics and Red Sox fan, but my interest is something else. I memorize the sports section of *The Guinness Book of World*

Records and torture neighbors with stray facts about quarterbacks who caught their own passes. Mom and Dad have season tickets to the Oakland Raiders, but I'm too young to go. (Or so they tell me.) I listen to the three-hour pregame show and then watch the game with a babysitter.

The Raiders are my heroes. One day while Dad is gone I see an ad in the *Oakland Tribune* for a charity fundraiser featuring future Hall of Famers Gene Upshaw and Art Shell. I beg a neighbor to take me. He says no at first, but I turn on the waterworks and he gives in. Upshaw and Shell are the first black men I've ever touched or talked with. It is the greatest day of my life. But Dad isn't there. He isn't there when I burst into tears when the Raiders lose to the Steelers on something called the Immaculate Reception. But Mom is there.

"It's only a game. Jesus. Don't be a baby."

She tries but doesn't understand. I'm starting to get it. Dad's never there. I learn a new term: workups. This means Dad gets up at five or six in the morning, throws his duffel bag in his car, and vanishes for three weeks at a time. He explains it to Terry and me one night.

"Before we can go on the big cruise, we need to do little cruises."

I don't know what a big cruise is. Let's face it. I have some issues. School is *so* hard. I am seven and I can barely write my name and I definitely can't ride a bike. And I can't tie my shoes. I sit on my bed, practicing for hours, but never get my fingers to move my laces up and around. I go purple and cry.

I do the same thing at school, especially during art class. One day, we are making tepees for Thanksgiving. The other kids cut their paper, put on glue, and draw on their new creations with Crayolas. I spend a half hour trying to complete the first step, cutting a triangle out of my paper. There are no green-handled lefty scissors, so I try to cut with my right hand, more like my right claw. I bawl and tell my teacher I can't do it. She watches me fumble with the scissors. She then grabs my face and yanks it toward her own.

"Stop joking around and acting stupid."

It takes her a few minutes to catch on that I'm not acting stupid. I just can't do it. She pulls out a manila envelope and stuffs my crappily cut-out paper inside and dashes a note off to Mom. I take it home on the bus. Mom reads the note and sighs.

"You know you're embarrassing me, right?"

Immediately, she regrets saying it. I can see it in her eyes. She's trying so hard. And I know she loves me. She cooks and cleans and listens to my long monologues about the Raiders and third-party presidential candidates. For hours, she listens. And then Dad comes home and I fly to him.

There are things I can do. I can read and I can run my mouth. Mom and Dad give me a boys' history of the United States for Christmas, and I memorize all the small-type bios in the back. Who's Alger Hiss? John Nance Garner? No one cares but me. There's not a subject that I don't have a thousand questions for: When was Halley's comet coming back? How could Joe Rudi hurt his shoulder while lifting a bag of groceries? Why did Ronald Reagan always look so happy?

This is California in the 1970s. My second-grade year is spent in a pod classroom where three teachers roam between ninety students. Everyone is always shouting with my voice rising above all the others until Mrs. Monaghetti loses it.

"Can you please shut up for a while?"

I try, I really do. My teachers don't understand. I take tests and finish in the top 1 percent, but I can't build a one-story house with Legos. At home, Mom says she's trying her best, but I'm driving her to the loony bin. I believe her. One afternoon, she puts bright red lipstick on and picks me up early from school. We drive the forty-five minutes to the base, me chattering away, her preoccupied with traffic and our destination.

I meet with a Navy doctor with tired eyes. We talk about Dad and what he does for a living. We talk about school and how boring it is. We talk about me getting along with Mom. After an hour, he pats me on the head, and Mom leaves the hospital with a bottle filled with white tablets.

It's Ritalin. I take one in the morning and then one from the school nurse around lunchtime. I can't tell you if they help or not. Probably not, because the school comes up with a new idea: I'll spend half the day with my regular class and half the day with special-ed kids.

This is a disaster. I spend afternoons with retarded boys and girls a half foot taller than me who outweigh me by sixty or seventy pounds. I cry and they cry too, but their tears come with rage. One day, a kid with a crew cut throws a Chinese checkers game at my head, marbles and all. I hide in a closet.

After that, Mom moves to straight bribery. Mom and the base psychologist come up with Snoopy Dollars; every day I keep my mouth shut and make my bed I get a fake dollar with a beagle on it. Once I reach twenty Snoopy Dollars I can buy baseball cards with the proceeds. It sort of works, and by summertime I have an almost complete collection of

1974 Topps cards, but Mom grows tired of keeping track. The contest ends.

"I shouldn't have to pay you to be good."

What does Dad say? Not much. He is a ghost.

ONE SATURDAY, MOM SAYS SHE NEEDS a break. She takes Terry shopping. Dad is in the garage working on his MG. He's wearing a white T-shirt and stained khakis. We live at the top of a hill in a new subdivision; I'm a little bit up the street riding my new blue bicycle. Well, riding it is a big fat lie. I'm six or seven, but still can't exist without training wheels. So I push-pedal up the street. I go by Mr. Lewis's house—the nice man who took me to meet Gene Upshaw—I've got so much new information for him! It's about Reggie Jackson and Fred Biletnikoff and that song "Seasons in the Sun." But he drops the garage door just before I get there. A couple of neighbor kids surround me. One boy starts in.

"You can't really ride that bike."

"Yes, I can."

"No, you're a baby. You need training wheels."

"Can too."

"Okay, ride it down the hill."

By now there are four or five kids around me. I hope for rescue, maybe the ice-cream truck? No, too early. Dad? Nope. His head is buried in the MG. I look down the hill. It is steep but clear, just one car at the bottom. The kids keep talking, crowding in on me.

And then I'm off. Did I jump or was I pushed? Doesn't matter. I'm flying down the pavement, picking up speed. I've never gone this fast in my life. And I'm not tipping over!

But then I start heading left. This isn't surprising. I do everything to the left. I'm heading straight for the car, actually a yellow pickup truck. I try to steer to the right, but I can't do anything to the right. I lean hard; maybe I'll miss it.

No.

How long have I been lying here? Thirty seconds? A minute? Ten minutes? Where did the kids go? My bike's front fender is twisted in. I see a small, sharp dent in the truck's grill. Mom isn't going to be happy. There are splashes of red on the handlebars. Where did that come from? I breathe in and hear a whistling noise. This is weird since I can't whistle. I feel a breeze on my gums. That's not supposed to happen. I put my hand to my mouth and touch teeth where there should be skin.

Only then does it hit me. My face is ripped open below my lip. Still, I feel calm. I never feel calm. I know Dad will kill me if I just leave my bike here, so I slowly walk it back up the hill. The bent front wheel scrapes and wheezes every time it turns. My red shirt is a darker crimson by the time I get home. I walk into the garage and put my bike where it's supposed to go. Dad is bent over with a wrench. I pull on his belt loop and he turns around.

"Dad? Don't be mad."

"Jesus Christ."

It's the first and last time I hear Dad swear. He picks me up and carries me inside. He wraps ice in a towel and holds it to my chin. For a second, he panics. What does he do? I see an opening.

"Dad, I just want to stay here and watch *Sesame Street*. Just one show."

That snaps him out of it. We're in his MG and the top is down. I don't even ask why we pass two hospitals so we can drive thirty miles to NAS Alameda. My chin is crusty and shredded, but I'm happy. I'm with Dad. We pull up to the base hospital and he half carries, half walks me through the doors. A nurse looks at me strangely. I know her from somewhere. Then it hits me: I know her from here. I've been here so many times the doctor told Mom that I should wear a helmet.

"Not you again. This is becoming once a month."

Dad blushes purple, just like me when I get angry! The nurse takes us into an examination room and peels off my blood-soaked shirt. I give up my towel and a compress is pressed against my chin. Someone comes in and gives me a shot. I look up at Dad. He gazes back, his face covered in a five o'clock shadow even though it is barely noon. He brushes the hair out of my eyes. I'm about to get nine stitches inside my mouth and nine more on the outside to close the wreck that is now my chin. And yet I'm smiling, so much that I can feel the crusted blood cracking on my face. I'm here with Dad and it's just the two of us. So what if I had to lose a pint of blood for it to happen? Doesn't matter. It happened. I drift away to sleep. I am happy.

BUT NOT FOR LONG. DAD GOES away for seven months. This makes me a minor celebrity at my non-Navy school. The idea that a parent can vanish for most of the school year seems like an episode of *The Six Million Dollar Man*.

Mom announces after Christmas that she's going to Hong Kong to visit Dad. Mrs. Borris, my second-grade teacher, offers to look after me. (Terry goes to a neighbor.) Every day after she finishes grading papers, we head off to a park with her soon-to-be-husband. We fly kites and eat ice cream. In the morning, I stand outside her bathroom and listen to her taking a shower wondering what could be going on behind all that steam. Mrs. Borris actually seems to enjoy talking to me. I don't want it to end. But Mom comes back. All Mrs. Borris gets is a cheap Chinese abacus as a thank-you. I don't want to go home.

Months later, Dad comes back. We drive to meet him at the base. We wait in a hangar full of balloons and moms talking about being horny, a word I don't understand. The sun begins to set and then Dad's plane touches down. He steps down from the jet—there he is!—and takes his helmet off. Terry and I run toward him, but Mom gets there first. She jumps into his arms just like Gene Tenace did with Rollie Fingers when they won the World Series. Finally, Dad scoops me up in his arms. He smells the same, Aqua Velva and sweat.

We go home and my parents stay in their bedroom for two days, emerging only to pour us more cereal and settle TV disputes. We head off to Mass that Sunday. Mom has a big smile on her face. There are guitars and the recessional is Woody Guthrie's "This Land Is Your Land," a choice that Dad complains about the whole ride home. I don't care. He is home and making me waffles for lunch.

And that's when my parents tell me we are moving next month. They mention a place called Whidbey Island and a new plane called a Prowler. I've never heard of them but I don't care. I'm seven and ready to move on.

Chapter Eight

TUPPER AND THE BLACK RAVENS FLEW their Prowlers on board the *Nimitz* on July 19, 2009. Or at least that was the plan. This being the Prowler, they flew two down and had to wait another day for the other two because of mechanical problems.

Tupper and Vinnie Johnson were getting along well. Vinnie loved Churchill and the Greek stoic Epictetus, while Tupper was working his way through Malcolm Gladwell and a Horatio Nelson biography. They both could babble endlessly about leadership and organization building well past the saturation point of their men, so it was good that they had each other.

Vinnie had started as a helo pilot, transitioning to Prowlers after he turned thirty. Switching platforms in midcareer wasn't easy, and Vinnie was known as a hard worker and a blue-collar pilot, the last part a backhanded compliment. As a junior Prowler pilot, Vinnie had been flying the second jet in a four-Prowler formation approaching NAS Oceana in Virginia Beach. The lead jet slipped out of the pattern and dropped down on Vinnie. The jet wash forced his plane down onto the runway. His Prowler landed hard on its nose gear and then bashed both wings into the runway before sliding another 2,000 feet. Somehow the entire crew escaped, but the Prowler was totaled. Vinnie was absolved of blame—his CO was relieved for approving a dangerous flight pattern—

but questions remained about his flying skills under duress. Tupper would have to keep an eye on him.

But the XO and the CO didn't spend a lot of time talking about flying tactics in the first days of cruise. Instead, they worked on motivating an officer corps beaten down by Doogie. Depending on who was coming and going, the Black Ravens had about twenty naval aviators in the squadron. Only five of them were actual pilots; the rest were electronic countermeasures officers (ECMOs) handling navigating and jamming from the Prowler's other three seats. The pilot-to-ECMO ratio wasn't a bad thing from a civility point of view. Most carrier pilots are megalomaniacs with adrenaline addiction issues. The ECMOs cut the machismo and delusions of grandeur to a more manageable level. Prowler squadrons had more decent folk and fewer assholes than the Hornet community simply because they had fewer pilots.

But there was a downside to four-man crews. Prowler inertia was a well-known joke throughout the Navy. Prowler guys were world-famous for not reaching consensus on anything, whether it be the best way to approach the carrier or which Taco Bell combo meal to buy while drunk in Anacortes.

Tupper and his men had heard all the jokes. They were accustomed to shitty planes, the Northwest rain, and being forgotten up in the far corner of Washington state. But Doogie's reign had been different. The men hated coming to work.

The first step was making things right with his department heads, the lieutenant commanders just below Vinnie and him. The cliché of naval aviators relentlessly cruising the skies looking for bad guys was mostly myth. Now all the lieutenant commanders had day jobs running departments within the squadron. Some of them were crucial—operations (ops) wrote the flight schedule, safety made sure no one got killed, and maintenance (mo) made sure planes were flyable. Some were bullshit—administration (admin) seemingly existed purely to plan parties and write up awards for the sailors, while legal was a clueless officer counseling a clueless in-trouble sailor on his constitutional rights.

All the departments had one thing in common; they were time-consuming pains in everyone's ass. A Black Raven might spend thirty hours a week briefing flights, flying missions, and then debriefing. The rest of his time was spent doing a ground job that made him want to blow his brains out. (The Air Force has ground officers handle their paperwork. Of course, Navy guys thought the Air Force was full of pussies, but, secretly, they were jealous.)

The *Nimitz* was spending a week in San Diego working out final kinks before heading west. Tupper wanted the squadron to hang out together on one of their last nights, but the younger officers succumbed to Prowler inertia and couldn't get their shit together. They splintered into smaller groups and wandered off. This was merely a gang of twenty-six-year-olds not agreeing on a bar, but Tupper took it personally. He was now forty and "back in my day" crankiness was settling in. He grumbled that it never would have happened when he was a junior officer.

So Tupper and Vinnie took the department heads out to the South Beach Bar and Grille for beers and fish tacos. Tupper knew his department heads from his XO tour. They were like his children: smart, ambitious, and complete mysteries all at the same time. There was Todd "Beav" Zenter, the hard-charging Jerry Mathers lookalike, a small man who drove a big truck with "USNA 99" license plates. Beav was the squadron's top pilot and hardest worker—a fact Beav was not shy about repeating. Sitting next to him was the admin officer, Silas "Shibaz" Bouyer, a regal African American with a sharp mind and a droll sense of humor. Tupper knew Shibaz was going places. The Navy lagged far behind the Army and Air Force in senior African American officers and the Navy brass was trying to catch up fifty years in a single decade. Shibaz just needed to fly straight to possibly make admiral.

Nursing a beer and looking glum was Blake "Stonz" Tornga, a red-haired, freckled-faced father of five. His call sign came because his hairiness gave him a slight resemblance to a caveman. Stonz's oldest boy was a nineteen-year-old Marine who would be boots on the ground in Afghanistan while his dad was flying in the skies overhead.

Tupper liked Stonz personally because they shared a dark view of the world: something bad was always about to happen, might as well prepare for it. Stonz had done everything the hard way, working his way up from sailor to an NROTC scholarship at the University of Nebraska. Now he was taking over maintenance, a thankless job made nearly impossible with ancient Prowlers making their last cruise before hitting the bone yard. If it went well, Stonz would make commander; if not, his career would be done.

Then there were two middle-of-the-packers, Robert "Turd" Peterson and Chris "Linda" Lovelace. Rumor was Turd earned his nickname simply because a chair he sat in back in flight school had the word "turd" scrawled on the back. He was a good man with a charisma deficit and wouldn't make command. He deserved better, and Tupper made a note to look out for him. Linda was a Citadel grad who had the misfortune of getting airsick on a third of his flights. Tupper had no idea why he hadn't been detoured to a desk job. Tupper already knew Linda and Turd would be disappointed with their end-of-cruise fitness reports, but he needed to keep them from dropping their packs. That kind of attitude could be contagious.

That left Lieutenant Commander Doug "Crapper" Crane, the Black Ravens' safety officer. The Ohio-born Crapper never told anyone where his call sign came from, which fit his image as the squadron's enigma. He had soft blue eyes and a dim view of the Prowler's mission. He was an electronics wiz who knew the Prowler's jammers better than anyone, and he was building his own light plane in his spare time. But Crapper was an odd egg, never quite meshing with the rest of the men, irritating everyone by turning paperwork in perfectly—an art form, really—but weeks late.

The dynamics of every Navy squadron are generally the same. The department heads always think the junior officers are slackers and work half as hard as they did when they were junior officers. The JOs bond together as the Junior Officers Protection Association and think the front office are ass-kissing dipshits. To VAQ-135's JOPA, Doogie's reign just confirmed their ideology. Now it was up to Tupper to change all of that in the sixteen months he had as skipper.

He ordered a round of beers for his department heads and proclaimed it was a new day. Contrary to the previous regime, he wanted their input on how to make the squadron better. He told them his door would always be open. In his early speeches to his sailors, Tupper stressed a simple three-point goal: always do your best; always do the right thing; and take care of your fellow sailors. Tupper told his department heads that this applied to them as well. If they found themselves in a situation where the choice was between protecting their sailors and an arbitrary Navy quota for mission completion rates or some other bureaucratic mumbo jumbo, they should always put their sailors first. He said the Black Ravens should be more than a squadron to the sailors; it should be their second family.

This was all sunshine and rainbows in theory, but the department heads each had ten to fifteen years in the Navy. They'd heard happy talk before. Besides, some of them had seen Tupper's dark side when he was XO, a temper and impatience that ran counter to the soothing words now coming out of his mouth. They'd watched Tupper enforce Doogie's draconian orders without a word of protest. That might have been the XO's job, but it didn't fill his senior officers with confidence that things would really change. Tupper would have to prove it to them.

Their skipper tried to steer the conversation toward how to remotivate the junior officers in VAQ-135, but the department heads didn't have any quick answers; they were just as shell-shocked from Breining's command as the young guys. They all agreed that the Doogie scar would have to heal naturally with time.

A few days later, the *Nimitz* pulled into NAS North Island across the bay from San Diego for one last day of R & R. This time, the squadron hung together as a unit, drinking beer and playing volleyball at cabanas on the beach. Tupper walked around slapping backs and joking with the men. This is more like it, he thought; we're coming together.

Then he went back to his room. He called Beth and the girls and then his parents. One of the perks of being skipper was having a phone in his stateroom and he could call home whenever he liked. But this was the last chance on a clear landline. Saying good night to his girls filled him with an unspeakable sadness. The *Nimitz* pulled out of North Island the next morning, the California coast fading in its wake. Tupper and the Black Ravens wouldn't touch American soil again for 237 days.

◇◇

Chapter Nine

We leave California the same day Richard Nixon leaves Washington. Dad just shakes his head and turns off the television in our hotel room, and we start the nine-hundred-mile drive north. We arrive on Whidbey Island two days later, crossing Deception Pass Bridge in the fog.

I can't figure it out. Fog in August? Where are we, the moon? But then the skies clear. We drive through roads carved into lonely forests. I wonder if there are any people at all.

Then we hit town. "Welcome to Oak Harbor, population 10,445" reads the sign at the city limits. There is a five-and-dime, a furniture store, a broken cinema, some ball fields, and a burger joint called the Arctic Circle. We pull into the parking lot and order dinner. Dad heads off our doubts.

"Arctic Circle is as good as McDonald's."

Of course we don't believe him. But the burgers are good. We finish them and then head south out of town, a mile or so. We take a left onto a dirt road and there's a circle of almost-homes. Dad stops the car in front of our property, just a cement foundation and bundles of wood. Terry and I scramble out of the car and chase each other through the sawdust and nails. Dad flew up a month ago and bought the place without Mom. I've never seen him look this nervous.

"Barb, what do you think? They're going to call it Crosswoods."

Mom smiles and hugs Dad. There is light in her eyes.

"If you're here, then I want to be here. But I get to pick out the next one."

Dad smiles. He says that sounds like a good plan.

IT IS JUST A NEIGHBORHOOD, BUT it is my neighborhood. It is just a house, but it finally feels like a home. There are four bedrooms; mine and Terry's on the left of the stairs, Dad's study and master bedroom are to the right. Mom makes a never-ending rotation of pork chops, spaghetti, fried chicken, and marinated flank steak. There is a living room we never use and a family room with a twenty-six-inch Zenith color television that gets four channels and a stereo console that holds Johnny Mathis, John Denver, and Simon and Garfunkel.

It isn't base housing, but it's close. There are fifty houses in Crosswoods and probably forty of them are Navy families. Some fly the A-6 Intruder, but most are new guys here to fly the EA-6B Prowler. What the Prowler does is a mystery to me. I read enough war books to know that bombers like the Intruder drop bombs and fighters like the Tomcat fight other fighters. But the Prowler is a radar jammer, whatever that means. All I know is it seems crowded; two guys up front, two guys in the back.

Every morning Dad rises at six, showers, shaves, jumps into his white MG, and makes the five-mile drive to NAS Whidbey Island. He's gone when I wake up and sometimes gone when I go to sleep.

It really isn't that bad. Behind our home are endless trees stretching for miles. My parents let me roam. I head out in the morning and wander the days away. I find a moss-covered log and make it my second home. Every day, I lie on my belly, peer inside, and watch the ants and worms go about their business. What are they thinking? Where are their daddies?

I'm not lonely. There are kids everywhere. I join Cub Scouts and play tag and kickball with Billy and Eric for hours. The sun stays up well past nine in the summers and we ride our bikes until then, collapsing in dusty clothes on unmade beds. And then we do it again.

But then there's school. Now I'm eight and everybody but me can write cursive. I try but produce chicken scratch. My teacher laughs and says I'll make a good doctor. What is she talking about? I don't want to be a doctor. I want to be president. The same teacher brings out a typewriter and suggests I type all my papers. She gives up after two lessons.

In the spring, I join Little League. Dad drops me off at the sign-up meeting where all the kids are assigned to a team. He says he'll be back in an hour. I make him promise. The hour passes. Then another. I sit down, my legs trembling. Somebody's mom comes over and puts her arm around me.

"You're an Apache now, but where's your chief?"

Dad finally returns, screeching his tires like in the movies. He says he's real sorry and blames it on airplane joint parts.

Then it is opening day. Mom and Dad come to my first game. I wave to him from the on-deck circle. Somehow, I get hits in my first two at-bats and then line out hard to the pitcher on my third. I can do this! But it was a mirage: I don't get another hit for the rest of the season. Matter of fact, I don't get another hit in my three years of Little League. I am a left-handed batter, a strange and weird thing for third-grade pitchers. An outside pitch to righties is a ball in the ear hole of my helmet. Balls plunk me in the shoulder and in the leg, game after game. My on-base percentage soars, but I am so scared. I start having nightmares where I get hit in the face by the ball repeatedly. Dad works with me once or twice after school, but I can see him looking at the gold Timex on his wrist. He has other things to do. I tell him to go do them. I'm not even that mad.

He's gone more and more. Our house becomes two different homes: Dad is here home and Dad is away home. The Dad is here means supper at six thirty sharp when he's not night flying. Elbows are off the table and there's a smack if we sass Mom. My bed is always made—and made again if Dad doesn't approve—and bedtime is always eight thirty even when twilight still fills the perfect summer sky.

Dad is gone features a breakdown of civilization. There might be bacon and eggs for dinner. Maybe even Frosted Flakes! Laundry piles up and Mass is missed. We fall into the rhythms of his coming and going, slacking off and snapping back when he reappears. This pisses Mom off. She thinks she looks like a fool with Dad because she complains about us in letter after letter, but then Dad sees two scrubbed and behaved kids and wonders who is telling the truth.

We rent cabins near Mount Baker in the Cascades when he's home. Dad loves to ski and so does Terry. One day she'll race in high school. For me, it's baseball all over again. I snowplow five or ten feet, list to my left, and face-plant into a snow bank. Then I can't figure which way to swing my legs so they'll be parallel to the hill so I can stand up again. I usually just leave my legs and poles in the yard sale position until a grown-up takes pity and hoists me up.

Mom and Dad are desperate. They buy me plastic skis not

much longer than snowshoes. You don't even wear ski boots with them, just regular boots. The day after they arrive, I fish the box out of the trash and see that the skis are recommended for children ages four to six. I'm ten. My cousins visit from Michigan; all three of them are great on the slopes. They stare at my red plastic skis and then look away. I ask them if they will ski with me on Heather, the bunny hill, in the morning. They all make excuses and change the subject.

The next morning arrives too soon with fresh powder and blue skies. We drive up the winding road to the lodge, everyone chattering excitedly about moguls and jumps while I pray for a serious but survivable car wreck. Dad is driving fast without chains. It could happen.

No luck. I slip on my plastic torture sticks and head over to the beginner's towrope with both Mom and Dad. The problem is the skis are so short I can't pick up any speed. I go twenty feet and then come to a complete stop before toppling over onto the packed snow. I pick up the skis after the fourth or fifth fall and chuck them, almost beaning a toddler schussing by me. I scream at my parents.

"These are for babies! I'm not a baby."

Mom's jaw juts out of her fake-fur hood. She cracks her gum loudly.

"You certainly are acting like a baby."

Dad slips his tongue out of his mouth and bites it, a sign that he is trying not to lose it.

"Now, Barbara."

Mom has a point. I crumple inside my red snowsuit. Something tells me I am on the cusp of a brand-new level of humiliation, so I stop crying. I tell Dad that I'll keep working at it with Mom. She plays along with the charade. Relieved, he pats me on the head and skis away, searching for my sister and my cousins.

Mom and I wait until he is out of sight. And then we take off our skis and hike to the lodge. I fish out a Judy Blume book that I'd stashed at a back table—I knew I'd end up here—while she sits a few rows away staring out the lodge's big bay windows. She is a lousy skier too and quits for good that year after being run over by two Canadian hotdoggers. But we never talk about our shared misery. Instead, she starts staying back at the cabin leaving me alone in the lodge with my books.

I don't mind until the sun begins to fade. That's when I get nervous. The mountain closes at four so I sit near the window and watch for Dad's black jacket and powder blue ski hat with the word PROWLER written across the front.

I wait a long time. Pete Rodrick always skis the last icy run, carving down the mountain with the ski patrol and the other toasted stragglers. I stare out into the dark, petrified he's crashed. I relax only when I see the white ball of his ski hat. Life can go on.

The shitty thing is that sports are all that matter to me. I let them torture me. I beg my parents for a subscription to *Sports Illustrated*, and there's Archie Griffin on the September 9, 1974, cover of my very first issue. Every Thursday, I sprint from the school bus to the mailbox and then to my room. I read everything, even stuff on gymnastics. The thing is, I don't need to be great at sports; I just need to be decent. But I am nowhere close. I need Dad to help or tell me that stuff doesn't really matter. But he is always half a world away.

Only in my room do things turn out okay. I come home, close my door, and correct the record. I lie on my bed tossing an orange Nerf off the ceiling, staring at my pennants, and reconstruct an entire season in my head. I always win, but there are hurdles to overcome. My team gets off to a great start, but then I'd break my arm or we'd get jobbed by the officials and have to claw our way back for the playoffs. I always play quarterback, a master of the short-passing game, working the sidelines and moving the chains. Soon, I branch off into other dream worlds. I run for president and lose the New Hampshire primary but slowly battle my way back, winning the Republican nomination at a deadlocked convention.

I daydream for hours. This drives Mom crazy. Every hour or so, she throws my door open trying to catch me doing something bad.

"What are you doing? Go outside."

"I'm just thinking. I'll go outside later."

She slams the door shut. Our fights are getting longer and louder. I start thinking that my very presence puts a sour look on her pretty face. She signed up for the Navy life, the kids, and the moves, but she didn't sign up for me. She doesn't understand it. Terry is good as gold and she sees her girlfriends with their happy sons. Then she looks back at me and I can tell she feels that she got screwed. I am a problem she cannot solve.

Everything I do confuses her. I dread playing sports, but then I watch the NFL for six hours without moving. It's sunny outside and I am in my room reading about Iwo Jima or Earl Morrall. She won't hold dinner for two minutes while I finish a *Sports Illustrated* story or try to catch the end of part 17 of *The World at War* on PBS.

"Just one more minute, Mom."

"Stephen Thomas Rodrick, why must you always defy me?"

Then again, her behavior confuses me, so we're even. She has patience with everyone but me. We scream and holler at each other, my tears of rage only stoking her own. But then the doorbell rings—Navy folks are always dropping by—and she rubs her eyes hard and pushes her hair back into place. Mrs. Barbara Rodrick, Pete's wife, magically reappears. She pinches her cheeks for color and answers the door with a smile. She is a different woman.

There aren't a lot of grown-up things to do in Oak Harbor, so my parents' social life revolves around Dad's squadron. The couples host progressive dinners in Crosswoods, with each house preparing a different dish. My mom bakes Cornish hens and piles her hair high on her head. I watch her get ready, always waiting for the grand finale: the ceremonial swirl spraying of Aqua Net. She slips into a red miniskirt with a white turtleneck and heads down the stairs.

The other wives love her southern charm as she plays a sillier version of herself, making fun of herself for not being able to figure out the lawn mower when Dad isn't around. Why does she do that? After dinner and drinks, the couples play bridge, sometimes at our house. I watch from the top of the stairs and marvel at the beautiful woman who has taken Mom's place. She plays the wrong card and my parents do a Disney version of *The Bickersons*.

"Son of a biscuit eater, Barbara, what are you doing to me?"

"Judas Priest. Was that the wrong suit? Sugar Ray Robinson."

Everyone laughs and so do I. This is a blunder. She catches me watching from the stairs. It is past my bedtime. She freezes me with her death glare. Busted. I blink in surprise like I've just eaten a Larry Holmes jab. But then I look again, and she is back cracking wise and smiling at everyone around the table.

I retreat back to my room and wonder what the hell I'm doing wrong. It would be easier if Mom were a crazy lady, not feeding me and screaming at the neighbors. I'd understand; I know there are not nice people in the world. But Mom isn't that at all. She volunteers for the Red Cross and bakes cookies for the neighbors. Her friends long to spend time with her. She's kind and warm and people love her.

I am her one true mistake.

Chapter Ten

THE MORNING BEFORE THE *NIMITZ* LEFT North Island, Doc told Tupper that one of his sailors was going to kill himself if he had to stay on cruise. Tupper had twenty minutes to decide whether to send him off or keep him onboard. It was an unwinnable choice: leaving him behind rewarded malingering, but he didn't need dead weight either. He sent the sailor off.

The next morning, Tupper ended the career of a fifteen-year sailor. Back on Whidbey, one of Tupper's petty officers had signed paperwork saying he had checked Prowler maintenance performed by a junior sailor. That was a lie discovered when a hubcap on the wheel of a Prowler's landing gear popped off because it was installed wrong. If the hubcap had popped off during landing there could have been a catastrophe.

It was just one incident, but indicative of a larger issue left behind by Doogie. Tupper's maintenance crew were like teenagers screamed at one too many times by a jackass stepdad. They fought back in a passive-aggressive manner, cutting corners wherever they could. It was obvious the bosses didn't care about them, they reasoned, so why should they give a shit?

The petty officer's faked paperwork was just the incident that was caught. Tupper had two options. He could give him an informal reprimand, put a nasty letter in his file, and leave it at that. Or he could take him to captain's mast, one step below a court-martial: the guilty sailor is forced to stand at attention in front of the squadron while the commanding officer reads off the offense, berates the sailor, and then strips him of rank or pay.

The petty officer was just five years short of retirement and took care of a special-needs son who desperately needed Navy insurance coverage. He begged Tupper to cut him a break. Tupper slept on it for a night. His approach to discipline had been shaped by his years at the academy. He'd arrived in Annapolis in 1988 with a chip on his shoulder, still pissed about his initial rejection. He decided he hated the place but would conquer it all the same. Like all the plebes, Tupper had someone screaming in his ear every day for that first year.

"Midshipman, how many carriers does the Indian navy have?

"I do not know, sir! No excuses. I will find out immediately."

"Goddamnit. Do it now!"

Tupper hauled ass to the library and dug up the information. (The answer was zero.) By the time he reported back, the upperclassman had forgotten he'd even sent him. He knew it was all a game to see who would crack under pressure, cut a corner, or commit an honor violation.

A fellow plebe committed suicide by jumping out of a window in his first year. Tupper's mother wanted to pull him out. Tupper set her straight.

"Mom, they're not yelling at me personally. They are trying to see whether I can handle stress. I can."

He detested the upperclassmen who got their jollies out

of terrorizing him for cheap pleasure. One upperclassman rode him his second year until he couldn't take it anymore. Tupper challenged the smaller man to a fight. They wrestled in a hallway at Bancroft Hall, and the smaller man kicked Tupper's ass. Turned out the guy was an all-state wrestler. He still didn't regret it.

But Tupper respected the less sadistic upperclassmen, the ones who were trying to teach him something. He thrived in a place he professed to hate. He rose to the rank of brigade adjutant his senior year, third in command of the entire brigade. A newspaper photographer snapped a picture of Tupper getting in the face of a scared-shitless plebe. His parents cringed, but Tupper loved it. He was teaching the kid something.

And now he had to teach his sailors a hard lesson. Shitty maintenance and cutting corners was going to get someone killed. It wouldn't be tolerated. At captain's mast, he busted the man from petty officer first class to petty officer second class, a move that would cost the sailor $1,000 a month in pay. Tupper's decision meant his sailor would be drummed out of the Navy long before he hit twenty years.

Through the cruise, Tupper would see the demoted sailor mopping floors in the mess and wondered if he had done the right thing. His decision weighed heavily on him and he wasn't great at hiding it. CAG pulled him aside after their daily staff meeting.

"Are you okay?"

Tupper blinked hard.

"Absolutely."

It was not the kind of attention a skipper wanted. He went back to his room and started an email to Beth. He wrote,

"I've never felt so alone" but deleted it before sending it. Beth had enough to worry about.

THERE WAS LESS THAN A MONTH before the *Nimitz* would be on station in the Gulf. Tupper had to sort out the maintenance issues fast. The air wing upped their tempo and there was a recurring refrain in the *Nimitz*'s launches and recoveries: Prowlers not getting airborne. One day the radios weren't working; the next day it was the regulators pumping oxygen to the crew. Then the slats on one of the Prowlers wouldn't come up after taking off. On and on it went. It was the cost of ancient planes, but CAG didn't want excuses; he wanted Prowlers in the air.

Tupper tried to tune out the white noise when he was flying. The cockpit was the one place where he felt at peace. He'd been flying Prowlers for twelve years, and there was a comfort that came with settling into the rickety pilot bucket of the EA-6B. It made all the other shit seem meaningless.

But flying as a skipper had its drawbacks. The Black Ravens were filled with junior pilots and ECMOs making their first cruises, and they couldn't all fly together for safety reasons. Well, they could, and some skippers insist on only flying with senior ECMOs, but Tupper thought that was asking for a mishap.

At night, a Prowler pilot needed a trusty ECMO next to him feeding him information and communicating with the carrier. But there was no way to become a trusty ECMO without experiencing some hairy nights that made your pilot want to punch you through your mask. So it fell to Tupper to fly with the junior guys.

A week out of San Diego, Tupper launched on a dark,

mist-filled night with Lieutenant Steve "Buttons" Murphy in the seat next to him. Buttons was a California boy and a former enlisted guy who'd made the transition to officer and was making his first cruise as an ECMO. Buttons' primary responsibility was assisting Tupper in his approach and "calling the ball," letting the *Nimitz*'s landing crew know that they saw the lights of the meatball and were lined up to land. But the creaky Prowler was filled with built-in booby traps. The cockpit fogged up on humid nights. If you waited for the first wave of condensation on the window before you flipped on the defog you were already screwed; you'd spend the next few minutes rubbing at the window with your flight gloves.

Buttons forgot to hit the defogger. The cockpit fogged up. Tupper cursed. Buttons tried to adjust the defogger while the landing signals officer on the *Nimitz* asked him to call the ball. Buttons didn't respond, his head down over the instruments. The deck asked again.

"Call the ball."

Buttons hesitated, confused. Tupper waited as long as he could, but then he aborted his landing and flew around the *Nimitz* for another approach. He slammed his fist against his seat and screamed at Buttons.

"You are fucking behind the jet."

Next time around, Tupper called the ball himself. The Prowler's tailhook dropped but skipped over the *Nimitz*'s four arresting wires. They had to circle again. They didn't land until their fourth try, a humiliation to Tupper. Pilots are graded on their landings and ranked against each other; he'd take a ton of shit for tonight's fiasco.

He stormed away from the jet talking to no one as he walked back to the Black Ravens' ready room, the squadron's office. He glowered at Buttons during the debrief but said nothing.

The silent treatment was one of Tupper's less successful leadership skills. He'd forgotten he had been in Buttons' flight boots many times. On his first cruise, his squadron was enforcing no-fly zones over southern Iraq. Their basic mission was flying circles over the country, daring Saddam Hussein's air defense to fire a surface-to-air missile so that the Americans could use it as a pretext to crush his missile sites, radar stations, and munitions factories.

Hussein wasn't quite that dumb, and the Lancers flew circle after circle above the desert. That was okay with Tupper. The Prowler didn't have a GPS navigational system like the Hornets and Tomcats, and its inertial navigational system was unreliable and often broken. Prowler crews were constantly on the radio trying to figure out exactly where the hell they were in the sky. Tupper would launch into the Gulf haze and try to find a Hornet to tag along with so he didn't miss his tanker rendezvous.

Landing on the USS *Constellation* was also a mind game. He couldn't quite figure out the Prowler. You could line up the A-4 from flight school behind the boat and it would stay level. The Prowler was an out-of-alignment pickup truck, drifting up and down, left and right without provocation. He couldn't keep it on speed. Tupper would give his Prowler power, but the jet wouldn't immediately react, so he'd give it more power and the plane would lurch forward and down, then he'd pull back on the stick to try and slow it down. On and on it went, Tupper lurching the Prowler around while his ECMOs sighed into their masks.

On final approach, he had the landing yips. His brain told him he had too much power and he was about to overshoot the carrier, so he'd throttle back too soon and the Prowler would land a second early, catching the number one wire and pissing off Tupper's skipper.

But that was long ago and Tupper didn't feel like cutting Buttons a break. Soon, they would be flying six-hour missions up to Afghanistan and landing on a pitching carrier in the Arabian Sea. It was best to scare someone straight now, not in October.

Besides, Tupper didn't have time to babysit. He had a squadron to run. He spent the next few days meeting and talking with his senior petty officers in the Goat Locker. He met with them down in the hangar bay and took their questions for hours as he tried to get them to buy back into giving a damn about maintenance. Most of them were still bitter from Doogie's reign, but he thought they were softening, nodding along when he spoke. He didn't tell them there were rumors that the *Nimitz*'s deployment might be extended to ten months because of maintenance problems with the USS *Enterprise.* There was no reason to crush what was left of their fight.

Tupper walked back to his room at night and tried to figure things out. He couldn't let his guard down with anyone. The sailors could bitch to each other, JOPA had JOPA, and the department heads could commiserate, but he had no one. Sure, he talked with Vinnie, but even with the XO he only said so much. He knew squadrons that went to hell because the men saw fear and indecision in their skipper's eyes. That wasn't going to happen to him.

So he called Beth and the girls. He knew he was waking them up, but he needed to hear their voices. Beth sounded like she was in her element, busy with her job and raising the girls. She didn't have time to miss her husband. Not yet anyway. Tupper understood that. Her voice was enough.

Chapter Eleven

THINGS CHANGE WHEN DAD'S AROUND. HIS buddies come over on Sunday afternoon and rehash the night before. They drink Coors smuggled back on cross-country flights in their Prowlers. I play with my Hot Wheels and listen to them talk about a pilot who lost his wings after attempting a landing without his wheels down. It sounds dangerous, but they are all laughing, so maybe landing without wheels is no big thing.

There are moments when we are like everyone else. Every other summer, Dad takes extended leave and we pile into our Buick station wagon for long road trips. We stay at Holiday Inns and giggle when he orders clam chowder and it arrives red and thin instead of white and creamy.

He turns highway drives into scary trips. He thrills at pushing another forty miles after the gas gauge reads empty, particularly in thunderstorms that force cop cars and eighteen-wheelers to the side of the road. Mom and I watch in white-knuckle horror. She whispers to him as she glances at the driving rain, "Peter, please," but Dad drives on.

Mom might let us skip Mass from time to time, but it never happens on Dad's watch. When we visit my grandparents in Alabama, we drive sixty miles through the Deep South to find a Catholic church. At home, there is a weekly battle. Dad is a devout Catholic but an equally devout sleeper. Every Sunday, Terry and I move stealthily around the house, hoping he will sleep through 10:30 Mass, the last one of the day. But then he arises at 10:07 and has everyone out the door in twenty minutes.

Even at church, Mom is the center of attention. She sits out communion because she is on the Pill, a mortal sin. My parents only argue about one thing when I am little: Mom's insistence that two kids are enough. Dad protests, but she won't give in. She tells him she can't take on more if he's going to be gone so much. But I know it's something else. It's me. I've scared Mom off.

At home, we have a picture Bible, but that isn't good enough for me. I find an old Bible of Dad's and start reading it cover to cover. My classmates read *The Hobbit*. I'm reading the book of Revelation. Dad always said the Bible is the word of God, so I take what I read literally. That means things aren't looking good for me. Stealing is a violation of the commandments and a mortal sin. Those who steal are going to burn in hell. This frightens me because I steal almost every night.

I wake up around 3:00 a.m., starved, and sneak downstairs. I grab a handful of Chips Ahoy!, sneak back upstairs, and eat them in my bed while listening to Larry King on the radio. If I die before I confess my sin I'll burn forever. Fortunately, I am a bumbling altar boy known throughout the parish for ringing the bells at the wrong time. One Christmas Eve before midnight Mass, the priest offers to hear the altar boys' confessions. He says we can talk to him face-to-face rather than behind the screen since we all know each other. This seems like a really bad idea. My turn comes and I sit in a chair facing Father Massie and begin crying hard.

"What is wrong, young man?"

"I'm a thief, I'm going to hell. Every night I steal."

"What do you steal? Money from your mom's purse?"

"No, I steal cookies. Chips Ahoy! cookies. Every night."

The priest sighs and hands me a tissue.

"God will not send you to hell for eating cookies in the middle of the night. If he does, you'll see me right beside you. God knows you're a growing boy. Tell your mother you get hungry at night. Go say two Hail Marys."

I say my prayers but I don't tell Mom. I'm not crazy.

She's already pissed about my grades. Every quarter, there's a mishmash of checks and check minuses. Mom stores them in a drawer and then throws them on Dad's lap when he comes home.

"See what's your son's doing? Absolutely nothing."

Dad doesn't say much. He looks at Mom and me like we're both retarded.

"Barb. It'll work out."

I don't quite believe him. I already know from books how hard it is to get into the Naval Academy. Dad must have already had his act together when he was my age. He is always in control. Was he born that way?

One day, he comes home early with a big smile on his face and a bottle of champagne.

"I screened for command."

Even I know what that means. He's going to be skipper of a Prowler squadron in a year or two. He is thirty-three. This is a big deal. But there's bad news. Before he can take command, he tells me, he needs to learn how to be a leader, so we have to move to the Armed Forces Staff College in Norfolk, Virginia, for six months.

We take a train across the country. My beloved Oakland

Raiders finally win the Super Bowl but I miss it, hearing the score at a Montana train station. In Norfolk, we live on base for half a year and the strangest thing happens: Dad is home every night for dinnertime. He plays in a softball league, does the dishes, and helps with homework. It's like we are on a long, glorious vacation.

But something is wrong. Mom has tears in her eyes every day. This never happens when Dad is around. At dinner one night, Dad says he has an announcement. Terry and I look at each other, wondering who died. But then he breaks into the widest smile.

"Your mother is pregnant. You're going to have a baby brother or sister."

My reaction is swift.

"I'm going to be sick."

I run into the bathroom and dry-heave for five minutes. I get that from Mom. We both panic at good or bad news. I come out and Terry and my parents are still sitting on our couch. In Dad's eyes, I can see the light: he looks so happy. But Mom looks like me. Dad puts his arm around her and smiles, but she says nothing. Late at night, I hear them talking. Mom sounds like she's crying.

"Barb, this is going to be different. In two years, I'm done with sea duty. I'll be there this time."

My reaction to the news continues to be less than ideal. Mom's belly grows and I get squirrelly. In my twisted head, the presence of new life makes me realize I'm going to die. I don't like that. I do the math; under the best of circumstances I might make it to 2050. That doesn't seem that far away. At night, I think of my grandparents: they must have been young once, right? Now they smell of mothballs and Avon and Budweiser. Soon, they'll be gone, and then my parents, and then me.

It's one of the first days of Lent. I've given up sweets, and one afternoon I pace the rooms in our house alone battling sugar withdrawal. Mom comes home from the grocery store and I'm crying in the kitchen.

"What's wrong with you? Did you hurt yourself? You weren't whittling, were you?"

"I don't want to die. Mom, I really don't want to die."

She drops herself into a chair and exhales loudly.

"Christ almighty, I can't deal with this. Wait until I talk to your father."

That can't happen.

"Please, don't tell him. I'll be good. I promise."

She nods and starts putting the groceries away, her left hand supporting her belly.

"I won't say anything, but grow up. I'm having a baby. I don't need you acting like a baby."

I can see her point. We move back to Whidbey in June. Two months later, Dad wakes me up in the middle of the night.

"You have a sister. We named her Christine Marie."

I'm groggy and don't quite understand.

"Who delivered her?"

Dad laughs and digs his two-day beard into my neck, equally ticklish and painful.

"Who do you think, knucklehead, the paperboy?"

But then Dad turns serious.

"You have to look out for her, okay? No matter what."

I tell him I will. I am nearly eleven and feel grown up.

"I promise."

◇◇

Chapter Twelve

NAVY AVIATORS LIVE ON THE LINE between bravery and stupidity, science and idiocy. One day you're planning a complicated twenty-eight-jet air strike over Afghanistan, the next your buddies are urging you to take a shit on a Dubai boulevard after your tenth Jack Daniel's. It has always been that way, fly hard, get drunk, and chase skirt. Tupper wasn't against it. His days with the Gutter Rats were filled with idiocy. He knew that naval aviators had the capacity to instantly toggle between the heroic and the moronic.

His Black Ravens were no different. There were rock stars like Beav and lovable goofs like Lieutenant Al Delvecchio. The son of a Reno cop, Delvecchio was a muscle-bound, well-meaning lout not afraid to call you a pussy if he thought you weren't drinking your fair share of Irish car bombs at a squadron bachelor party. Last year, Delvecchio had launched on a five-hour mission over Afghanistan without a piss tube, a piece of plastic you shoved into your flight suit when you had to urinate. He was dying in the backseat when his seatmate offered up a Ziploc bag that she'd brought a sandwich in. Delvecchio grabbed the bag gratefully and filled it to the top. His fellow backseater pulled out a cell phone to take a picture. Delvecchio triumphantly held up the bag and began waving it around like a water balloon.

That was a mistake. He caught the bag on a switch and it ripped. Urine spilled across the dashboard, shorting out circuits and the jamming pods. The plane limped home, and Navy accountants calculated the damage to be near $40,000. Delvecchio had his call sign: "Ralph," aka "Retarded Al Pissed Himself."

Tupper preached to his men that in the new, uptight Navy you had to pick your spots: one DUI, one blown assignment, and your career was dead-ended. But they didn't always listen, just as he hadn't listened when he'd been a JO. Everyone had to learn the hard way.

A few days after Tupper's flight with Buttons, a Prowler managed to get in the air with no problems. Flying the plane was Lieutenant Carl "Hot Carl" Ellsworth, a fun-loving South Carolina boy with a quick smile and a knack for finding mischief where others found monotony. Hot Carl had Turd next to him and Crapper in the backseat.

They were running the Prowler through some mandatory checks and were bored out of their skulls. But then they saw a shiny bauble just a few miles away. It was Midway Island. The location of one of the United States' most important naval battles wasn't even a naval air station anymore, just a deserted speck of coral surrounded by endless blue ocean. It was late afternoon and there were no other planes in the area. They had fuel to burn. Hot Carl turned to Turd and asked him if he wanted to buzz the place. Turd said, "What the hell," no one had told them not to.

It wasn't even much of a buzz. Hot Carl took the Prowler down to 1,500 feet and flew over the island, blasting his twin Pratt & Whitney engines. They noticed a deserted-looking airfield and a lot of birds. Crapper jumped on the radio.

"Man, what a hole."

They made one more pass and then headed back to the *Nimitz* and landed with no problem. The following morning, Tupper was awakened by a call from a pissed-off CAG. Hot Carl's Midway pass had everyone's panties in a twist. Midway's airfield wasn't active, but there was a controller on standby in case a civilian or military plane had problems while crossing the Pacific. The controller had already gone home for the day but rushed back after Hot Carl's first pass, thinking the Prowler was in distress. He put the airfield on high alert.

That was the least of Tupper's problems. The bigger shit sandwich was that Midway Island had been rechristened Midway Atoll National Wildlife Refuge in 1993. Midway had gone from world's largest naval battle to home of the world's largest gooney bird refuge. Someone at the refuge had snapped photos of the Prowler flying low and scaring the hell out of the gooneys. That guy complained to his boss at the Department of the Interior. The Department of the Interior then complained to the Department of the Navy who complained to the fleet in Honolulu who complained to the *Nimitz*'s CO. The shit ran downhill until it reached CAG.

Now he was hammering Tupper. He listened to CAG's complaints, but his initial response was a flashback to his JO days. He didn't say anything except "Yes, sir," but he thought "You've got to be fucking kidding me." Sure, no one had said they could fly over Midway, but no one had said they couldn't. If you couldn't blast your jet over a hunk of coral every once in a while, what the hell was the point? Let the men have some fun.

This was a mistake. That afternoon, CAG called Tupper and the crew into his office. He told them about the complaints. A smirk crossed Hot Carl's face. CAG let him have it.

"You think this is a joke? You think this is fucking funny?"

CAG ripped the crew a new one for twenty minutes. All Tupper could do was keep his hands clasped behind his back, saying nothing. The crew was dismissed, but Tupper lingered behind. He wanted to ask his boss a question.

"Did you chew them out because you didn't trust me to chew them out? Because I can chew some ass."

CAG said that wasn't it, but Tupper didn't believe him. CAG's punishment was making the crew chart and file new air maps for flights over Midway taking into account the gooney birds' nesting sites. (In the end, Tupper wasn't happy with the crew's work and did the maps himself.)

To Tupper, it was a ridiculous situation—a deleted chapter from *Catch-22*—but he noticed a change in CAG's attitude toward him. Gone was the "We're all in this together" bonhomie; in its place was "What are you doing now to screw with my air wing?"

The *Nimitz* hit Yokosuka Naval Base outside of Tokyo a week later. It was the ship's first port of call, but that didn't mean the work stopped. Tupper held another captain's mast, this time over maintenance leaving a small wrench in a Prowler cockpit. It sounded inconsequential, but when the jet started twisting and turning at five Gs, the wrench could fly up and bean the pilot or smash his instruments. Tupper busted three more sailors, but he didn't restrict any of them to the ship for the port call. Everyone needed to blow off some steam.

Tupper was no different. On their last night in port, Tupper and the department heads jumped on a commuter train and headed to the suburb of Kanagawa and a Korean barbecue dive recommended by Stonz who had been stationed up the road in NAF Atsugi a few years back.

They were miles from the ship and they cut loose, the sake disappearing faster than the beef. They talked shop for a while, made fun of CAG, and grew quiet when Stonz worried about his son on his way to Afghanistan.

They closed the restaurant and missed the last train home, leaving them with five hours to kill until the first morning service. The men were dressed like software nerds, in khakis and loud Tommy Bahama shirts, and the locals gave them a wide berth. There may have been some public urination. Tupper was particularly hammered. He mumbled that it would be awesome if there were a base with a Bachelor Officers Quarters (BOQ) nearby. The men staggered around a corner and found Camp Zama, a sprawling U.S. Army base. Magically, his wish was granted. The men high-fived each other; they couldn't believe their luck. They flashed their IDs at the guard station, and the MPs called for a van to take them over to the BOQ. They were all drunk and profusely grateful, none more than Tupper. While checking in, he asked the desk clerk a question.

"I want to personally thank the base commander for his hospitality. What's his phone number?"

The clerk wasn't sure if Tupper was serious.

"Uh, sir, it's 2:00 a.m. I think he's asleep."

Tupper would not be denied.

"Wake him up. I HAVE to thank him personally."

Eventually, Vinnie steered Tupper away from the desk. The men went up to their suites and changed into BOQ-issue kimonos and slippers. They hung in the hallway bullshitting for a while. Tupper was still pissed off.

"I want to thank the base commander. It's the fucking right thing to do."

Vinnie let out a sigh.

"Skipper, we can call him in the morning."

Tupper wandered away while his men kept talking. Then they heard the door to the stairs slam at the end of the hallway. That popped them out of their stupor. They looked around and Tupper was gone.

In their inebriated state, it took a few seconds for them to understand the implications. Turd and Vinnie sprinted toward the door. They stumbled down the stairs and were now outside. At first, they didn't see anything. But then Vinnie spotted a familiar-looking man a few hundred yards away hightailing it in kimono and slippers. It was Tupper and he was making a break for Zama's officers' housing. They gave chase.

By the time they caught up with him, a military police van had sidled up next to Tupper. The skipper was still on his mission.

"I just want to thank the base CO for his hospitality. Can you help me out? Which one is his house?"

The MPs were flummoxed. But then Vinnie flashed his ID. He sweet-talked the MPs into letting them walk Tupper back to the BOQ. Upstairs, Vinnie made sure his boss was asleep before he went back to his own room.

The morning came quickly, and the massively hungover men caught a ride back to the train. Nothing was said about Tupper's midnight run. They all understood. Sometimes, you just had to light your hair on fire.

But this was different. Tupper wasn't a junior officer pissing into a glass in a hotel room. He was in charge now. If he had found the base commander's house and awakened him at two in the morning that would have brought down more shit than a dozen flights over Midway. This was the new Navy. One call from the MPs to the *Nimitz* and Tupper's command tour might have ended before it really started.

Chapter Thirteen

MOM AND DAD COME HOME FROM the hospital empty-handed. Christine stays behind for an extra day because of a bad case of jaundice. What they do bring home are some hospital brochures on sudden infant death syndrome. That night, I read the words a hundred times. Could this happen? Could Chrissie just go to sleep and not wake up?

I remember Dad's words to watch over her. He leaves on workups a few months later. Mom is home alone, this time with three of us. She rocks Christine to sleep and then places her in the crib. I sit quietly in my room and wait. Mom drifts off to sleep, and I slip back into Christine's room and make sure she is sleeping on her back and hasn't thrown her blankets over her head. I do this every night before and after my cookie raids. Mom catches me one night and tells me I'm banned from Christine's room after dark. I disobey her the next night.

I'm in junior high now. I come home, toast up two blueberry Pop-Tarts and wait for the *Seattle Times* to be delivered. I pore over every page from "Dear Abby" to "Dondi." One day, I hear another Navy kid is moving away and the paper is looking for a new paperboy. Dad had a paper route when he was a kid. I can do it too! Mom agrees, reasoning correctly that anything that gets me out of her hair is worth a try. Dad is skeptical.

"You realize that you have to do it every day, even when you don't feel like it, right?"

I tell him no problem. The next Monday, giant stacks of papers are sitting in our driveway when I get home from school. Sundays are the worst. I have sixty customers on my route, but I can carry only ten or twelve Sunday papers in my sack without falling over. Dad walks the route with me in the mist and rain one Sunday, just the two of us. He tells me about buying his mother her first dishwasher with his paper money. I laugh out loud.

"I'm not going to buy Mom a dishwasher. No way."

Dad stares me down. He looks so disappointed. I try to backtrack.

"She already has one. She doesn't need one."

We walk in silence for a while. Then he tells me to save my money for something else. He's leaving again in the spring. But this time when he comes back I can meet him in Hawaii and ride the carrier with him from Honolulu to San Diego. There is one condition: I have to buy half of my plane ticket. I tell him it's a deal.

But that's so far away. My twelfth birthday is just six weeks away. Dad goes away for a month, but he makes it home just in time. There's going to be a party with Billy and Eric and Timmy. Then something terrible happens. There is a boy down the street named David Bruce. He is a year younger than me and has the only buzz cut in the neighborhood. I know he wants to be my friend and we play one-on-one football in his front yard, one of the few games I can win since I outweigh him by thirty pounds. I meet his dad after one of our games, working in his garage. He doesn't smile.

But then David and I have a falling-out over something stupid, or maybe he just gets tired of me being mean to him.

I see him on the school bus but we never really talk. Then, a few days before my birthday, David's father is killed in an A-6 accident off the USS *Ranger.* I hear the news, but it doesn't register. Dad comes into my room on the morning of my birthday.

"I want you to invite David Bruce."

"C'mon, Dad, he'll ruin it."

"I'm not asking you, I'm telling you."

I call David's house. His mother answers in a shaky voice. I ask her if David could come over later for my party. She starts crying on the phone, babbling thank yous through tears.

David shows up a few hours later in a too-big blue windbreaker that belonged to his dad. He gives me a hastily wrapped stapler as a present. I begin to roll my eyes and Dad shoots me a death look. I say thank you. We have cake and then we play football in the backyard. Dad makes sure David scores a touchdown.

MOM AND DAD LEAVE FOR A weekend in San Diego the next morning. We are left in the care of an elderly babysitter who smells of grape juice. The next day is Monday, October 2, 1978, momentous because that afternoon the Boston Red Sox and the New York Yankees are playing a one-game playoff. The only problem is the game starts at 11:30 a.m. Oak Harbor time. I'll miss it if I go to school.

So I hold my breath until my face goes red and tell the babysitter that I'm sick. She calls my parents down in San Diego. I sneak upstairs and pick up the other line. Dad listens for a minute, relays the information to Mom, and tells the sitter I can stay home. I can hear Mom in the background.

"He's faking, you know that, right?"

How does she know?! I watch the game propped up on my parents' bed on the $35 black-and-white television we bought at a garage sale. Carl Yastrzemski pops up to Graig Nettles to end the game and I run out of the house to do my paper route, miraculously healed. My parents come home a day later and Mom stares me down.

"I hope you're feeling better."

Mom keeps asking me what I'm doing with my paper route money, and I can't honestly tell her. Poor accounting is swallowing up my profits. I can't keep straight who I've collected from and who I haven't. I ring a cranky neighbor's doorbell one night and he barks at me that I'd just collected from him a week earlier. He threatens to call my boss. Now I collect just enough to pay for the papers and have some cash left over for movies and ice-cream sandwiches.

But Mom is convinced I have a secret stash of fifties somewhere and I'm up to no good. Dad comes home exhausted one night, and before he can open a beer she starts in with the questions.

"Pete, where is the money going?"

Dad's eyes glaze over. Sometimes, he spends a few minutes trying to help me figure out my bills, but once he becomes confident I'm not swindling anyone or hoarding big money, he lets me go back to doing it myself.

He is more concerned with my paper route's cleanliness. Dad hates litter. More than once, we'll be driving somewhere and he'll point out a pile of garbage and pull over and pick up the trash. He then turns to Terry and me.

"That's not acceptable. You will never do that."

Like most things, I agree with Dad in principle but not in action. I have giant plastic bags full of rubber bands for my papers and they start multiplying around our house. I'm watching television one night when my neck is hit with a fierce pain. I spin around, ready to punch Terry. But it's Dad. He's holding three rubber bands.

"Every time I find one, you're getting shot."

He shoots me another half-dozen times over the next week. For some reason, I don't get angry like when Mom is on my ass. I learn my lesson.

Some weekends, I get my friend Billy to deliver my papers so I can head up to the mountains with my parents. We just bought a condo up in the Cascades with Dad's friend Laddie Coburn and his wife, Ulla. Laddie is everything my dad isn't: a smart-ass who does what he wants. He's got an opinion on everything, even things he knows nothing about. He's cool. We show up with strollers and bags and Laddie waves from the couch and doesn't offer to help. That seems awesome. He also has a stash of European porno magazines that I discover. I worship him.

Terry and I head off to the condo's clubhouse every day to swim in the pool while Dad retreats to a log cabin owned by the condo association with a black briefcase full of papers. He's got fitness reports to churn out. Mom is left alone with Chrissie; she doesn't even have a television or phone. By dinnertime, she is exhausted. She complains and Dad does the dishes quietly.

Every night, he sends me to take the trash over to a dumpster about a hundred yards away from our property. One pitch black evening I make my way with a Hefty bag slung over my shoulder. I'm about to throw the bag in when a black shadow cuts me off.

"BOOOO!!!"

My heart explodes in my chest. I drop the bag and piss myself a little. Is it a murderer? Could be, Ted Bundy's back on the loose. Nope, it's Dad! He must have snuck out behind me and run ahead. His face is purple and a freaky smile is on his face.

"Did I get you?"

He did. But I don't understand. I could see Laddie doing something like this but not my father. I'm scared. I start crying.

"That's just mean."

We walk home in silence. Dad puts his arm around me and says he's sorry. I tell him it's okay. He opens the door and whispers in my ear.

"We don't need to tell your mom about this."

And we don't. It's our secret.

THEN DAD LEAVES.

I drift off at school. In science class, I write down all the bones of the human skeleton on seven Juicy Fruit wrappers, get an A on a test, and feel ashamed. Dad would kill me for that. But I can't help myself. I keep doing stupid things. I bring rubber bands to school and try to shoot a buddy, but I miss and hit my crusty science teacher in the neck. He walks over slowly and smiles.

"I think it's time for a swat."

Out in the hall Mr. Renegar gets ready to bring his paddle down on my bony ass. But first he tells me he's drilled holes in his paddle to make it more aerodynamic. Then he hits me twice. I scream and swear. That gets me another.

Mom is less than sympathetic. Christine has constant earaches and she is exhausted. She reads the note sent home from school and then tosses it on the dinner table.

"Good for them."

She immediately regrets it and tells me that came out wrong. I tell her I know. I go out into the rain and deliver my papers and on it goes.

I do nothing to lighten her load. The deadline to raise $250 toward my Hawaii trip comes and goes. I have $43 in my pockets. In my spare time, I teach my baby sister to walk into a room slamming her hands on her head screaming "Dopey me" in honor of something Robin Williams did on *Mork & Mindy*. I go on a father-and-son Boy Scout camping trip with someone else's dad. David Bruce moves away. Last I heard, his mother had been diagnosed with multiple sclerosis.

I taunt David Tapia in English class about how I'm heading to Hawaii and he's not. I turn thirteen and get a note from Dad: "Happy 13th. Welcome to Being a Teenager. Yuck!" Mom forgets and then makes me a cake at the last minute.

We barely speak. I stop constructing sports fantasies in my head and begin a new one: how great life would be if Mom were gone. I figure out what relatives would watch over us while Dad was at sea and how our life would be full of glamour and mystery. I'd be in charge of Christine; that part I could handle.

And then the opposite happens.

THE HELOS ARE NOT LOOKING ANYMORE. Mom takes Terry and me into the kitchen away from the chain-smoking wives bearing deli trays.

"It's just us now. We're used to that. Your dad's watching us now. Let's show him how strong we can be."

We're sitting at the kitchen table where Dad served waffles on Sunday mornings. She gets up, straightens her blouse, and walks back toward the grown-ups. I can hear her gasping for air. I don't know what to do so I do nothing.

The next day, a priest stops by. I am upstairs in my parents' bed staring at the ceiling. The priest is tiny and peculiar-looking with moppy hair. He sits down on the bed and puts his hand on my head and prays. He tells me to call him at any time; he'd be happy to have me over to the rectory or maybe we could go skiing. He says Dad was a great man and a good Catholic; he'd want me to be close with his priest.

I nod blankly, promising that I'll call him, but I know I never will. He gives me the creeps. (He'll be busted for pedophilia twenty years later.) The priest asks me to remember something.

"Remember all the good times you had with your dad. Those memories can last you your whole lifetime."

I try, but what do I have? I remember the drives to church and the lectures about littering. I remember a man who made others snap to attention. And I remember him gone. I remember a man who made Mom happy while I make her miserable. I know I do not carry one ounce of his decency in my bones. I wished Mom dead and God punished me by taking Dad. Simple as that. But I don't say anything.

The priest tells me one last thing before he puts on his hat and heads downstairs.

"You're the man of the house. Your mother is counting on you."

Chapter Fourteen

TUPPER AND HIS MEN SETTLED INTO the routine of a naval aviator at sea, vast hours of tedium punctuated by seconds of terror. A few days out of Japan, Tupper had one of the terrible moments.

The frightening contradiction of carrier flying is that a pilot has to reduce his plane to the slowest speed possible short of stalling for the last quarter mile of an approach to the carrier. Watching from the tower, it looks like the plane is suspended, barely floating, for the last few seconds before wheels and tailhook hit the deck.

On a windy day north of Singapore, Tupper's Prowler was at that tenuous instant when a gust whipped around the *Nimitz*'s tower. For a moment, the wind looked like it was going to push Tupper's Prowler down into the *Nimitz*'s backside. But Tupper anticipated the gust—known in the Navy as the burble effect—by a half second and went to full power. His Prowler surged up fifty feet and caught the two wire.

His legs quivered as the plane captain on the deck directed his Prowler to its parking space. He knew he would have been a goner if the same problem had arisen when he was a young pilot. But that night, he checked his email and found out Brenna had been cast as the lead in *The Nutcracker.* Tupper went back to the ready room and didn't talk about cheating death; he talked about his daughter's dancing skills.

The Ravens' ready room was an 800-square-foot windowless space just below the flight deck that served as the squadron's workspace and clubhouse. There was a small cubbyhole of an office for maintenance and operations and a front desk where a duty officer fielded phone calls. The rest of the room was a series of leather chairs pointing toward a podium at the front of the room where Tupper spoke about squadron business. But the star attraction was the giant plasma-screen television. Each night, the men settled in and watched the television show *Top Gear* and the movie *Beerfest* on an endless loop.

Tupper and most of the men were hanging around the ready room one afternoon when they were told that Captain Paul Monger, the *Nimitz*'s commanding officer, would be making an announcement over the ship's closed-circuit television system. His round, bald head popped up a few minutes later and told them the news the men had been dreading: owing to problems with the USS *Enterprise*'s nuclear reactor, the *Nimitz* would be extending its cruise from six to eight months. As usual, the guys on board were the last to know. Tupper had received info from folks back in Whidbey that *USA Today* had already reported the *Nimitz*'s extension.

Tupper and the men pulled into Singapore for a port visit a couple of days later, but there was a gloom about them. As usual, the officers rented an admin suite in a posh hotel, a sprawling 1,200-square-foot place that seemed more luxurious before twenty naval aviators moved in and filled one of the tubs with cheap beer and booze. Sure, there was the requisite binge drinking and Tupper ended up sleeping on the floor with just a bathrobe as a bed—the actual beds were first come, first served—but there was blackness to everyone's mood. The Navy was screwing them again.

Back on board, Tupper thought he had turned a corner on the maintenance issue. The sailors seemed to have warmed to him once they realized he wasn't going to be Doogie redux. They invited him down to the fo'c'sle—an area in the front of the ship that houses the anchors—for a chief indoctrination where three seamen were being promoted to chief petty officer. The sailors were blindfolded, spun around, and given hypothetical situations, and then they had to shout their answers. The petty officers let Tupper slip in front of the sailors, and they were screaming instructions back and forth. Then they whipped off the blindfolds and the new petty officers saw they were trading spittle with the skipper. Everyone laughed and Tupper thought: "This is why I joined the Navy."

He went back to his room and checked his email. Caitlin had sent him an essay she'd written about learning to kayak. He was amazed by how grown-up she sounded. But then he read the line, "I wish my Dad was here to see me, I miss him." His eyes clouded over. Tupper wanted to call her so badly. But it was the middle of the night back in Anacortes.

A WEEK LATER, THE *Nimitz* ARRIVED on station in the Arabian Sea, two hundred miles south of the Pakistan coast. Tupper and his men had their first flights in-country.

The Prowler mission was both critical and absurd. To reach Afghanistan, the Black Ravens flew almost 1,000 miles north—up the boulevard, in Navyspeak—over Pakistan before entering Afghan air space. The Command and Air Operations Command at Bagram Air Base would dispatch them to different quadrants where American troops were moving. The Prowlers would fly the route and see if the pulses coming from their pods could explode radio-controlled mines and IEDs before they blew up Americans. Then they would try to jam the cell phone and radio communications of the Taliban fighters before they could tell their comrades that American troops were on the way.

There was no way of knowing whether you'd jammed a Taliban warning call or blown up an IED before a Marine stepped on it, so the Black Ravens flew 2,000 miles daily not certain whether they had helped or not. All they knew was that the guys on the ground didn't want to move without the Prowlers' protective blanket. For Tupper that was an easier burden than the one borne by the Hornet guys—a Prowler squadron would never go to sleep wondering whether they bombed a schoolhouse by mistake.

The missions lasted six hours, but only two or three of them would be doing actual jamming. The rest of the time was spent on the commute and hitting Air Force tankers for more fuel. There was a solution to all the coming and going: place the Prowlers at Bagram in northern Afghanistan. (The Air Force had discontinued the EF-111 Raven, its radar-jamming plane, in the 1990s, leaving the entire mission to the Navy.) From there, it was just a forty-minute flight to the fight.

But that contradicted the Navy mission. The modern Navy was all about carrier warfare: the ability to put five acres of sovereign American soil on an enemy's doorstep. If you started taking parts of a carrier's air wing and stashing them on Air Force bases, the next thing you knew Congress might start reassessing whether the billions spent annually to maintain the Navy's eleven carriers was really necessary.

So the Prowlers stayed on the *Nimitz*. The borderline lunacy of the situation struck Tupper on that first flight back from Paktia Province in northern Afghanistan. He was hitting the KC-135 tanker for the third time in six hours and turbulence pitched his Prowler up and down, hundreds of feet at a time. Five miles up, Tupper had to maneuver the refueling hook of the Prowler into a magnetic basket connected to the KC-135 refueling hose. It was a terrifying illusion as a pilot: it was hard not to think the basket was going to fly through your windshield.

An hour later, Tupper landed back on the *Nimitz*. His back was killing him. He'd hurt it when he was a twenty-year-old Middie running from a rent-a-cop in the catacombs underneath the Naval Academy, slashing his spine against a heating duct. Now each long flight reminded him of his crazy days. He sat down in the squadron's maintenance shack and signed in the jet. Twenty minutes later, he asked a petty officer to clear the room. Once the room emptied, Tupper whispered, "I can't stand up." His sailor nodded and gingerly lifted his skipper to his feet.

But it was okay. His back might ache, but at least he was now doing something real, something that justified his family's sacrifice. That night, he got his first good sleep in weeks.

THE GOOD FEELING DIDN'T LAST LONG. Doc called him early the next morning. One of his sailors had been gravely injured.

The Prowler used nitrogen cartridges to blow down wheels and flaps if a mechanical failure prevented the plane from doing it the normal way. Seaman Ryan Headden was up on a ladder manning a hose refilling nitrogen through a

Prowler's nose wheel. When he was done, another sailor was supposed to cut off the nitrogen and then Headden would unscrew the hose. But something went wrong. No one turned off the nitrogen. Headden twisted off the pressurized hose and it whipped around and smashed him in the left eye, an eye unprotected because Headden had pushed his safety goggles to the top of his head.

At first, the injury didn't seem too bad. Navy doctors bandaged Headden up and sent him back to his room with ice and a Percocet. But Headden woke up the next morning and couldn't see out of his left eye. The eye socket had swelled and exploded, detaching his retina.

Tupper was furious. Where was the veteran chief who was supposed to be supervising the kid? Why was the most junior sailor performing tricky maintenance on a ladder while his superiors waited below? Why didn't someone insist he wear his goggles correctly?

But he pushed those thoughts out of his head temporarily. They needed to get Headden to an eye specialist as soon as possible. The nearest air base was in Oman, a two-hour flight away. Headden was bandaged up and prepared for a COD flight. Tupper dispatched a trusty chief to travel with the kid so he would be less afraid.

Then the phone rang again. The COD was broken. Tupper cursed. The damned CODs were always broken. They were worthless. The *Nimitz*'s command then made a compassionate decision. The 1,092-foot-long nuclear aircraft carrier with 5,600 sailors in the middle of combat ops turned west and hauled ass for six hours until the *Nimitz* was within helicopter range of Oman.

Tupper was grateful, but he also knew he was screwed. A sailor in his command had been injured while performing unsafe maintenance, forcing a warship to divert from wartime operations. Sure, the air wing kept flying missions to Afghanistan, but every pilot had to fly longer, every plane had to burn more fuel, every sailor had to work that much harder. It had happened on Tupper's watch. It wouldn't be forgotten.

Headden was eventually taken from Oman to Bagram where an ophthalmologist specializing in battlefield injuries unsuccessfully tried to save the vision in his eye. Headden was medevaced to Germany and then back stateside to Walter Reed Hospital. Back on the *Nimitz*, another Raven sailor put his hand into a still-spinning jet engine, resulting in thirty-three stitches. Tupper and Vinnie met in his stateroom and tried to come up with a new strategy. They lowered their goals. Instead of being the best Prowler squadron in the fleet, they talked about getting through one day without kicking themselves in the balls.

And he kept flying. On the long flights up and down the boulevard, some of the pilots and ECMOs bullshitted the whole way. On one flight, four Black Ravens spent five hours debating how they could introduce anal sex into a relationship after a no-anal-sex first year. But Tupper's flights were filled with silence. He watched rivers, sparse forests of pine, and small valley towns pass below him, saying nothing but what was required.

Back in his room, he stared at pictures of Beth and the kids and some Churchill quotes he'd taped above his medicine cabinet for inspiration. He started dealing with an emotion he hadn't felt since he was eighteen. It was a dark thought he had not let enter his head before, not when he was at the academy, not when he was a test pilot, not even when he was Doogie's XO. The feeling was doubt.

But then he received an email from Brenna. She was stuck on an algebra problem and Mom couldn't help. Tupper typed up some math tips he'd learned as a boy. A little later, Brenna emailed him back. "Thank you, you're my hero."

That helped.

October burned by. It was supposed to be the midway part of the cruise, but with the extension they were barely a third of the way through. Still, Beth and the wives went forward with their midcruise dinner back on Whidbey. Tupper had all the officers write letters to their wives and girlfriends that would be placed on their dinner plates. Tupper struggled with what to say in his note. He settled with describing him and Beth as two proud trees whose roots had grown intertwined. He knew she would think it was corny, but it was true. It was also true that it was hard to find new ways to say I love you after twenty years.

Beth passed on some new school pictures of the girls and Tupper saw how much they had changed in just three months. A week later, he awoke to an email from Beth announcing in a sentence that Brenna and Caitlin had been baptized at the church the family had started attending two years ago. In an earlier time, Tupper would have been pissed at the unilateral decision making. But things that once seemed worth controlling simply didn't seem that important now. He hoped they would gain strength from the water.

Besides, there wasn't a lot of time. One moment he was

reading about his kids being baptized in Anacortes, the next he was 25,000 feet above 85 Charlie kilo, thirty miles north of Kandahar, listening to an out-of-breath tactical air controller huffing his way to the top of a hill so he could direct Tupper's Prowler on an aerial path to support troops under attack.

Naval aviators talk endlessly of mastering situational awareness, knowing where you are and knowing what comes next at all times while in the cockpit. But on the long flights back from Afghanistan, Tupper's mind would toggle furiously between home and war, mission and family. He'd approach the carrier and his laser focus would return, but then he'd see his kids' faces swim before his eyes as he parked his Prowler on the edge of the deck. Tupper knew his situational awareness was seriously fucked.

Chapter Fifteen

We lingered in Oak Harbor for just five months. There was an unspoken rule for widows: move on. All we did was remind our neighbors of the worst-case scenario. Besides, Mom said she didn't want to drive down roads decorated with homemade welcome-home signs. That was a homecoming she'd never know again. I completely agreed. I loved Oak Harbor as much as a thirteen-year-old uncoordinated, fatherless ADD boy could love anything, but now I wanted to get the hell out.

Mom considered moving us to her hometown of Virginia Beach, but that was a Navy town too, still too much blue and gold. Her sister Nancy insisted that we move near her in Flushing, Michigan, just outside of Flint. They were not particularly close, but she stepped up after Dad died—neither of Mom's parents made it out for the memorial service—so Mom listened.

Nancy was a tanned type A personality always changing in and out of tennis whites. She'd worked as a stewardess before marrying my uncle Larry, a suave dentist with a Clark Gable mustache who waltzed into rooms like he was starring in a movie only he knew about. They lived in a mansion and told Mom there was plenty of room until we found a place of our own. I delivered my last papers on April 25, 1980, the day of the failed mission to rescue the hostages in Tehran. We boarded a dumpy turboprop at a grass airfield just outside of Oak Harbor.

Our plane took off and banked south toward Seattle-Tacoma Airport. Crosswoods grew smaller and smaller in the airplane window until it was gone for good.

We arrived in Flint just as the auto industry was collapsing, but you wouldn't have known it from my uncle and aunt. There was a Cadillac and a Jaguar in the five-car garage and a lake house up north. Mom hoped my uncle would serve as a surrogate father to me. It didn't happen. I was thrown off by his constant presence. He came home for lunch every day, eating a sandwich and then dozing for a few minutes on the couch in his powder blue shirt as a game show droned on in the background. That seemed unnatural to me.

We moved to Flint before our house was finished because Mom hoped I'd make some friends before summertime. Unfortunately, Flushing Junior High was populated with kids in Reo Speedwagon T-shirts, known by a previously unheard term: burnouts. They smoked weed and cigarettes before gym. Back in Oak Harbor, it was hard to buy candy cigarettes. Here, no one cared what Dad did or how he died. At lunch, I substituted chocolate shakes for my ice-cream sandwiches. I drank them alone and then wandered the hallways, trying not to be noticed.

In June, we moved into a subdivision called Hidden Creek Drive. The subdivision's name was a lie; the creek was pretty easy to find since there were no trees. GM middle managers filled the tract homes. There were two cars in every driveway, most religiously washed on Saturday afternoons. I'd ride my bike around the neighborhood alone—most of the kids were much younger than me—and wonder about people who waxed and shined up metal just for the rain to fall and wash away their hard work. Maybe they had nothing else to do.

Mom kept it together for a while. Her father came out and the two of us finished our basement, which consisted of me hammering the occasional nail and then Grandpa following behind me, pulling out the nail, and redoing my work. The walls of our new home were decorated with old pictures and plaques from my dad's career, while models of his planes sat peacefully on the mantelpiece. But we never talked about him. Whole calendar years could pass without a specific mention of him. Dad's parents came to visit when I was fourteen, and his name was not spoken.

I no longer spent hours in my room conjuring up season-long triumphs on the football field. Instead, I devised narratives where Dad wasn't dead. No bodies were recovered after the accident, so the rest was easy. They had ejected in the Indian Ocean and were immediately picked up by an enemy spy ship, probably Soviet. They were taken to a secret prison and locked away.

But, somehow, Dad led a prison break. He took his crew across a no-man's-land of mountain ranges and deserts until they staggered, barely alive, to a friendly border. We received a phone call in the middle of the night and through the crackle we could hear Dad's voice.

"I'm alive."

The story usually ended with me sitting at a table with Dad's arm around me as he did an interview with the *Today Show.* The fantasy lived in my mind for years.

That first summer, we drove to Cape Cod and shared a house for three weeks with my father's sister, Lyn, and her four kids. One afternoon, I took the ferry from Woods Hole to Martha's Vineyard to see my Oak Harbor buddy Billy who was visiting his grandmother. Billy had two brothers, but this trip was just him and his dad, something I never experienced. I watched with glee as they short-sheeted each other's beds and talked about their Pinto having 4-60 air conditioning; four windows down at sixty miles per hour. I didn't want to leave.

We drove back to Flushing a few days later, and the following Sunday just Mom and I headed to Mass. We parked and I told her there was something I wanted to discuss.

"Billy's dad said I could live with them back in Oak Harbor. Or maybe we could move back."

Mom slapped me hard.

"You wanted to move here as much as everyone else did. Why don't you try helping for once in your life?"

She was right. That summer, Mom sold Dad's MG to her probate lawyer. Minutes before he arrived, she stared at Dad's car, still shrouded in canvas. I didn't know what to say, so I rode off on my bike. That night, Mom was stone silent. At dinner, she stared at me through bloodshot eyes.

"What?"

"Why did you make me do that by myself?"

I had no answer. Soon, September was here. I determined there was no way I would get out of Flushing High School alive. I begged Mom to shield me from the criminal element and send me to Powers Catholic, Flint's parochial school. This was a bit counterintuitive, as Powers was located in a sketchy neighborhood of Flint, the murder capital of the country. But then again, Mom had just moved us to a city with 20 percent unemployment; faulty logic was the family ideology. I told her Dad would have wanted me there. She couldn't argue with that.

Powers was not the sanctuary I imagined. Most of the kids had attended one of the county's K-through-8 Catholic schools. Many had friends dating back to first communion. I didn't know anyone. This wasn't new for me, but no one else was Navy, so they were more guarded. Strangers were intruders.

I went out for freshman football. In Oak Harbor, I'd been decent in football because the league was done by weight, so I was thirteen playing against ten-year-olds. Here I was a 104-pound fifth-string defensive back on a team of seventy. I stretched one of my dad's Naval Academy T-shirts over my shoulder pads for practice thinking it made me look tough, but I wasn't fooling anyone.

A wide-eyed redheaded sadist named Mr. Duncan was one of our coaches. He taught science, but Bunsen burners and splayed frogs were just the price he paid so he could stalk the sidelines like a Viking on a killing spree. Duncan lived for a football drill named Bull in the Ring. We'd all gather in a circle, start running in place, and make animal noises until Duncan screamed out two names, supposedly at random. Usually, he'd pair two kids of like size and talent. Other times, he went for sadistic comedy.

"Artis!" "Rodrick!"

Bill Artis was already six feet tall and weighed 200 pounds. I tried to go low on him, but Artis went lower. I was flipped up in the air—a rodeo clown getting the horns. I landed in the dust with a thud. No one made a sound for a moment.

The trainer checked my pulse. He assured everyone that I was not dead, and laughter became permissible. I would have laughed too, but I couldn't breathe. Bill apologized after practice but also suggested I might want to consider cross-country. I should have listened. I got in for eight plays all season.

I was placed in a number of honors classes because of my acute skill at filling in circles with a pencil. I found my people, so to speak, in Mr. Winchester's history class. One of them was Gordie, the fair-haired boy of our class. I'd seen him on the football sidelines—he smartly nursed a wrist sprain for the entire season—but he seemed out of my social class, aka the untouchable new kid. He was blond and an expert soccer player, the Flint equivalent of an Ibiza playboy.

In a strange bit of synchronicity, we shared a heritage: his dad was also a Navy pilot, if a distant one, living in Washington, D.C. We never really spoke about it, but any accredited child psychologist or sitcom writer could have predicted what would happen next. Together, we embarked on an unintentional competition to see who could have the most spectacularly underachieving high school career.

It was the fall of 1980 and we had an unhealthy affection for Ronald Reagan. I'd grown up in California and Reagan was the governor when I was a little boy. On TV, he seemed cool and handsome. When he ran for president in 1976, I read everything I could, rooting for Reagan with the desperation I usually reserved for the Raiders. I cried when he lost to Gerald Ford. Now he was running against Jimmy Carter. Carter was an Annapolis guy but not an aviator, and Dad and his squadron mates hated him, blaming parts shortages on his White House. Oh, yeah, he also turned the *Kitty Hawk* around, indirectly leading to Dad's death. I was not a fan. Gordie and I drew up business cards that read the Conservative Liberation Organization, ripping off Yasser Arafat. We celebrated Reagan's landslide by toasting milk cartons in the lunchroom.

Things at home started slipping away. Mom managed to keep us fed and chauffeured us to our various school activities, but her brave face was gone. Most days, she struggled to keep it together. I'd do puzzles with Chrissie while she fixed dinner with a furious clatter, banging pots and slamming glasses. We'd eat in silence, then we'd all go our separate ways: me up to my room to work on Dad's escape, Terry to talk on the phone with her new friends, and Mom to put Christine to bed.

My first-semester grades were a clot of B minuses with a single A in history. I gave them to Mom after dinner one night. She stared at the page for a full minute, as if she could make the letters change by sheer will. Then she threw the card at me, stormed upstairs, and slammed her bedroom door.

I could hear her sobbing. Terry came out of her room, rolled her eyes, and took Christine down to the basement to play. I sat outside Mom's door. I could hear her talking to someone.

"Why did you do this to me? Why? I can't do this. Why did you leave me? Why? Please, please come back."

I knocked softly on the door.

"Mom, I'll do better. I promise."

"GO AWAY."

THE THING IS, I DIDN'T DO better. At school, I learned that the quickest way to stop the other kids from making fun of you was to make fun of yourself. In religion class, I memorized passages from the book of Job and started doing impromptu readings to spice things up.

"My soul is weary of my life; I will leave my complaint upon myself; I will speak in the bitterness of my soul."

The other kids would laugh with or at me. I didn't care. I soon dropped out of honors classes. Mom took me to an adolescent therapist that spring. I sat through one session and couldn't get over his awful wine-colored suit. I was no fashion expert, but I knew no one dressed that badly could help me. At school, a sweet, harmless counselor came up to me in the hallway. He took me into his office and we talked for a few minutes.

"I want you to write a letter to your father. Tell him everything you want to say."

I told him I would, but I never did.

Chapter Sixteen

THERE WAS A BRIEF PORT CALL in Bahrain, but by late October the *Nimitz* had passed through the Strait of Hormuz and was back on station. On Halloween night, Tupper was back in his stateroom emailing the girls about their costumes when he got a call that his men were in trouble.

Earlier in the afternoon, Beav Zenter's Prowler had launched for a standard six-and-half-hour flight up to Afghanistan and back. All had gone well and they had dropped to about three hundred feet for their final approach to the boat. Beav murmured "dropping the gear," flipped a switch, and then glanced at the gear gauge. It should have switched from a barber pole to a wheel symbol after a few seconds, but the left one remained a barber pole. Beav tried again but the landing gear on the left wing refused to drop. He aborted the landing and told the *Nimitz* he needed some time to troubleshoot.

Tupper was notified. He'd flown the same jet the day before and had landing-gear issues, but maintenance had promised him that everything had been fixed. He ran down ladders and hallways to the Carrier Air Traffic Control Center (CATCC, pronounced *cat-see*), a labyrinthine room that serves as the *Nimitz*'s night-flying nerve center. The CATCC was kept cinema cool to protect its stacks of tracking devices and navigational computers. Tupper stepped into the room and saw officers from each squadron sitting on two rows of benches, a sort of Star Chamber for those in the sky. A large glass computer screen was illuminated with the numbers of each jet in the air. Once a plane landed, its number vanished from the screen. Soon, all that was left on the screen was Beav's Prowler. Vinnie was on the radio with the crew. Tupper took over.

He tried to remember quickly who was next to Beav in the Prowler. Vinnie told him Chicken was in the front seat, and he exhaled. Matt "Chicken" Choquette was his best ECMO, a rock star in the making. He was already legendary for reaching over and pushing the throttle to full power when a rookie pilot he was training almost plowed into a flight deck. If anyone was going to have a shitty night, Tupper was glad it was Chicken and Beav.

A tanker was launched and gave the Prowler more fuel and did a visual inspection of the jet. It was no joke: the wheels were not down. Beav took the Prowler up to 10,000 feet and began throwing it around, tilting the wings and dropping altitude quickly, the aerodynamic equivalent of kicking the vending machine in hopes your Twinkie will fall. Nothing worked.

The *Nimitz* had three options, none of them promising. The flight deck could rig a barricade of net and cables and let the Prowler do a controlled crash landing. But there could be a fire or the barricade might not hold. Another choice was to have Beav pull the jet parallel to the *Nimitz* so the crew could do a controlled ejection. Hopefully, the helos could pick them up within ten minutes. But it was a dark, moonless night. A lot could go wrong with an ejection—a parachute could not deploy or the force of the ejection might knock one of the crew unconscious so he drowned.

The third choice was safer if equally daunting: gas Beav's Prowler up and send it 650 miles southwest to Masirah Air Base in Oman. There were dangers in sending a bone-tired crew to a strange airfield in the middle of the night, but Masirah had a 10,000-foot runway with an arresting wire that could stop the Prowler in about 200 feet. That would forgive a lot. After a quick discussion, CAG sent Beav to Masirah.

Tupper stayed on the phone with Beav for the next thirty minutes. He told them this had happened to a buddy of his and suggested they try landing on the right side of the runway since once they hit pavement the lack of a left wheel would naturally drag them to the left. Beav and Chicken said they were on top of it.

The *Nimitz* launched Mongo Koss, a Hornet skipper, to fly with Beav to Masirah and help him figure out the airfield. After an hour, both planes drifted out of the *Nimitz*'s radio range. The CATCC went silent. Tupper thought of Navy chaplains having to visit wives back on Whidbey. He said a silent prayer.

About an hour later, Beav and Chicken found Masirah and woke up the controller—battling a language barrier until he finally turned on the field's landing lights. They made a low pass, sussing out the field. Satisfied, they circled back around and prepared a final approach.

Beav told his crew this might be the time to get right with God. They quickly briefed over what to do if the landing went south. The Prowler was a tank of a plane that didn't have a record of flipping even on crash landing. Everyone decided if the Prowler hit a truck or a shed they were going to stick with the bird and ride it out.

A minute later, the Prowler landed on its right wheel, bouncing a bit, before listing to the left and grinding to a stop—sparks flying—a mile down the runway. They were safe.

About an hour later, Mongo's Hornet came back to the *Nimitz* with the good news. A quick cheer went up in the CATCC. CAG came over to Tupper and shook his hand. He told him that Tupper and Beav's coordination of the emergency had been flawless, much better than a Hornet squadron in a similar situation. Tupper said thank you.

He went back to the ready room and high-fived some of his men. He then walked to CAG's stateroom and called Beth. (CAG had the best phone line on the boat.) He wanted her to tell all the wives that there had been an accident but everyone was okay. But he got Brenna instead. His oldest daughter listened carefully and took down the names of the aviators involved. She double-checked the spelling and told her father she'd make sure her mother got the information right away. Tupper hung up the phone and took a deep breath. Somehow his men were safe and his daughter was now a young woman. He wasn't sure how it all had happened.

CRAPPER CRANE SEEMED LIKE AN UNLIKELY candidate to screw up Tupper's command tour beyond all recognition. He had a soft smile and kind eyes and his Navy career had been a series of horseshoes found in beds of four-leaf clover. Crane was commissioned a naval aviator in 1997, and his career became a series of diminished dreams. He wanted to fly Tomcats; he got Prowlers. He wanted to be a pilot; the Navy slid him over to ECMO. He handled the disappointments gracefully—there were some side benefits to being off the fast track. He was assigned to VAQ-134, the first Prowler squadron that went expeditionary, aka land-based. There was no JO jungle—an eight-bunk, fart-filled room on a carrier housing junior officers—for Crapper. Instead, he flew missions enforcing the no-fly zone over Iraq for six months from Incirlik, Turkey, a gig so lush that when the CO said a flight crew could go home to Whidbey a month early, no one volunteered.

Crane was then accepted into the Naval Postgraduate School in Monterey, California, to earn a master's in aeronautical engineering. But the month before he was supposed to start, NPS eliminated the aeronautical engineering major. The Navy felt bad, so they sent Crane off to an air force program at Ohio State University, an hour from his boyhood home.

His luck didn't end there. After graduating, he was sent to NAS Point Mugu in southern California, where he helped design new jamming pods for the Prowler. The great thing about the Point Mugu job was that few in his department had a Prowler security clearance. Crapper worked in a building separate from his bosses. He enjoyed five years of shore duty while the rest of the post-9/11 Navy did cruise after cruise.

Even the backwater job broke his way. Most of the eggheads in his department were getting out to take lucrative jobs in aero defense fields, so when it came time for his fitness report, Crapper was competing against no one. He was promoted to lieutenant commander and made department head.

And that's where Crapper's gravy train left the rails and plunged into a canyon, taking innocents with him. His first misfortune was being assigned to Doogie's squadron. The Black Ravens were on the *Nimitz* when Crane joined, and Doogie and Tupper were baffled when they learned that Crapper had no experience flying around the boat at night and no experience managing sailors.

Tupper watched Crane bumble his way through a tour as safety officer. A department head's job is to make sure the work gets done and, hopefully, foster leadership skills in his men and women. Sometimes, you had to drop the hammer on sailors underperforming and cajole or scare them into doing better. Crapper would do the exact opposite. He'd show up outside Tupper's office pleading the case of a chronically late sailor or other screwup and write Doogie memos pleading for leniency. Doogie responded by writing WTF in red ink all over the page.

Tupper spent an exorbitant amount of time trying to figure Crapper out during his XO tour. They both owned Harleys, and Tupper invited Crapper to ride with him from Whidbey to Reno for 2008's Tailhook Convention, the annual gathering of naval aviators. They drove through the Cascades, waited out rain storms in underpasses, and drank whiskey past midnight. Three days and 1,600 miles later, Tupper thought he had a handle on Crapper. He was a smart and decent guy—just not someone cut out for military leadership. No one had mentored Crapper, so how could he know how to lead men? Everyone else had cut him slack and now Crapper was hanging himself. But Tupper decided Crapper was essentially harmless, he just had to surround him with good people and keep an eye on him. If everyone else in the squadron was tough and tight, they could carry Crapper.

Tupper knew he had underestimated the problem after the cut-and-paste incident. Crapper had moved on to admin department head. He was writing a fitness report for a sailor up for a promotion but was having trouble downloading the form from the chronically frozen Navy computer system. Frustrated, he took a picture on his computer of the form, converted it into a pdf, printed it out, and typed in the information.

He gave Tupper the fit rep and Tupper did a double take. The words and fonts didn't match up. It looked like a ransom note written with words cut out of a newspaper. Tupper tried not to lose it. Did his department head really think they could send this into the Bureau of Naval Personnel?

"Doug, we can't send this in."

"Why, skipper? All the information is there."

"Doug, get the hell outta my sight. I can't talk to you right now."

Crapper's face crumpled. A few days later, Tupper fired him as admin officer. He reassigned him back to safety, a semi-bullshit job where you made sure everyone wore a helmet on the flight deck and didn't drive drunk when back on Whidbey. The only real responsibility he had was writing an accident report if the Black Ravens had an accident involving one of its planes. Fortunately for Tupper, VAQ-135 hadn't had a mishap in a decade.

Then came Oman. At first, it was a triumphant moment. Beav and the crew returned to the *Nimitz* to hugs and jokes. Tupper sent a maintenance crew out to fix the Prowler. On board, Crapper began writing the accident report. Navy mishaps are ranked as either class Alpha, Bravo, or Charlie in descending order of damage. If an accident is ruled an Alpha or a Bravo, the flight crew is grounded until a full report is reviewed by senior command. It's up to the safety officer to get a damage estimate from the maintenance crew repairing the plane and make a call on the accident's classification. Tupper asked Crapper where the Oman incident fell and he confidently answered, "Definitely a class Charlie."

Beav, Chicken, and the rest of the crew were cleared to fly. Meanwhile, Crapper dragged his feet on the safety report. Tupper started getting a bad feeling in his gut. A few days later, Crapper came down to Tupper's stateroom with some bad news. The evaluation of the Prowler's damage had just come in from Oman. Upon further review, the accident was definitely a class Bravo.

The veins on Tupper's head started to throb. Now he would have to tell CAG that Black Ravens were flying who had no business flying. CAG's response was typical. He barked at Tupper.

"How the hell do you not know that? You really have a shitty safety officer."

"Yes, sir."

Tupper started the painful process of getting Beav and his crew waivers from fleet command for flying when they shouldn't be. On a whim, Tupper ran the numbers on the accident. Turned out, Crapper had done the math wrong. The accident was actually, still, a class Charlie. Tupper had humiliated himself with CAG and the Navy brass for no reason. He had to make another call to CAG telling him everything was okay.

Tupper wrote an official letter of reprimand for Crapper

that would have ended his career if he had submitted it, but he kept it on his laptop. A few weeks later, Crapper finished the accident report. Tupper read it with admiration; it was a magnum opus, the most thorough investigation of a class Charlie mishap he'd ever read. But by then it didn't matter. Tupper joked that the Gutenberg Bible published in the twenty-first century goes out with a whisper.

By then, Tupper had fired Crapper again. Crapper would have no further responsibility for the rest of the cruise except to fly and compile the standard cruise video that would serve as a memento for the Black Ravens at the end of the deployment. (Three years later, the squadron was still waiting on the cruise video.)

Tupper was furious at Crapper, but he was angrier with himself. He'd put his fate in the hands of someone else.

◇◇◇

Chapter Seventeen

My sophomore year, Gordie told me about an after-school scam called Model UN. Four or five nerd students picked a country—any would do—you researched the country, and then in the spring you'd go to a fancy-pants hotel and pretend you were that country at the United Nations.

Our principal signed off provided we found a teacher who would serve as our chaperone. Gordie and I immediately thought of Mr. Richardson, our pipe-smoking European history teacher. His thick glasses and droopy mustache made him look like a warlock. He found out Dad was a Navy pilot and exhorted me to look for old manuals in the basement and bring them in for him to copy and digest. I thought he was a god or a spy.

Mr. Richardson agreed to be our chaperone by simply arching the bushy brows that set off his dilated pupils. We picked Norway and did some cursory reading in encyclopedias and almanacs. They had icebergs and the band a-ha. That seemed like plenty of information. We needed some girls to balance out the delegation, so we drafted the Dodson sisters, some brainiac odd ducks who lived out near me in Flushing.

Mr. Dodson gave us a ride to the parking lot where a chartered bus waited to take us cross-state to the Kalamazoo Hilton for the four-day session. He was an auto exec and rattled on about the decline of the auto industry and how it was all Reagan's fault. I interrupted him, offering him an opinion from *National Review* that I'd recently started reading at school.

"Autoworkers make too much money. Twice as much as schoolteachers. Layoffs get rid of the lazy ones. American cars suck."

Mr. Dodson shook his head.

"You are the most cynical fifteen-year-old that I've ever met."

I went red. I didn't quite know what cynical meant, but I knew it wasn't a compliment. No one ever described Dad as a cynic.

We registered at the Hilton a few hours later. Mr. Richardson signed his name to the chaperone list with a flourish. He shook our hands and promptly left town. Mr. Dodson's words still stung. I went up to our room and began chugging vodka I had smuggled inside a shampoo bottle. I then staggered downstairs for a committee hearing. Next thing I remembered, the blue-blazer guys from Shaker Heights, Ohio, were screaming at me.

"Norway is voting out of character, out of character!"

Apparently, I'd cast a crucial vote making Norway a supporter of the Soviet police action in Afghanistan. I switched my vote but the Shaker Heights guys still eyed me suspiciously. The next three days went by in a blur. The conference threatened to throw us out because of Mr. Richardson's vanishing act, but we begged and told them Model UN participation was a crucial component to our Georgetown School of Foreign Service applications. The chaperones relented and we promptly thanked them by skipping out on a crucial General

Assembly vote so we could go watch *Das Boot*, the first foreign film I'd ever seen.

The final night vanished with Gordie wooing a lass from the Romanian delegation while I passed out with my arms wrapped around our toilet. The bus ride home was torture, but I somehow convinced my mom that I had the flu. I lay in my bed that night cotton-mouthed and fuzzy-headed, knowing there was more to life than just Flushing, Michigan. I just had to find it.

But Mom seemed hell-bent on stopping it from happening. I started subscribing to the *New Yorker* and the *Village Voice* after hearing Gordie and his friends casually name-drop them at school. Mom complained about the mess they created. I started reading about film and built a Sunday around watching Peter Weir's *Gallipoli* on cable. It was a sunny day and Mom banged plates around muttering that I should be outside. Dinner hit the table about ten minutes before the Australians made their last, futile charge. She walked over and snapped off the television.

"It's dinnertime."

I sat down at the table and glared at her. She slammed my steak down in front of me. My sisters stared at their plates. I seethed inside for a minute before exploding.

"Just because you're so unhappy doesn't mean you have to make everyone else unhappy."

She slung a fork at me. It shattered my milk glass, white droplets drenching everyone. Mom stood up with her fists clenched.

"I thank God every day that your father is not here to see what you've become."

She bolted to her room and slammed the door. This time, the sobbing lasted all night long. For days, she made us dinner and took care of Christine but did it in virtual silence. Once Christine was put to bed, she'd lock herself in her bedroom and we wouldn't see her until the next morning.

It got so bad Aunt Nancy drove over one Sunday. I was mowing the lawn when Nancy burst out of the house and grabbed me by my collar.

"Do you know what today is?"

"No."

"It's Mother's Day. And you did nothing. No card, nothing! What is wrong with you? This has to stop."

I stared at the ground while she drove back to her perfect home on the perfect golf course with the perfect kids who remembered Mother's Day. I tried to apologize to Mom, but she was already sequestered in her room.

There were times when the only frayed strand holding our family together was Christine. She was now five, with big brown eyes perpetually dazed in a state of wonder. Her innocence could make you cry; there was joy in her every move, in her recitation of her favorite Smurfs. The rest of us could agree on nothing except our love for her. We found happiness playing Candyland or taking her for vanilla chocolate swirl cones and watching her dribble ice cream down her shirt. It was blessed light amidst all the darkness.

My grades continued their long slog to the bottom. I wouldn't show up until third period some days, clutching a poorly forged note composed by the Dodson girls claiming extensive dental work. No one seemed to notice I never wore braces. I wasn't getting stoned in the parking lot; I was at the

Flint Public Library, reading back issues of *Rolling Stone* and *Melody Maker*, devouring stories about New Romantic bands. I wanted to be part of a different world, any other world.

The school was complaining to Mom about my behavior on an almost weekly basis. The problem was the old story: I'd sit in the back of class and daydream or bullshit rather than add anything constructive. The calls usually came late in the afternoon. I'd hear Mom pick up the phone and I'd eavesdrop. She'd hang up the phone and come looking for me, her voice breaking as she started swatting at me with backhands that were more comical than brutal. I'd laugh and she would lose it.

"I don't know what game you're playing, mister, but this is going to end. You're going to leave this house and I'm not going to feel bad about it."

She slammed my door. I came home the next week to military school brochures scattered on my bed.

WE AGREED ON THAT ONE THING: the idea of getting me somewhere far away. Mom saw me in a uniform getting screamed at by some tyrant. Me? I wanted to be somewhere like the places I read about in the piles of magazines and books that filled my bedroom.

That fantasy world I dreamed about was vaguely British for some reason. I'd become an Anglophile, which in early 1980s Flint made me a jackass. I blamed it on Gordie and another buddy named Jim. Despite the fact that they both grew up on the not always happy-making streets of Flint, the two of them had developed an obsession with the United Kingdom. Gordie even looked like Sebastian Flyte as played by Anthony

Andrews in the BBC's *Brideshead Revisited.* Except he wasn't gay and it's doubtful Sebastian ever placed his face against a yellow legal pad and said, "Man, look how greasy my face is!" Jim's take was more rock 'n' roll, perhaps most tragically summed up by his insistence on wearing a Clash T-shirt from their *Cut the Crap* tour, which was actually just crap.

Somehow, the American version of Anglo mutated into preppiness. We all wished we went to a prep school. They just seemed cooler. Jim and I almost picked up two blondes at a Catholic teen dance by saying we were lacrosse players from nearby Cranbrook.

No human being better personified the American prepster-as-Brit than William F. Buckley Jr., *Firing Line* host, spy novelist, and former New York City mayoral candidate. Buckley spoke in a clipped, hesitating manner accentuated by arching eyebrows. This was quite exotic to us. We worshipped him from our Conservative Liberation Organization days.

That spring, the Flint chamber of commerce disregarded the double-digit unemployment rate, pooled their savings, and announced that they were paying Buckley to speak at the Whiting Auditorium in downtown Flint. Afterward, he would attend a cocktail party at the home of a University of Michigan–Flint professor.

We scored tickets to the speech and reception, but that wasn't enough. We gamed the extremely limited flights arriving at Flint's Bishop Airport from New York City and cut our afternoon classes to meet Buckley at the airport. Some guys blew off class to get blow jobs. We cut out of choir class so we could accost an old man in a Brooks Brothers suit at the airport.

It seemed right at the time. This was celeb-free Flint and three camera crews showed up at the airport. WFB, as his friends called him, made some brief remarks, none of which touched on his 1960s support for segregation. He was rushed away after a few minutes, declining our offer of a ride. We barely touched the hem of his trench coat.

I don't remember much from his Whiting speech. He used a lot of words I'd never heard before. The reception was held in a professor's drafty, rapidly depreciating Tudor. It was a momentous night for me: my first cocktail party. Now I know every cocktail party is exactly the same—intolerable made bearable by creeping drunkenness—but at the time it seemed like something out of, well, an Evelyn Waugh novel.

Buckley was pounding vodka and grapefruit and had a frozen look on his ruddy face that I now realize was half public persona, half get me the hell out of here. Waves of assistant professors shook his hand and asked him what he really thought about Gore Vidal, whom I'd never heard of. I don't know if it was the spring weather, the open bar, or just middle-aged smart folks starved for a little intellectual glitter, but all the grown-ups got stinking drunk. After an hour or so, Buckley had had enough. His blue eyes began searching for his designated driver. He found him, but the hapless professor was wasted beyond even the lax Michigan DUI standards of the mid-1980s.

He then turned to us and stage-whispered.

"Say, are you boys still good for that ride?"

It was pronounced *rhiiide.* We nodded yes. Then Buckley grabbed his coat and muttered, "Let's get out of here, then."

He said good-bye to no one, which seemed quite British and awesome. We went out to my car. Buckley blanched for just a moment when he noticed it was a two-tone Chevy Chevette. He piled into the passenger seat and placed his black loafers down on a sea of Taco Bell wrappers and a boom box holding a Smiths cassette. I lurched the car into drive.

Gordie asked a complicated question about Reagan and Thatcherism. Buckley answered with a bon mot drenched in alcohol and a plummy American accent not known to common men.

Overstimulated, I floored the Chevette through a blood-red light. Buckley didn't lose his cool, offering just a cautionary stuttering of "Ah, ah, ah," as he pointed his patrician forefinger toward the next potentially lethal intersection.

Maybe it was luck, maybe it was Buckley's Yale-educated and old school Catholic God waving off the traffic, but we didn't get broadsided by a Chevy Blazer. Buckley was staying at the recently opened and soon to be shuttered Hyatt Regency. As we pulled into the circular drive, I screeched the Chevette to a stop and shut down my V-4. Buckley smiled at me.

"Now, now, that was an adventure."

I asked him if he could sign something as a memento for me.

"I, I think I can do better than that."

He reached into his coat pocket and pulled out a small, blue velvet case. His manicured fingers popped the case open. Inside was a gold key. The inscription read, "From the Citizens of Flint, Michigan." Buckley pulled out a fountain pen and a scrap of paper and signed, "To Stephen, Best Wishes, William F. Buckley." He shook my hand, gathered his trench coat and stepped out of the car. He quickly disappeared into the revolving doors.

The next day, I told my government class about my night. My teacher overheard and told me he didn't believe me. I went to my locker and returned with my blue velvet trophy. He squinted at the handwriting and sadly shook his head.

"Rodrick, how do I know this isn't fake?"

I didn't say anything. Inside, I knew the Buckley encounter meant something. There *was* a whole world out there. Maybe I really could find it.

FORTUNATELY, A MUGGING AND A QUIZ show intervened on my behalf. One afternoon in history class, I was providing unwanted commentary to a filmstrip discussing the root causes of World War I when Mr. Winchester had enough.

"Rodrick, you're not helping here. Go across the street and get me some cigarettes."

I jumped up. There was a 7-Eleven across the street from school and I headed there with Winchester's $20 bill in my hand. The 7-Eleven was a hangout for lowlifes and minor thugs who nominally attended the public high school next door and spent their days playing Asteroids. I tried not to make eye contact. I bought the cigarettes and some Hostess cupcakes as my tariff. I'd barely crossed the street back toward Powers when three Asteroids kids jumped me and threw me down on the grass. I popped up, disoriented. The ringleader jabbed me in my palm with a rusty jackknife just enough to draw a drop or two of blood.

"I'd like your money."

I gave them my change and they pushed me back down

again. Then they sprinted away. I staggered to my feet and walked back toward my class. The filmstrip was just ending. I paused for a second and smeared some extra blood across my ripped yellow button-down shirt. I was ready for my close-up. I stumbled into the room and slammed the smokes on Winchester's desk.

"Here are your cigarettes."

Winchester's face went white. He marched me to the nurse's office where a Band-Aid was placed on my very minor wounds. The principal called Mom. She immediately threatened a lawsuit. We were a united front, if only for a moment.

The school offered to drive me home, an out that I would have jumped at on any other day. But today was tryouts for Quiz Bowl, an academic extracurricular activity that required no study but merely a reservoir of useless information and a twitchy trigger finger. A moderator asked semi-intellectual questions, and you could buzz in as soon as you had an answer even if he was still talking. I rolled up the sleeves of my ripped shirt and bashed through questions about Roger Maris and William Henry Harrison. In the end, I was the only underclassman to make the four-man team.

Finally, something I was good at! Every Saturday, four eggheads and a chaperone headed off in a van to nearby Alma College for the state tournament. By the time the host read "It is held every April in Augusta, . . ." I was ringing in "The Masters." This was not really a marketable skill, but it did bring our school glory and provide me with a get-out-of-jail-free card. I was close to being drummed out of school before Quiz Bowl, but now I was essential to Powers' delusions as the Notre Dame of Flint.

We won the state championship and earned Powers $8,000 in scholarship money that, inexplicably, wound up completely in the hands of a tobacco-chewing quarterback who tortured me in trigonometry. The Quiz Bowl team was introduced at a pep rally, and everyone went nuts when one of my tall teammates dunked a dictionary. Sure, they were laughing at us, not with us, but I didn't care.

It's not an exaggeration to say Quiz Bowl changed my life. Mom put the military school brochures away. She now viewed me on sporadic occasions as not being without some merit. At school, teachers rolled their eyes a little less. I could have taken the change and built on it a more mature version of myself. That didn't happen. Instead, I analyzed the situation and saw myself now as untouchable by Powers' management. I decided to press my luck.

IN MY SENIOR YEAR, GORDIE AND I were trapped in the English class of Ms. Otten. English was a dangerous place for us. We fancied ourselves young men of a literary bent, largely based on our consumption of back issues of *Harper's* stolen from the library. In European history class, our knowledge of the Black Prince would never match that of Mr. Richardson, so he had our respect. But this was not the case with Otten. We already believed ourselves more learned.

She quickly sensed our condescension but did not concede the premise. Possibly born in plaid slacks, Otten had black Spock bangs and reading glasses that swung back and forth across a rotating flat-chested foreground of unisex turtlenecks. She was on to our game early and placed us at opposite ends of the classroom. She also made regular sly remarks about the crummy colleges we would be attending, that is, if we managed to avoid the state pen in Jackson.

Otten was an odd duck. In addition to her classes, she was adviser to the *Powerline*, the school's newspaper. We didn't write for the paper—that would have been too constructive—we just made a series of cracks about its suckiness. The school's colors were blue and orange, and Otten had a similarly colored, shaggy-headed stuffed animal perched on a shelf above her desk. For reasons lost to history, it was named the Moofla.

Moofla was the paper's mascot and Otten's closest confidant. During class, she would address her fuzzy friend with asides like "The Moofla doesn't like dangling prepositions." As the semester wore on, the conversations became more frequent. Once, when a hapless student suggested an unsuitable essay topic, Otten turned to the creature and asked, "What do you think, Moofla?" She paused, apparently considering his reply, and then declared, "We don't think that will work."

This was disturbing. Most of our teachers tuned out our bratty prattle and counted the days until we were out of their domain. Otten engaged us in a long-running low-intensity conflict. She reveled in mocking Gordon's writing in front of the young women he was trying to woo. One day, I turned in an essay extolling the virtues of Ronald Reagan's Strategic Defense Initiative. It was quite late. This I blamed on a confluence of mononucleosis and an implausible automobile accident. Otten went into investigative reporter mode. She ferreted out my lies and called my mother.

"Your son is the most manipulative student I have had in all my years of teaching."

Mom's response was succinct.

"Tell me something I don't know."

Gordie and I were pissed but powerless. Then Otten made a crucial mistake: she called in sick. On an early winter afternoon, her class descended into anarchy. A substitute sat at Otten's desk with her face in her hands. *Crime and Punishment* paperbacks whizzed through the air. Gordon went on an extended walkabout with a bathroom pass. I plotted how I could interest the impossibly tall Sarah Torri in any of my romantic scenarios.

This depressed me so thoroughly that I put my head on my desk and began to doze. Then Gordon returned. I awoke to see him frantically snapping his fingers in the doorway. He mouthed one word.

"Moofla."

I immediately understood. Casually, I rose from my seat and made my way to the shelf holding our raggedy nemesis. A couple of hockey players wrestling on the floor in a homoerotic way provided a diversion. I grabbed the Moofla from behind the near-tears sub and pivoted toward the door. I then tossed the blue-orange fur ball sidearm to Gordon. He tucked the creature under his sweater and stashed him in the safe house of his locker. That night, the Moofla was smuggled to Gordon's home in an L.L. Bean book bag.

The next day, Otten returned. She eyed us coldly as we smirked into her classroom. She had an announcement.

"The stealing of a teacher's property is grounds for expulsion. Those of you who know what I am talking about should act accordingly before it's too late."

We chose a different path. Gordon had an unhealthy interest in the Red Brigades' 1978 kidnapping of Italian prime minister Aldo Moro. He had an idea: ransom the Moofla back in exchange for a public apology from Otten for not acknowledging our literary greatness. Like most radical kidnappings, this was bound to fail. Still, we hatched a plan: we would photograph the Moofla at various Flint locations and mail the Polaroids to Otten, whose home address was unwisely published in the White Pages.

It was now mid-December. We set upon our mission with a zeal that could have perhaps been better utilized conjugating the verb *être.* On a succession of Fridays, Gordie and I bought a bottle of Riunite at a Flint bodega, put the Smiths on the boom box, and set out in the most unsubtle of vehicles: Gordie's 1963 Buick LeSabre.

We logged many miles. There was Moofla on a chairlift at the local ski hill. There was Moofla being ravaged by other stuffed vixens on Gordon's bed. There was Moofla reading *Playboy.* There was Moofla holding a current edition of the *National Enquirer* to prove he was still alive. And our favorite: Moofla spooning the baby Jesus in St. Paul Lutheran's nativity scene.

We mailed the photos. Soon after, Otten began a class with another announcement.

"It is a federal offense to send threatening items through the mail. These are serious crimes."

This seemed particularly unrealistic in a place like Flint; the FBI was going to pursue the kidnapping of a Muppetesque animal while the entire city was a Beirut-style war zone and drunk driving was considered a civic right? Not likely.

Still, things were getting too "hot," as they said on *Starsky*

& Hutch. It was time to unload the Moofla. We would return him to his mama—with one significant alteration. The Moofla would be hairless.

Why? Who can say? It seemed right at the time. One snowy evening, Gordon brought the Moofla into his living room, lovingly placed him on a towel, and broke out his brother's electric razor. Then he proceeded to mow off his synthetic blue-and-orange hair with the sideburn trimmer. Gordie's mom walked by, prepared to speak, gave a sigh, and went upstairs to bed. His older brother then made a cameo. Matt asked if that was his electric razor. Gordon said yes. His brother shook his head and whispered, "You'll be sorry, chump."

These were more words than I had heard Matt utter in three years. Our original idea was to stick the shorn Moofla in Ms. Otten's mailbox. But then Heineken intervened. We stopped at a hardware store. We bought some rope. We drove over to Otten's apartment complex. We drank more beer. We stepped out of the car into the cold, hard Michigan night.

I put the rope around Moofla's neck and tied a sailor knot I almost learned in Webelos. Gordon finally put his athleticism to proper use. He lassoed the excess rope like a rodeo cowboy. He then skillfully hurled the Moofla high onto an upper branch of an oak tree by the building's doorway. Moofla swayed gracefully back and forth under the starlit sky. He didn't look like he was in pain.

For a moment, Gordie and I stared wide-eyed at each other. A faraway siren sounded and then seemed to draw closer. There was a moment of conscience mixed with fear. Should we take it down? "Nah," we cackled simultaneously.

We jumped back into Gordie's car and peeled off into the darkness.

The following Monday, Otten didn't mention the shaved Moofla or the hanging. Actually, she never mentioned the Moofla again. This earned our grudging respect, if not our remorse.

Why did we turn it up a notch? I can't say for sure. Why do boys set fire to ants? Why do grown men start wars over barren pieces of land? Boys do things that are not explainable, especially boys without dads. The only thing I knew was Mom was right for once; it was good that Dad wasn't around to see it.

Somehow, both Gordie and I managed to graduate the next year. After the ceremony, Mom had tears in her eyes. This seemed normal. The beautiful woman I'd watched a decade ago from the top of the stairs was gone, replaced by someone I didn't know. She held my little sister's hand with one hand and wiped her eyes with the other. My grandmother tried to comfort her, but Mom couldn't stop the tears. Finally, she spoke.

"The vice principal told me you were the student who had the most potential but did the least with it."

She was trembling. Christine, now six, looked up at me with giant brown eyes. She was frightened and wrapped her tiny arms around Mom's waist. In front of me was Dad's Holy Trinity, his mother, his wife, and his little girl, the last, best thing he created. Classmates rushed by me, a blur of shouts and blue robes. I didn't know what to say.

Chapter Eighteen

LIFE KEPT HAPPENING WITHOUT the Black Ravens. The Nimitz was floating in the Arabian Sea when Vinnie's wife, Marci, went into labor back in Whidbey. He woke up the next morning to a son named Henry. That evening, the whole squadron celebrated with cigars on the fantail.

Tupper watched his men bullshit and joke and thought this was how it was supposed to be. But he missed his family. With the seventeen-hour time difference, he kept getting Beth's voice mail. His parents had just finished a visit to Anacortes, but now they were gone. Caitlin was heartbroken wondering who would read her bedtime stories now that Grandpa Jim was gone. Tupper's mom emailed him details of their visit, describing his daughters' jokes and smiles in the vivid detail he could never get from his wife.

He finally got Beth on the phone. They talked a bit, but he realized he didn't have much to say, a common problem after they'd been apart for months. But he could hear the rain pounding on the roof of her car, 8,000 miles away. He just listened. Tupper had not heard rain in three months.

All there was to do was work. Tupper could feel Crapper's incompetence spreading like a pesticide-resistant fungus. All naval aviators had to stay current in their swim and survival qualifications: once every four years they had to demonstrate that they could still swim a hundred yards in their flight gear, just as they did back in flight school. It was up to the safety officer to make sure everyone was current before deploying. Crapper had missed Beav's deadline and he was out of qualification. Beav was going to have to fly off on the COD to Bahrain and then make the twenty-four-hour trip back to Whidbey unless CAG called NAS Whidbey and asked for a waiver. He went to see his boss, hat in hand. CAG wasn't sympathetic.

"The policies are there for a reason. You have to send him home."

Tupper decided to chew some ass. He made Crapper produce a chart that showed where every officer was in his swim and safety qualifications. If there was any doubt, Tupper yanked the aviator off the flight schedule. The result was that Prowler sorties were canceled because of insufficient flight crews. It was a clever but efficient fuck-you to CAG. Suddenly, CAG was on the phone, frantic. He didn't mean enforce *all* the policies.

"CAG, I'm just trying to make sure everyone is current."

"Well, don't go overboard."

All the pissing and moaning was enough to make him forget that it was Thanksgiving. General David Petraeus, the head of United States' Central Command, flew out in the morning from Bahrain. He got a ride in a flashy new Hornet—typical, thought the Prowler guys—and then served turkey to the sailors.

In a military filled with bullshitting middle managers Tupper thought Petraeus was a guy who did what he said without worrying about his image. (Then again, Tupper wasn't shocked by Petraeus's fall in 2012. He'd seen it all. The public face. The private lie. Nothing surprised him.) Like most officers, Tupper supported the wars in Afghanistan and Iraq, but he was baffled by the lack of an end game. At least Petraeus had gone into Iraq and executed a troop surge that brought a sliver of stability. Maybe he could do the same in Afghanistan and Tupper wouldn't have to spend more Christmases away from his girls.

In the evening, Petraeus stopped by the Black Ravens' ready room and spoke for a few minutes, joking that Tupper didn't have enough gray hair to be a skipper. Tupper told him he didn't know the half of it.

Tupper went back to his stateroom and flipped through a book on Churchill that Vinnie had loaned him. He loved how Churchill never gave up whatever the odds. But then Tupper's dark humor took over. Churchill never had to skipper a Prowler squadron.

THE NEXT DAY, THINGS GOT BETTER. The squadron completed seven sorties out of seven. Their time in-country was becoming more productive. Some of Tupper's officers had begun communicating directly with CAOC in Bagram about where the Prowlers should be flying and what troop movements needed protection. Before, CAOC called CAG's staff and told them their needs, and then the information was relayed to the Black Ravens. The end result was high-tech telephone tag with something always getting lost in translation. Streamlining the process and speaking to the source directly was making the missions more effective.

There was only one problem. CAG didn't like being cut out of the loop. He called Tupper early one morning.

"Are your guys talking directly to CAOC?"

Tupper was still half asleep.

"Yes sir."

CAG slammed the phone down. That was a first for Tupper, a superior hanging up on him. He thought he had just been streamlining the process, and his boss thought he'd disobeyed the chain of command. Now he didn't know what to do. So he did nothing. Tupper knew he should apologize or explain, but screw it, if CAG didn't want to listen he wasn't going to show up outside his stateroom like a naughty schoolboy begging the Mother Superior for forgiveness.

So the Black Ravens went back to doing things CAG's way. That night, Tupper took his Prowler over Farah Province in northern Afghanistan. They arrived on station, but because of a communications foul-up, they just circled the sky for two hours doing nothing. It was six and half hours of burning dinosaurs, Navyspeak for wasting thousands of dollars in man-hours and jet fuel. Tupper watched shooting stars in the Afghan sky and thought of Brenna making her debut in *The Nutcracker* back in Anacortes. He lined his jet up behind the *Nimitz* on a pitch black night a few hours later and thought: what a waste.

The next day, he saw CAG at the morning meeting. They exchanged maybe five words. It was the week before Christmas and there was a holiday dinner that night for the *Nimitz*'s senior staff in Captain Monger's private dining room. There were assigned seats, and Tupper noticed he was at the far end of the table away from the CO and CAG. He would have needed a can and some string to join their conversation. He didn't mind.

Soon it was December 25. By chance, all of Tupper's

deployments as a junior officer had begun in the spring and brought him home for the holidays. This was the first one away from Beth and the girls. Maybe it was the blues, maybe he'd just had enough, but he told CAG that the Prowlers were being wasted, too much of their time was spent circling, waiting for assignments that should have been worked out before they left the *Nimitz*. CAG listened and said he'd take it under advisement.

Tupper went back to his stateroom and opened presents from the girls. He briefed that night and took off for Afghanistan. Again, the Prowlers didn't have a specific mission. In-country, Tupper put his Prowler on autopilot and began composing a Christmas poem at 25,000 feet for Beth on the back of his preflight checklist. He was still working on the first stanza when he saw a sparkle of lights down below. It was a firefight going on in Nuristan. Across the radio came the crackly voice of a tactical controller down on the ground. "Can you jam them?"

"Roger that."

Tupper's crew flipped on the four jamming pods underneath the wings. An ECMO turned a knob and sent out a blizzard of electronic whiteout. A few minutes later, there was a coordinated series of explosions. Tupper guessed American troops had responded to a nighttime attack with a slew of artillery. Had the Prowler prevented Taliban lookouts from relaying information to their men about where the fire was coming from? Probably, but he would never know for sure.

On the way home, the sun was coming up as the Prowler passed through the mountains. Tupper could see the small huts of villages located at about 10,000 feet. Someone had told him that the villages held blue-eyed blond Afghanis, the descendants of earlier invaders. Tupper thought that soon the United States would be gone too. Will we have done any good?

THE *NIMITZ* PULLED INTO BAHRAIN JUST before New Year's Day and the squadron held a belated Christmas party at the Marriott. The afternoon before the party, Tupper wrestled with what to say to his sailors. He liked to prep his speeches days in advance, but this time he didn't. Instead, he went out with his men and got hammered at the pool. That evening, Tupper took the microphone in front of his sailors and held it for a moment. He thought of quoting Churchill or some other leader. He went in another direction.

"I only want you to remember one thing," shouted Tupper. "You have one thing that the rest of the Navy will never have." He paused for effect. "You are Black Fucking Ravens. Black Fucking Ravens. Never forget that."

He then did a rap about how other squadrons wished they were as awesome as VAQ-135. At the end, Jim and Cindy's son tossed down the mic, MC-style. For a moment, there was just shocked silence. Then his sailors started whooping it up.

"Allrrrigght, Skipper!"

Tupper worked his way through his men, high-fiving officers and seamen alike. His face was flushed red. Then he stepped out of the pool area and puked into a garbage can. He'd violated his own promise not to get shit-faced while CO. But nobody blamed him for it. It just made him seem more like them.

TUPPER FLEW HIS LAST MISSION OVER Afghanistan at the end of January. Barring a series of unlikely circumstances, he would never fly in harm's way again. He thought he would be emotional, but he was just too exhausted to think about it.

On board, his management responsibilities were crushing him. He was working on the fit reps of his junior officers, and his choices would decide who made department head and who would be dumped into an unforgiving economy. After his performance in the seat next to Beav on the flight to Oman, Chicken was his future rock star; only an extraordinary act of buffoonery could stop his career.

At the other end was Rodney "Socr8tes" Williams, a teddy bear of a man: everyone loved him in the ready room, but few wanted to fly with him because of his stammering on the radio. When things go bad, a pilot wants a navigator speaking crisply with the tower. That wasn't Socr8tes, who had a hard time getting the plane's radio calls right. Tupper had him into his stateroom earlier in the cruise and asked him if he had considered speech therapy. Socr8tes—he got the "8" in his call sign because of his mispronunciation of the Greek philosopher's name on a port call—told him he'd been doing speech therapy since he was five. Tupper just nodded and patted him on the shoulder.

Socr8tes was African American and Tupper guessed that was why his stutter was probably overlooked, but he wondered whom exactly the Navy was helping by passing him through flight school and putting him and others in harm's way. Next up for Socr8tes was a stint instructing at VAQ-129, the training squadron. Tupper could only imagine the implications of a rookie pilot with Socr8tes next to him in shitty weather. Only Tupper had the power to stop the madness. He went back and forth over a sleepless night before ending Socr8tes' flying career, thinking it might save his life.

On it went. Tupper filled out form after form. He tried to remember all the stupid things he did as a JO and cut some breaks, but some things he couldn't take. It filtered back to him that Crapper and an ECMO junior officer, Lieutenant Devon "the Wolf" Benbow, had publicly grumbled that Vinnie's flying was unsatisfactory and they didn't want to fly with him.

They had a point. Vinnie's landing grades on the *Nimitz* were not great, and Tupper had paired Chicken with him after CAG complained. He'd even gone with Vinnie to an eye doctor in Bahrain on a port call. But for the men to go public with their misgivings undermined Vinnie's ability to lead the squadron in and out of the plane.

Tupper called Wolf and Crapper into his stateroom separately. He asked them if they had voiced their concerns to Vinnie in the debrief that follows every flight. They both said they had not. Tupper then asked if Vinnie was unsafe to fly with and should be taken off the flight schedule. They both answered no.

"Then shut the fuck up."

He had other things to worry about. Beth was coming to meet him in Hong Kong in two weeks. It had been seven months since he said good-bye to her back at NAS Whidbey. Their conversations had grown strained over the cruise as they lived separate lives connected only by their children. He looked himself in the mirror in his stateroom and worried. Was his face ruddier? Had his hair gone grayer? Would she still see in him what she saw when they were at Penn State?

But when she opened the door for him at the Renaissance Hotel it all melted away. They kissed and fell into delirious conversation, happy and nervous all the same. Tupper tried too hard at first. He took Beth to a posh Hong Kong tailor and insisted she order $2,000 worth of suits and skirts, clothes that she would never wear.

They went to the Stanley Market the next morning and walked hand-in-hand through the stalls. They Skyped that night with Brenna and Caitlin and Tup's parents, who had flown to Anacortes to watch the kids. The next night was the twenty-second anniversary of their first date, so Tupper bought an expensive bottle of French wine and took Beth to an Indian restaurant she'd read about in a magazine.

And just like that it was over. Tupper took his wife to the airport and watched her pass through security. He felt sadness sweep over him. But it was a happy sadness. It was comforting to know they could both miss each other after all these years. And he'd be home in a month. The hard days were almost finished.

Chapter Nineteen

I SPENT MY TWENTIES RUNNING FROM Mom and Dad.

Gordie's and my Georgetown fantasies were long dashed and we both ended up in ragged facsimiles of our actual dreams, Gordon at Catholic University in D.C. and me at Loyola in Chicago. Loyola fit my very loose criteria: it was Catholic, they accepted me, and it was in a big city. They didn't seem to mind that I'd finished in the gooey middle of my class. I received my acceptance letter in April of my senior year and didn't give it another thought until August.

I'd fallen in love for the first time. She was a preppy blonde who so entranced me I didn't mind wearing a homemade "Je t'aime" sweatshirt with her name on it to school on Sadie Hawkins Day. I'd stolen her away from a friend, getting drunk and making out with her for the first time as the poor guy pounded on the front door, crying on the steps of the house.

So I earned all the ensuing bad karma. On prom night, I drove across town to pick her up in Mom's brand-new Buick Century. It had just started to rain, and I reached down to adjust my cummerbund and looked up too late to see a red light. I hit the brakes hard and slid the car up and over a concrete curb. The Buick's alignment was never the same. Mom was not happy. We ended up driving to the dance in my Taco Bell–infested two-tone Chevette.

On a July night, we drove her Chevy Nova to a back

street of a new subdivision. That's where I lost my virginity. I looked up at the moment of consummation and saw through the windshield a yellow sign that read "Dead End." But that was before I did signs or metaphors. We were both consumed with Catholic guilt, and she spent the rest of the summer breaking up with me while I begged her to take me back.

There was universal relief when it was time for me to leave for college. Aunt Nancy agreed to drive with Mom and me to Chicago for the move-in. This was a wise and magnanimous move; a road trip with Mom and me alone together in a car for five hours would have likely ended with state troopers and sirens.

We reached downtown Chicago near twilight and forced our way north on Lake Shore Drive. We came around the curve near Oak Street and suddenly there were high-rises casting shadows onto green water. One of the buildings had balconies. I stretched myself around to get a final look before they disappeared behind us.

Mom and I were so giddy at the prospect of getting rid of each other that we didn't fight at all, tenderly stepping around each other for the last twenty-four hours, like soldiers checking our watches, waiting for a midnight armistice. We moved my belongings into the dorm and then said our good-byes on a busy street. We stared at each other with wonderment, both not knowing how we had made it through without killing each other. She gave me a peck on the cheek before climbing into the car. The light turned green. Maybe it was the tough merge, maybe it was nerves, but Mom and Aunt Nancy seemed to burn rubber pulling away from me. I wasn't offended.

But she was never far from my thoughts, largely because I'd merely replaced pacifying her with pacifying my girl, who promptly announced we were back together a week after I arrived in Chicago. She was a typical seventeen-year-old—one moment thinking it was cool to have a boyfriend in Chicago, the next deciding she couldn't do long distance for another day. I learned to keep her happy and smiling, apologizing for things I hadn't done wrong, coddling her to keep the peace.

Most of my classmates lived in the Chicago area and retreated home on the weekends. So did I, just further, trying to keep things going with my girlfriend. I'd ride a bus five hours to see her for a day and then head back. It drove Mom insane. I'd agitated to get out of her sphere of influence for years, and now I was coming back every chance I could.

We parked anywhere we could. One night, we drove the Chevette to the far side of an elementary school near her house, but I ran down the battery listening to Steve Garvey win game four of the 1984 National League Championship Series. We pushed the car back into the front of the school, but we still had to tell our parents. Mom was not pleased.

"Keep going, push your luck with the man upstairs."

I had profound separation anxiety every time I left. My girlfriend's parents drove me to Detroit one Sunday to catch a flight back to Chicago. At the gate, I wept and hyperventilated, barely able to get on my flight. Christine had it too. I'd come home and she would throw her arms around me, clinging like an octopus. When I left, she threw herself on the floor, crying inconsolably until she passed out from exhaustion. It was something Dad bequeathed to us all.

Loyola was a relatively liberal place, but I remained in the throes of harsh Catholic guilt, a theological residue from Dad. I believed anything that went wrong in my life was direct retribution from God for my laziness, low manners, and generally shifty personality. There was a pregnancy scare during my freshman year. After she told me she was late, I prayed hard and often, promising God I'd never have premarital sex again if he'd spared me this one time. She got her period and I kept my word, flushing a half-dozen condoms down the nuclear-powered toilet system in my dorm. We never had sex again.

SOMEHOW, ONCE I HAD THE FREEDOM to go or not go to class, I started doing well. I opened my first report card at our dinner table over winter break. Mom saw the three As and two Bs and nearly entered a state of shock. After a minute or two passed, she placed the paper on the same dining room table where she once threw forks at me.

"I'll be damned. I didn't know you had it in you."

And just like that, our war was over.

I HAD SOME FRIENDS AT COLLEGE, but the city was my best friend. I took the L to watch Cubs games and sat high in the bleachers, a silly smile on my face for hours. There were bands at the Cabaret Metro, *Hamlet* with Aidan Quinn, and Truffaut double features at the Music Box Theatre. My second summer I stayed in the city and got a job at Water Tower Place working in a gadget store that sold $1,400 massage chairs, gold-plated eyebrow clippers, and a thousand other things that suggested the American tax rate was far too low.

Next door was a Victoria's Secret where I ran into Jamie,

a friend of a classmate. She was home for the summer from Boston University. It was a fortuitous meeting because Jamie ran through jobs with alacrity: this was her second and last day selling lingerie. We went to Gino's on Rush Street for dinner one night. She announced halfway into our pizza that she was Jewish, an incomprehensible level of exotica for me. I was twenty and had never had a conversation with a Jewish woman in my life.

She talked of losing her virginity to her horse trainer on a pile of hay after an equestrian event. I blushed. After dinner, we walked down Michigan Avenue onto Lake Shore Drive. I asked if she wanted to take the train back north with me. I explained I was subletting a place on the North Side where one of the spare bedrooms was accompanied solely by grow lights and neat rows of marijuana. She said that wouldn't do. She took me by the hand and led me up the steps of a high-rise building that seemed oddly familiar. Then I remembered. It was the building from the August before, the one I had passed on Lake Shore Drive.

An elderly black man doffed his cap and held the door. The elevator raced up sixteen floors. We stepped off and there was an old woman dressed in Saks Fifth Avenue and Bonwit Teller, a layer of makeup artfully spread across her face like expensive frosting. She was Jamie's nana. Her husband was long dead and so were many of her friends.

"Watch this," said Jamie with a smile. "Nana, how's Rose Noodleman?"

Nana gravely turned her head and looked us in the eye.

"Dead, Rose Noodleman is dead."

Jamie honked a laugh. Before long, Jamie exiled Nana from

her own bedroom to a daybed in the sewing room. We had sex in one of the twin beds left over from Nana's marriage. Jamie kept eye contact with me through the whole endeavor, an unnerving concept for a Catholic boy. Afterward, Jamie got dressed and went into the kitchen to do her weekly discarding of outdated food from Nana's cupboard. I stumbled out onto the balcony, overwhelmed by the sex, the view, and a Coast Guard helicopter peering a spotlight down onto Lake Michigan. The pink light of the Drake Hotel beckoned in the distance. This was where I wanted to be.

I wandered into the bathroom and smiled at myself in the mirror. Something caught my eye. The bathroom had two toilets, a regular one and one that had no seat but featured a spigot. I stared at it for a few minutes. I got down on my knees and examined the contraption. There was a knob on the side. I turned it on and water shot into my face and onto the marble floor. I turned off the switch and mopped up the water with monogrammed towels. It was months before I realized it was a bidet.

The summer was a happy blur. We'd eat takeout pizza with Nana as she shushed us during *Wheel of Fortune*. She had a hard time remembering my name, so she just started calling me The Nice Boy. It wasn't exactly accurate—Jamie's sister once observed, "The funny thing about The Nice Boy, he's actually not always nice"—but it made me feel wanted.

We headed out on the train to her parents' house in Barrington Hills on the weekends. The walls were lined with modern art. I didn't know any of the artists, but in the study there was a giant, garish painting of a giant heart with an actual hammer embedded in the picture. I stared at it for hours on my first visit and her dad caught me ogling it.

"Do you like Jim Dine?"

"Uh, absolutely. He's one of my favorites."

I had no idea who the hell Jim Dine was. I suspect he knew that, but he let me babble. Steve Harrison was an ophthalmologist who after years of button-downed life was now letting his freak flag fly. He wore leather pants and let his hair grow down his back. Sometimes he liked to slip a bit of the tongue when greeting Jamie's friends. But her mom was a complete gem. Kathy cooked gourmet meals and kept all the kooks in the family on schedule. Her face lit up when I walked off the train: I don't think there has ever been another person on this earth who seemed happier to see me.

The Harrisons reveled in my goyness. They asked me about Wonder Bread as if it was caviar. Out by their pool, they would beg me to "Do Jesus on the raft." I'd jump on a raft, thrust out my arms Christlike, suck in my scrawny ribs, and say "Forgive them, Father, they know not what they do." They would laugh and laugh. The whole family spoke in shorthand and used made-up words that only they understood. They were weird and I loved them for it. Here was the family I always wanted! I didn't feel like an alien around them. I felt like I was home.

Jamie and I broke up a year later, but her parents didn't care. I vacationed with them in Longboat Key in Florida almost every year for decades. They started calling me son. Not that there weren't problems. Dad's absences and death left emotional scars, but it also left yawning gaps in my practical knowledge. One winter, I was house-sitting out in Barrington. The Harrisons were in LA visiting their daughters while I was sticking around for a day before heading to Iowa on a story.

Before leaving, Steve gave me a checklist of things to do. I watered their houseplants and took out the garbage. Upon returning from taking out the trash, I noticed one of their flowerpots was leaking water onto the floor. I grabbed some paper towels, cleaned up the mess, and—having already taken out the trash—flushed eight paper towels down the toilet.

We both returned to Barrington a week later on a Sunday morning. Kathy made some french toast with challah bread—my new favorite—and then loaded the dishwater. A few moments later, the sound of cascading water rumbled through the ceiling. A pipe burst and water gushed onto the Norwegian wood of their living room.

At first, I was a hero. I grabbed towels and called plumbers. The next day I headed downtown to Nana's condo to write while the plumbers came to survey the damage. That night, I received a call from Steve. There had been $30,000 worth of damage to their house.

"It's the damnedest thing," Steve told me. "The plumber says there was a clog of paper towels. We're going to have to fire the housekeeper—not because she did it but because she won't own up to it. It's too bad because she's an off-the-grid type, no Social Security number."

I hung up the phone and paced the floors for twenty minutes. Could I let the maid take the fall? I could not. I called Steve back and blubbered about how much their family had done for me and I paid them back by acting like a special-needs child. I told him I was sorry.

He forgave me. I wondered if Mom would have done the same.

DRIVING INTO CHICAGO FROM FLINT ON the Dan Ryan Expressway past the Robert Taylor Homes and the desperate South Side poverty purged me of my Buckley conservatism. I swung far to the other side, voting for Jesse Jackson in 1984. I worked out my dad issues at work. My boyhood fantasy of being a politician lingered, and I started working in Chicago politics while an undergrad. The men I worked for were memorable for all the wrong reasons.

I started as an intern in the Chicago office of Alan J. Dixon, a U.S. senator. Dixon was nicknamed "Al the Pal." He had a wicked comb-over and a politician's thousand-yard stare, looking right through you on his way to someone more important. His ideology was simple: take both sides of every issue. A rusty Irishman ran the state for him. Emmet O'Neill was an old ad exec who enjoyed the five-martini lunch and sometimes wore a yarmulke so his bald spot wouldn't burn in the Chicago sun. Before a meeting with a suitor, he'd growl, "Who's his Chinaman?" Chicagoese for "Does he have a powerful sponsor?"

He eventually hired me as a part-time aide. I performed momentous tasks like trying to get influential friends better postal service. Emmet fired me more than once via phone on his drunken drive home to Winnetka, forgetting all about it by the morning, more perplexed with why there was a bucket of fried chicken in the backseat of his Lincoln.

He called me into his office one afternoon and told me he was farming me out to work on the campaign of a congressional challenger. I'm pretty sure this was illegal for a government employee and, more important, a violation of the Chicago code of conduct because the guy was running against an incumbent.

But that didn't stop me from falling in love with the guy. Mel Reynolds was black and eight years younger than Dad, but I worshipped him in the same way. The only problem was he was flesh and blood, not a man in a photograph. Reynolds was a buck-toothed Rhodes scholar running against the appropriately named Gus Savage, a racist black congressman on Chicago's far South Side. A few days a week, I took the commuter rail to 103rd Street and walked into a storefront campaign office that was a galaxy away from my own small world. Volunteers stamped letters and made signs while subsisting on day-old doughnuts and takeout chicken. Gunfire could be heard on occasion. I loved it.

Mel was the son of sharecroppers, and his travels from Mississippi to Oxford to Chicago were catnip to a newly minted white Chicago liberal like myself. I now realize that I saw Dad in his Horatio Alger story. The incumbent was an old-school creep best known for fondling a Peace Corps worker and giving his son a no-show job. He was easy to hate. I wrote press releases and op-eds late into the night and watched Reynolds draw close in the polls a few days before the primary.

People were already talking about me being his twenty-four-year-old press secretary. But then Savage took to the pulpit of a South Side church on the Sunday before the primary. He read off the Jewish-sounding names of the contributors to Reynolds' campaign. In Chicago, this was known as rallying the base. Reynolds lost by a few points and I was crushed. I didn't understand. Were people really that stupid? Reynolds swore he'd try again in two years and I swore I'd be there for him.

But in the interim, I got a rude education. I moved to Washington in 1991 to work as Dixon's deputy press secretary. A few months later, Dixon was one of eleven Democrats to vote for Clarence Thomas's confirmation. He was up for reelection the next year, and he thought the vote would protect him from a Republican challenger. I played a minor role in drafting his floor statement praising Thomas and I felt like a whore. In the end, Dixon was defeated from the left in the Democratic primary, and I secretly rejoiced.

I kept in touch with Reynolds. He called me one evening for a favor. He told me he'd done all the coursework for his master's at Harvard's John F. Kennedy School of Government, but just needed some help with his thesis. Lots of help. Reynolds asked casually if I'd like to write the entire thing for $2,500. I stuttered a bit, half out of ethical outrage and half because Reynolds was already known as a debt dodger. A friend was still owed three months' back pay from the campaign. I knew I'd never see the cash. I begged off, blaming my own graduate classes, and got off the phone.

I saw Reynolds again a few months later when we shared a ride back from a speech at the Chicago Hilton. He elbowed me in the ribs as we drove down Michigan Avenue and pointed at two schoolgirls in plaid uniforms. He arched his eyebrows in the universal sign of creepiness.

"Steve, what do you think?"

My toes curled up in my loafers. True to his word, Reynolds won the next time out. The turning point was when Reynolds was assaulted while hanging campaign signs in his own neighborhood. This gained him great sympathy and favorable media coverage. My Spidey sense told me Reynolds faked the attack. After the election, he approached me about becoming his press secretary and I turned him down. It was a lucky choice since Reynolds was indicted for campaign embezzlement and statutory rape two years later. I watched Reynolds on *Larry King* trying to wriggle himself out of his corner, sweat beading on his forehead as he blamed his downfall on a conspiracy of white politicians. I clicked off the television. He was definitely not my father.

◇◇

Chapter Twenty

I'D BEEN ONBOARD THE USS *NIMITZ* once before as a ten-year-old holding my daddy's hand. He did his department head stint on the carrier's maiden cruise in 1976 and gave our family a tour while the carrier was in port in Norfolk, Virginia. I don't remember much about that day except the infinite ladders going down, down into the bowels of the ship.

Now I was going back on my own. I flew onto the carrier from Okinawa for the last month of the Black Ravens' deployment. CODs usually land on a carrier from a straight-in approach, passing the boat at a leisurely pace and then lining up eight to ten miles behind the boat. But the pilots had heard from the Black Ravens about Dad and told me they wanted to bring their COD in on a break and show me what it felt like.

I said sure. Ninety minutes later, I saw the *Nimitz* outside one of the plane's tiny windows, and then the COD tilted downward and to the left, pressing me back against my seat with a meager two Gs, about three less than a Prowler. We dropped our hook and caught the number two wire, my head slamming back against the seat.

Tupper was flying, so he sent a posse of Black Ravens to meet me: Beav, Shibaz, Chicken, and Jeff "Stoli" Stodola, a young pilot. Beav was concerned.

"Did that COD come in on a break? I've never seen that before. Didn't really look that safe."

I told him I was glad that I didn't know that twenty minutes ago. The guys grabbed my bag and led me back across the *Nimitz* through a dimly lit labyrinth of halls and then down ladders past CAG's office and on to the Ravens' ready room.

Tupper had set me up in a four-man room with Stoli and two ECMOs just down the hallway from the ready room. Stoli showed me where the head was and then pushed open the door to our room. The space was a perfect imitation of a shared cell at a minimum-security prison. There was a tiny living area dominated by a giant television and lined with a gray metal locker for each of the men. Playing Call of Duty with headphones on was Lieutenant Devon "the Wolf" Benbow. Next to him sweating from the gym was Lieutenant Chris "Lil Chris" Sutherland. Stoli started apologizing.

"It's small, but if you go see the enlisted men's quarters, they'd have eight guys in this space."

A blue sheet separated the living area from the sleeping quarters, which were two rows of bunks and some more lockers. Stoli pointed to my bunk and then dramatically pulled back the curtain that afforded a modicum of privacy.

"Welcome!"

My bed was filled with a dozen red and yellow balloons. A mint rested on my pillow. The guys started to laugh. Stoli explained.

"I know it seems gay, but we just wanted to make you welcome."

I was touched, but a part of me thought they were screwing with me. These were combat naval aviators, could they also be sensitive metrosexuals? The other thing was, they'd been at sea for six months and they were beyond bored. The arrival of a new guy—any new guy—was like three six-year-old boys with chicken pox getting new Legos. It gave the guys something new to talk about, someone new to prank. We spent the next few weeks hiding the deflating balloons in each other's lockers and shaving kits.

I quickly got their backstories. Stoli was a sharp new pilot from suburban Chicago. He was getting married in September and it was hard to tell whom he loved more, his fiancée, Jodi, or Bears linebacker Brian Urlacher. The Wolf was an academy grad and probably had twenty IQ points on most of the rest of the guys in the squadron, not always an advantage as a junior officer. His wife was a helo pilot flying in Afghanistan; they'd spent three months together since getting married two years earlier.

And then there was Lil Chris. He'd completed the Black Ravens' last cruise, but while everyone else was enjoying time back on Whidbey he'd been shipped out to Iraq for one of the dreaded IAs. He made it back to Whidbey last July, got two months at home, and rejoined the Black Ravens in October, just in time to be in the backseat for Beav's emergency landing in Oman.

The *Nimitz* was fifteen stories deep, a block wide, and over a thousand feet long. It was as unknowable to a newcomer as Manhattan to an immigrant. But like a great city it was broken down into a series of self-sustaining neighborhoods, ones where the locals all spoke the same language. A Black Raven could go weeks without leaving the block except to go up top to fly and down below to get a shitty haircut in the barbershop. The wardroom was spacious, but the squadron tended to eat together at one round table, cramming in extras as they arrived, the middle of the table becoming a compost of plates bearing half-eaten chicken fingers and a poor man's imitation of lettuce.

I first saw Tupper at dinner. His cheeks had gone concave and he was fifteen pounds lighter than last summer. The next day, he stopped by my room with something green tucked under his arm.

"If you're going to hang with us, you have to dress like us."

He handed me a flight suit and flight boots. I told him that men had worked years for the honor of wearing a Navy flight suit and I hadn't earned it. I tried to hand it back, but Tupper refused.

"Believe me, you've earned this more than a lot of us. Put it on."

Tupper left and I closed the door. My roommates were all out briefing flights or flying. I slipped off my khakis and shirt, stepped into the flight suit, and zipped it up.

It took me to another time. I'm eight or nine. I've just struck out to end a Little League game. My parents are not there. I'm pissed off and wondering how I'm going to get home. Then a hand falls on my shoulder. It is Dad in his flight suit. He is both kind and impatient.

"Don't worry. Everyone strikes out. Even Ted Williams. We'll work on it. But don't be a crybaby."

Stoli then burst through the door. I blushed, embarrassed, feeling like he caught me playing dress up at fantasy camp.

"It looks good. The thing is, they are so damn comfortable. They're like pajamas. By the time you leave, you're never going to want to take it off."

He was right. The flight suit had one giant zipper running from crotch to neck, much like the jammies I wore as a kid watching Mom and Dad play bridge. It was odd how one item of clothing could make me feel like a man and a child at the same time.

I WANDERED INTO THE READY ROOM after dinner one night early in my stay. The guys had finally grown tired of watching *Beerfest* and Vinnie was trying to rally them into watching an early season of *The Sopranos*. He was the XO, so no one was really going to say no, but the images of violence and intrigue didn't attract much of a crowd. I plopped down into a seat next to Lieutenant Commander Scott "Sherm" Oliver, a Black Raven I hadn't really met yet. Sherm had blue eyes and gray-blond hair, and one of the officers' wives had nicknamed him McSteamy after a stud doctor on *Grey's Anatomy*. He was discreetly spitting tobacco into a cup and staring right through Christopher and Paulie trying to escape the Pine Barrens.

We didn't say anything for a half hour. But then we started to talk. It was one of those Navy conversations that once it got rolling went straight to the pain. He told me that he grew up outside Atlanta and his father was a writer too, a speechwriter for Coca-Cola who had just retired. He started asking me how I do what I do and I told him my job was much like his: 15 percent cool, 85 percent drudgery. We laughed about that. He told me he'd gone to the Citadel in South Carolina. His call sign came from William Tecumseh Sherman because of his Southern roots.

"I acted like I hated it, so it stuck," said Sherm. "That's the secret. Act like you hate it. But I actually think it's pretty cool."

He asked me if I was married. I told him I was divorced. He perked up and gave a sad smile.

"My wife just left me. She's moving out of our house this week."

He unspooled the details. He had met her at the Citadel his senior year. She worked at the college and came from a military family. Her father was an Army paratrooper who was killed when she was a teenager; his chute didn't open on a training mission.

They fell in love and got engaged. Sherm couldn't believe his good fortune in meeting someone who already understood the hardship of being a military wife. They got married in 2001 and eventually did tours of duty in Whidbey and Pensacola. In 2006, they thought an instructor tour in Pensacola was a good time to start a family, but when she was five months pregnant Sherm was sent to Iraq on an IA to do anti-IED work. He learned he had a son, Grayson, via satellite phone while he was camped near Baghdad. Another son, Trent, was born in 2008 while he was doing a staff tour at Oceana Naval Air Station in Virginia Beach. He was home for that one.

Sherm then made department head, which meant they had to head back to Whidbey. But his wife hated it there, hated the damp, and hated being so far away from her friends in South Carolina. Sherm fell back on the old military trope that it wasn't forever. She knew differently. They'd be there for three years and then another three if Sherm made command.

Her husband tried to turn her around, finding a beautiful house in the hills above Anacortes. He tried to make it a home in the three months before he had to meet the Black Ravens midcruise, but he could feel things falling apart.

Sherm went to see his mentor, Captain Tom Slais, his first Prowler skipper. Slais had moved up the ranks and was now commodore of NAS Whidbey, overseeing all the Whidbey Prowler squadrons. Sherm told him his domestic situation. Slais wanted to help. The commodore called Tupper on the *Nimitz* and asked if he could spare Sherm and have him join the Black Ravens back in Whidbey after their deployment. But their conversation was classic militarese, both speaking in a code the other didn't understand. Slais didn't tell Tupper why he wanted to keep Sherm home and Tupper didn't ask. Instead, Tupper told Slais that if Sherm didn't make part of the deployment he'd have a hard time bonding with the guys once they made it back to Whidbey. He wouldn't have shared experiences with them, either in the air or in the ready room. Slais said he understood.

Sherm shipped out to the *Nimitz* in February, meeting the Black Ravens in Hong Kong. His wife left him a month later. When Tupper found out, he felt unwittingly responsible. He would have left Sherm at home if he had known.

"She told me 'I still love you, but I just don't want to be married to you anymore,'" Sherm told me. "What does that mean?"

I told Sherm I didn't know and that I was really sorry. My own feelings were confused. I tried to sympathize with his wife—I knew losing a father at such a vulnerable age can cause incalculable damage—but ditching a husband on deployment and moving his kids 3,000 miles away made me equally furious. I asked him, dumbly, how he was doing.

"I'm fine."

The ready room had filled with a few more officers grab-assing and waiting for "midrats," a fourth meal served on a carrier around midnight. He pointed at the other men dressed in the same green flight suits.

"These guys are my family."

Sherm had known most of them for less than a month.

SHERM TOOK ME UP ON DECK for afternoon recoveries the next day. We stood at the front of the boat with the landing signal officers as they talked to the pilots approaching the *Nimitz*. There was a rhythm to the chaos. A sailor shouted "foul deck, foul deck" in a singsong voice until the previous jet was cleared off the landing strip and then sang "clear deck, clear deck." I could catch snippets of the one-way conversations between the LSOs and the pilots. If the LSO was soothing it meant the pilot was on track; an urgent repeat of "power, power" at escalating volume meant hit the throttle hard so you don't strike the ramp and die. We stood maybe thirty feet away as Tupper brought his Prowler in on a smooth break and caught the number two wire. Sherm tapped me on the shoulder.

"You've got a pretty damn big smile on your face."

He was right. I was ecstatic, bouncing up on the toes of my flight boots looking for the next plane to emerge out of the clouds. For the next hour, I watched as planes emerged out of the darkness and, somehow, returned home to a tiny speck of America in the Pacific Ocean.

But then I went to a dark place. The idea that I never had and never would have a conversation with Dad about what it's like to land a jet on a carrier was unbearable. I thought back to how close I came to spending a week at sea with him. A week on board as a thirteen-year-old and maybe I would have followed in his flight boots, somehow triumphing over my lack of coordination. Would that have made him proud?

After the last plane landed, Sherm and I made our way back down to the Ravens' ready room. I told him I had a headache from the noise, but that was a lie. I went back to my room and slid into my bunk and closed my eyes. Mom always said after the accident that Dad was about to be rotated off flying to a staff position within a year. "God took him doing something he loved," she said. "Maybe God knew he wouldn't be able to live without it."

I always thought that was bullshit. Now I wasn't so sure.

I WAS PLAYING BACKGAMMON IN THE ready room when Tupper told me he had a surprise for me.

"We're going to get you up in a flight. I want you to see what it's like to come in off the break and catch a wire."

I thought he was joking, but he wasn't. VIPs flew all the time, he said. General Petraeus got up in a Hornet just a couple of months ago. There was just one problem: I wasn't the most powerful general in the United States. We were somewhere between Okinawa and Midway Island with no divert fields. I'd be ejecting straight into the Pacific Ocean if things went badly. This could be a slight impediment since I had no parachute experience, zero water survival information, and negative motor skills. It was typical Tupper—push the idea and don't sweat the reality.

"Don't worry. I can make this happen."

I did the math and calculated ten careers—from Tupper to the secretary of the Navy—that would be ended by a *Navy*

Times headline reading "Son of Dead Prowler Pilot Dead in Prowler Mishap." But it wasn't my call. Tupper was persistent and pushed the paperwork. Before long, I was down in the *Nimitz*'s hospital undergoing a physical. Blood was drawn, hearing was tested, and three chest x-rays were administered because the corpsman kept loading the film in backward.

Everything checked out. Tupper told me he was just waiting for CAG to sign off on the request. Finally, I believed him. That night, there was a nervous tingle in my stomach not completely attributable to my consumption of a vat of tater tots at dinner. I lay in bed thinking of a catapult shot and the water rushing below me. What would it mean to me? What would I now understand?

But the next morning, Tupper took me aside. He put his hand on my shoulder.

"It's not going to happen. The boss said no."

"No big deal. It was always a long shot."

"We'll get you up from Whidbey, I promise."

"Sure."

I smiled and walked away, heading back to my room. My roommates were either flying or briefing. I climbed into my rack, pulled the flimsy curtain shut, and cursed into my pillow.

Chapter Twenty-One

I DECIDED TO GET OUT OF politics when I was twenty-five and take a job mirroring the uncertainty of my childhood. I can't say I woke up one morning and decided I wanted a career where I was always the new kid, but that's exactly what happened.

I was in grad school at Loyola for political science and wrote a paper on Greece's entry into the Common Market. I was a little short on scholarly research, so I riffed a bit, throwing in a joke or five. My professor wrote, "The *Chicago Tribune* will pay you good money to write like this." It was the first time I thought about writing for a living. I began freelancing for an alternative weekly in Chicago. On a whim, I applied for a $200-a-week internship as a researcher at the *New Republic* in Washington. Somehow, I got it. I moved to D.C. a few weeks later.

I hadn't met more than two or three Ivy Leaguers in my entire life and now they surrounded me. There were weekly editorial meetings where English philosopher Michael Oakeshott was casually quoted and the predilections of Israeli politicians were debated. The people doing the talking were folks I'd seen on *The McLaughlin Group* and the meetings were presided over by Andrew Sullivan, who was also a model for the Gap. I had no idea what the hell they were talking about half the time. It wasn't until years later that I realized they didn't know either.

Eventually, the nausea about saying the wrong thing went away. I was lucky. No one expected much from me. The other interns were drowning under the weight of their expectations. There was an odd woman who was obsessed by my button nose. She remarked, "Every time I look at you, your nose gets smaller and smaller." She disappeared after a plagiarism scandal. The guy next to me had a terrible secret: he went to Penn for a year before transferring to Harvard. (I didn't learn this until a decade later.) And then there was the preppy fellow who was nicknamed Masthead Man for his photographic memory of the staff of every magazine this side of *Redbook*. Compared to them I was well adjusted.

These kids were all used to doors opening for them. I didn't even know there were doors. The staff didn't discourage their delusions of grandeur. The writer Michael Lewis was there at the time and took me to lunch toward the end of my internship. "I'm not sure why we can't pick up the phone and get you a job at *GQ*. Let me look into it."

I never heard back from him. But that was okay. A friend house-sat for Lewis and we threw a party where we built a shrine out of the eleven different language versions of *Liar's Poker* he had stacked in his living room.

Sometimes, I had to walk home because I was too broke for the Metro. The only lodging I could afford was the handyman's apartment off the trash room in a three-story building on a sketchy Capitol Hill street. I woke every morning to the landlord's mutt taking a squirt on the small, scarred windows above my bed that provided the only natural light to the place.

I learned other things, particularly the power of Dad's story. I wrote a column about visiting his marker at Arlington

National Cemetery. It was well received by the magazine's mercurial editor in chief, Martin Peretz. My reward was holding cellist Yo-Yo Ma's coat while he played tunes for Al Gore at a posh *New Republic* party shortly before the 1993 presidential inauguration. This seemed like a fair trade.

BY JUNE, MY INTERNSHIP WAS UP and I was down to my last $300. I was about to move back to Chicago when a friend told me of a job opening at *Boston Magazine*, a city monthly specializing in political profiles and clam chowder recommendations. I was flown up for the interview and put up in a posh hotel by a newish editor in chief just in from Cleveland. He was impressed by my *New Republic* experience and didn't seem to care that my job description largely centered on faxing an in-the-tank journalist's campaign articles to Hillary Clinton days before publication. He hired me over a third glass of white wine.

I wasn't being paid much, but it was enough to afford a one-bedroom apartment in a nice section of Boston's South End. Or so I thought. My first Sunday, there was a front-page *Globe* story about an unsolved gang-related murder from a year earlier. The photograph above the fold looked out from where the shots had been fired. It looked vaguely familiar. I then realized it was shot from my front stoop.

One night, I heard a rustling noise and saw a shadow in my apartment. I threw the light on. There was no thief, but something worse, a watermelon-sized rat. I shrieked like a Brownie at her first sleepaway camp.

The landlord came over the next morning and stuffed chicken wire into a hole between the refrigerator and the dishwasher where he thought the rats were coming in. He declared the problem solved. Not quite. I came home that night to a rat on my kitchen counter, forcing its way into my Jif peanut butter jar with just its fangs. I flung a can of SpaghettiOs at it; the rat skittered away to God knows where. I restuffed the hole with some old Graham Greene paperbacks. I came home the next night to find Greene's *The Quiet American* and a loaf of bread half-digested on the kitchen floor. I messengered my landlord the paperback with a note reading, "Thought you might enjoy this one. The rats obviously did."

He was not amused. Still, he installed some snap traps around the apartment. I came home a few nights later to a black rat flopping like a salmon on the deck of a fishing boat, his neck pinned by the snap trap. I shrieked some more and went for a three-hour walkabout hoping the rat would die while I was out.

I ventured back around midnight and found the rat completely still. Thank God! I took a shot of vodka and impaled the rat with a broom handle for disposal. This merely reanimated the rat. This time, it was the rat that shrieked as his little legs did a bicycle pump. I puked in the sink.

I opened my back window and hurled my rat-on-a-stick into the back alley. I hoped it might serve as a visual deterrent to his brothers, much like the Romans crucifying Christians along the Appian Way. Still, the rats came.

Times like that made me miss Dad so badly. I'd come a long way, but there were so many things I couldn't do, so many things I didn't understand. I could cold-call senators and lawyers, but simple things left me petrified and useless. Things a boy should have learned from his father.

Chapter Twenty-Two

TUPPER WAS TWO WEEKS FROM HOME when the Goat Locker told him that Seaman Cruz Roblero had stolen an iPod belonging to another sailor. Roblero was an East LA kid who joined the Navy to escape the gang violence that killed his brother, but he was constantly chafing at the Navy's discipline. He had a sneaky smile that made him look guilty even when he wasn't doing anything wrong.

Tupper had been patient through some of his earlier screwups—malingering, petty theft on shore—but stealing from shipmates was a near capital offense. The sailors slept in rows of stacked bunks with only a glorified high school locker to stash their gear. Stealing in such close quarters led to fistfights. It was unforgivable.

Tupper might have gone easier on Roblero earlier in the deployment, but he was sick of carrying dead weight. He met with Roblero and the sailor cried and told him he was just borrowing the iPod. Tupper told Roblero it was just a pathetic attempt to save his skin. There would be no mercy. Tupper went at him hard. He wanted him court-martialed, a move that would earn him a dishonorable discharge and cost him all his veterans' benefits. If convicted, Roblero could do a year in the brig, military jail, once the Black Ravens returned to Whidbey.

This wasn't a popular move with his men. Roblero was a crappy sailor, but he had his friends and they wouldn't look kindly on someone doing jail time for stealing an iPod. The *Nimitz*'s lawyer and his own officers weren't on board either. Tupper thought it was just because they didn't want to do the work. A court-martial meant a three-day investigation by the *Nimitz*'s military police followed by a trial with a jury of chief petty officers. A half dozen of Tupper's men would have to submit to lengthy interrogations—both time-consuming and nerve-racking—as they tried to get the planes ready for the fly-off.

The *Nimitz*'s lawyer leaned on Tupper to take Roblero to captain's mast, a move that would end his career but would avoid a trial and carry no jail time. She suggested it would be easier on everyone. But Tupper wouldn't budge. Captain's mast was for work screwups and dereliction of duty. This was a criminal act. Besides, it was *his* squadron. If he thought Roblero warranted court-martial that should be it.

The next day, the lawyer told him it wasn't his decision anymore. There would be no court-martial and there would be no more arguing about it. Tupper was furious. Was it really his squadron? If so, why was he taking orders from a pissant lieutenant lawyer?

He took his frustration out on Roblero the next morning. At 8:30, the squadron was assembled below deck. The sailors were in their blues, their hands behind their backs. The officers were in khakis and flight jackets. Tupper entered in his dress whites and everyone stood at attention. Roblero was brought in from the brig by two MPs. You could hear him before you could see him. His arms and legs clanked as he shuffled in. He was wearing leg and arm irons. The MPs undid Roblero's shackles and he stood in front of the skipper. Tupper began to speak.

"Seaman Recruit Roblero, I want to be clear about why you are here, and why you are not here today in an open mast before the Black Raven team. You are *not* here to be publicly humiliated, degraded, or embarrassed."

Of course, this wasn't true. The whole point of a captain's mast was to publicly shame a sailor and persuade his fellow shipmates not to screw up lest they suffer the same humiliation.

"You have had a tough life before the Navy. I could say that about dozens of sailors in this audience. But you are the one who did wrong. The Navy was your ticket out of the barrio, the street gangs that claimed the life of your brother."

A couple of officers exhaled and shifted on their feet. Another rolled his eyes. Tupper had pronounced "barrio" with an over-the-top guttural inflection, like a Caucasian news anchor saying "Nicaraguan contras" back in the 1980s.

His officers were exhausted; they just wanted to do their jobs and go home. They were tired of Tupper's speeches. But Tupper wasn't done. His cadence moved to controlled shouting. Small flecks of spittle radiated from his mouth as he spoke.

"YOU HAVE AN HONOR PROBLEM. Maybe you can fool a bleeding heart, game a sympathetic ear from someone in religious ministries or medical, but not here. You won't fool the Old Man. I'm a sailor. And these are all sailors. You can't fool your own."

A woman in the ranks began sobbing. Tears rolled down her cheeks as she fought to remain at attention. Tupper looked at her with disgust and kept speaking.

"The only expectation that I ever had for you was the same

expectation I have for every Black Raven: do your best, do the right thing, and take care of shipmates. You not only did not take care of shipmates, you tried to HURT shipmates. And for that, you're going back into the box. You don't like the box? Don't steal. I am sorry you failed. But I am not sorry to see you leave. May you forever regret what you have lost here today."

Roblero shuffled forward and gave Tupper a stiff salute. The MPs chained his hands again and he was led back to the brig, his chains clanking behind him. He would receive only bread and water until the *Nimitz* pulled into port.

Tupper knew his sailors were mortified. Roblero was a fuckup, but few thought he deserved the full disgrace of Tupper's words. He tried to win them back.

"Ravens, do not be discouraged! This squadron is a winning team, and for every bad sailor, there are 167 others striving for excellence. Keep your eyes on the prize: safe, up aircraft, and caring for each other. The tide is turning, and it turns in our favor!"

But the tide wasn't turning in Tupper's favor. That evening, I was in my room with Stoli, Wolf, and Lil Chris. They had decided to have a final *Date Night* of the cruise. We all watched Colin Farrell misplay Alexander the Great on the screen while we feasted on goodies sent from home. Lil Chris produced a giant packet of smoked salmon and Stoli rustled up some gourmet crackers. We drank some awful Bahraini fake beer and laughed at Farrell's attempt at gravitas. Wolf was in a better mood, but he thought Tupper had been wrong.

"That didn't have to go like that," said Wolf. "He put on

that whole show for your benefit. He loves an audience. He can't help himself."

We bullshitted for a while, and then there was a knock on the door. Lil Chris jumped up. He'd become my protector of sorts, warding off the *Nimitz*'s public affairs guys who kept checking up on me, wanting to see if I wanted to tour the nuclear reactors or some other godforsaken part of the boat.

"If that's the freak public affairs officer again, I'm going to tell him to fuck off."

But it wasn't the public affairs guy. It was Tupper. He looked pale and uncertain, the exact opposite of this morning's command performance. He asked me if I could come down to his room.

I thought I'd done something wrong. I followed him down the dimly lit hallway. He pushed opened his door, and I took a seat on his couch. Tupper slumped into a chair.

"CAG shot me. I'm done."

TUPPER'S PHONE KEPT RINGING THAT AFTERNOON while he was meeting with one of his chiefs. He finally picked up. It was CAG asking him to stop by his office as soon as possible. Tupper headed down a few minutes later. CAG offered no small talk. He told him he wasn't going to get one of the top two fit reps among the squadron skippers. Tupper just nodded, expressing no emotion. Finally, he asked a question.

"If there's an area I haven't seen or an area I should have focused on, can you let me know what that is?"

CAG nodded. He quickly ticked off the cruise lowlights: Seaman Headden's accident, the Midway Island fiasco, and Crapper's botched accident report.

Tupper didn't respond. There wasn't anything to say. CAG told Tupper to call Beth and let him know in the next forty-eight hours his preference for his next duty station.

Tupper knew this was a farce. He was destined for Navy middle management, which meant more sea duty. He would retire with full benefits and there was even a chance he could still make captain if he stuck it out for another five years. But he'd never run his own ship or command sailors again. He had gone from Top Gun to Willy Loman in five minutes. Two hours later, he still couldn't quite believe what had just happened.

"I thought I was going down for I don't know what. It was literally like a drive-by shooting." He referenced the ill-fated Black Raven flight over Midway. "I can't believe Hot Carl and some below-average electronic countermeasures officers are going to sink my career."

I could see he regretted trashing his guys the moment after he said it. But he was crushed. He had already called Beth. She was pissed about the timing. Couldn't they have waited a week? Couldn't they let him enjoy his fly-in and his home-coming? But they both knew the Navy didn't work that way. Timing, feelings, and emotions were civilian luxuries. All he could do now was catch his breath.

"I think CAG underestimated how far we've come," he said quietly. His eyes were glassy. "I'm completely unprepared to deal with this."

I asked him who he thought was going to get the top slot between the COs. He let himself slip back into bitter-ness.

"It's going to be Mongo Koss, the Hornet guy next door.

Everyone always knew he was the golden child. He's a great guy, but he's got the newest jets on the flight deck."

A thousand thoughts were rushing through Tupper's head. Should he apply for an IA slot in Afghanistan or Iraq? Maybe he could do that for a year; that would bring him right up to twenty. That would allow the girls to stay in the same schools. Or maybe a ground job in Pax River? But that place had so many bad memories from back when the girls were small and Beth was sick. Should he tell Vinnie? Or maybe that just made him a lame duck.

I tried to make him feel better. I told him of jobs I didn't get, contracts not renewed, assignments killed. I didn't think it was much solace, but Tupper was touched. It wasn't until later that I realized it wasn't anything specific that I'd said, but just another man admitting failure wasn't something he was used to hearing from the Navy.

We talked until there was nothing else left to say. It was midnight and Tupper still needed to pack up his room. I told him to get some sleep, but I knew he wouldn't.

I walked back to my stateroom. The combined stench of smoked salmon and American men in an unventilated room hit me the second I opened the door. It was strangely comforting. Stoli, Lil Chris, and the Wolf were all asleep in their bunks, dreaming of wives just a few days away. I lay in my bunk thinking of all the sacrifices Tupper and Beth had made. All the time away from the girls. I wondered if Dad had reached this moment of diminishing returns. Would he have returned from that last cruise, seen me a head taller, and said, "My God, what have I missed?"

TUPPER WOKE UP TO EMAILS FROM Caitlin and Brenna, telling him they'd love him promotion or no promotion. The messages simultaneously lifted his spirits and pissed him off. He thought he'd told Beth he wanted to tell the girls himself when he got home. It was just another in a long line of misunderstandings.

Tupper's face was gray by the time I saw him at lunch. It was only twelve hours since he got shot and his body had already dropped its pack.

"I'm coming down with the ship crud. I'm losing fluid from both ends."

I asked him if he was well enough for the fly-off the day after tomorrow. It seemed overly cruel—even by Navy standards—that he'd miss flying home with his men. He told me he was going to be fine. Walking off the boat when the *Nimitz* pulled into Bremerton was an indignity he couldn't take. He then excused himself and raced for the head.

That night, the air wing held *Focs'l Follies*, an end-of-cruise series of skits and awards ceremony. It didn't go well for the Black Ravens. They didn't win anything and CAG's staff, fearful that I would see something shocking, ejected me. Afterward, Tupper briefed the flight crews on the fly-off. He told a funny story about spinning a Prowler while taxiing on an icy runway in Colorado, emphasizing that unsafe flying this close to home could be deadly.

But he didn't take his own advice. The next morning, Tupper made it to CAG's daily meeting but then went back to bed. No one saw him for the rest of the day. Around dinnertime, Doc stopped by his stateroom. She took one look and sent him down to sickbay, where he got hooked up to an IV. His flight was a half day away and he could barely stand up. But he would fly anyway.

Chapter Twenty-Three

I'D FINALLY FOUND SOMETHING THAT I was good at with magazine writing. Stories about everything from John Kerry to teenage killers to New Kids on the Block reunion tours tumbled out of me. The rats disappeared, but Boston never felt like home. I was lonely and Boston was full of eggheads and indie rockers on the make. If you weren't part of their scene, you didn't exist.

Then a friend told me she had someone she wanted me to meet: an Australian woman of Lebanese descent, dark-haired and olive-skinned. Like me, she came from nowhere. She was at Boston University on a Rotary scholarship and was wide-eyed and ravenous for her new country. We made each other laugh, but that was it. I walked her home after our first dinner and nothing happened. (Her sisters called me No Zing for years because of our initial lack of chemistry.) This went on for a couple of weeks until we went to see *The Piano.* I'm not sure if it was the antipodean story or Harvey Keitel's dangling member, but something happened that night.

After that, we were inseparable. She was charismatic and would go to any extreme to sell a joke, once stuffing an entire orange into her mouth and then trying to speak. This mattered. We walked home on a December night and leaf-size snowflakes began dropping from the sky. She began dancing and skipping down the sidewalk. "I know I'm acting like a girl in a douche commercial, but I can't help it," she told me through happy tears. It was her first snow. An hour later, we lay on the ground and made snow angels.

We fell in love. We were both essentially fatherless, broken people, but broken in the same way. Her dad had walked out on his wife and five children. He only gave money to his one son. Her mom tried to make a living the best she could by working at bars and restaurants. Somehow, my girlfriend earned a degree while working collecting debts for a department store. Her three sisters had proven less adept at throwing off the family trauma. One was married to a sketchy businessman; the other two were permanently single. I was the first man in the family's history not to be seen as a total asshole.

I can honestly say I never gave her personal history and the impact it might have on our relationship a single thought in the first six years we were together. Our past was not prologue. But her dad's abandonment and my father's death had left understandable scars; any attempt by either of us to negotiate our relationship was met with accusations that we were trying to take things away from the other. She said the thing she loved most about me was that I never let her go to bed mad. It was true. No matter what the dispute, I'd be there with a joke or an elaborate gag to make her laugh before the lights went out. These were skills I learned as a boy.

BOSTON BECAME OUR BATTLEGROUND. FOR HER, it was manageable and offered a sense of security that she lacked as a child. I was bored senseless. I was freelancing for national magazines and my home and work life separated at a ridiculous rate. On the road, I had great adventures with no-hope presidential candidates and boxers on their fourth comeback.

At home, I was a regular at the 10:50 a.m. Friday showings of every new movie that played on the postage stamp–sized screens at Boston's Copley Place. The Navy brat in me grew restless. Things got bad enough that I moved for work first to Philadelphia and then to New York and commuted home on the weekends. I told myself the moves were for better jobs, but I was now thirty and repeating Dad's life in another way: 100 percent faithful in a part-time relationship.

So we decided to get hitched. Why? That was my bright idea. I was a good Catholic boy. And I guess I thought once we were contractually bonded she would understand my commitment to her and would be amenable to moving somewhere else. We were married in an Australian Navy chapel with giant windows on a bluff overlooking Sydney Harbor. (Her father wasn't invited.) We exchanged vows as a military jet passed outside the windows and, according to the Harrisons, waggled its wings as we said "I do."

It seemed meant to be. But she had just been offered a job at *The Boston Globe*; it was too great an opportunity for her to pass up. I moved back to the town I loathed, but we agreed it was just for a year or two. That was at the end of 1998. Within a year, she was covering John McCain's presidential campaign. We both thought this was somewhat hilarious since McCain was a Naval Academy grad of my dad's era and she had only a tenuous grasp on American politics. I wrote her up a 3,500-word annotated history of the New Hampshire primaries, helped her pack up our Sentra, and she headed north.

She spent most of the next year on the road covering McCain; this made me alternately miserable—I missed her terribly—and ecstatic—her absence allowed me to flee Boston for friends in Los Angeles and Chicago. But even the 2000 campaign eventually ended. She was now a star at the paper and all talk of moving to New York or Los Angeles ceased. And she wanted to start a family.

Our arguments left me bitterly reflecting on my own childhood. Dad had given up nothing for his wife and children. Not his dangerous profession, not his career climbing. And now, having endured that, I was supposed to be the postmodern man, sinking my own ambitions for a wife and unborn child? I faced some of the hardest decisions of my life. As usual, I felt unprepared and alone.

THERE ARE TURNING POINTS IN LIFE that you don't notice at the time. The dissolution of my marriage wasn't one of them. I can tell you exactly when it imploded. It was in a third-floor room of the New Orleans Ritz-Carlton. I was profiling a seventeen-year-old jockey and we had just flown in from San Francisco for the Eclipse Awards on an interminable flight where we took turns stealing liquor bottles off the airline cart. At the airport, a horse owner picked us up with an open case of Coors on the backseat of his Cadillac. An hour later, I had just fallen into a hard, drunken sleep when the phone rang. I heard the Australian accent that still killed me eight years after falling in love with her. She was excited.

"I found the perfect house."

I expected to hear the tale of another overpriced condo we could barely afford in the Back Bay or the South End.

"It's in Nahant."

Nahant is a lovely town on the north shore of Massachusetts, surrounded on three sides by the Atlantic Ocean. It was home to our best friends and their two kids whom I desperately loved. Often, I would make the thirty-minute trek from Boston to soak up their food, play on their backyard tire swing, and have a swim. But I had no desire to live there. Nahant is nearly all white, houses one pizza joint, and is fifteen miles through horrible traffic and strip malls from the limited possibilities of Boston. I saw a Stephen King existence in my future: not that of the wealthy writer but of a man driven slowly insane by isolation.

"Nahant? I thought we agreed I didn't want to live there."

A forty-five-minute monologue followed. I don't remember the particulars except for a repeated phrase: "If you don't want to buy the house, you were never committed to this marriage."

I could have said no, but I was never good at that, not in that relationship, not in my life. I could feel her slipping away from me, so I did what I always do with loved ones who threaten to slip away. I surrendered. I said okay and hung up.

I FLEW HOME THE NEXT NIGHT on a red-eye that was caught in a blizzard, so I didn't land at Logan until 10:00 a.m. We had to make an offer that afternoon. In a haze, I walked through the wood floors, saw the distant sea view, noted my wife's enthusiasm, and signed the papers. I just wanted her not to be mad at me anymore.

We moved in two months later. Shortly after the moving truck arrived, a friend stopped by and found me wandering aimlessly through the rooms. "Dead man walking," he quipped. It wasn't too far from the truth.

I spent the next year in a deep depression. I lived a double life there. I'd jet off to wherever and interview a quarterback or a murder suspect or the occasional Colombian rebel. In some ways, I was living the big life I always wanted. But at home, I struggled to get out of bed before ten. On a good day, I'd fall into my rusting Honda and drive three miles to the YMCA in nearby Lynn, a dying industrial town. The Y on a weekday morning was populated with retirees in their sixties from a nearby General Electric plant. They were a rough bunch—there was a sign in the shower that read "Cleaning habits that may be acceptable at home may be considered offensive by other patrons"—and the regulars would blast CNBC and trot on treadmills without bothering to change out of their flannel shirts and deer-hunting orange hats. I'd move quickly toward the pool where I'd share a lane with a mildly retarded man who eagerly awaited my arrival with a lopsided smile and a propensity to scissor-kick me in the ribs every lap or so.

But in the water I'd lose myself. Swimming lap after lap, I'd envision an escape to Los Angeles or New York. No more lunches at Wendy's on the Lynnway, no more being awakened by the lobsterman's backfiring truck as he headed off to tend his traps at four in the morning. My fantasy woman was a lot like my wife, but without the picket fence fetish. She would be a slightly bohemian type with an artsy job who wanted to raise boho kids in a shambling, run-down apartment in Brooklyn or Santa Monica.

Every day, I wrote for a couple hours, called friends across the country, and then slipped into a two- or three-hour nap. Some days, I wandered the deserted roads of our town. Nobody walked there, so this led to my being hassled by the cops. This did not improve my attitude. By the time my wife arrived home, I wasn't fit company for anyone. Surly and sarcastic became my default settings. There were ultimatums and timetables given for my improvement. I entered therapy. I took Paxil. She became convinced that I wasn't going to be a fit husband or good father until I came to grips with the death of my own father.

I agreed, but how?

THEN 9/11 CAME. THE PLANES THAT destroyed the World Trade Towers took off from Boston Logan, passing over our little town before making a U-turn and heading south. When it became clear what had happened, she headed into work. For some reason, I drove to the T and took it to Logan. The once bustling terminals were now quiet except for a woman sweeping the floor while crying quietly to herself.

The *Globe* sent my wife to Pakistan a few weeks later. I returned to Flint for Thanksgiving. The country's buildup to war triggered something long buried. The night I arrived, Mom and my sisters watched the news and footage of planes taking off from faraway carriers. I lay on the couch and felt a physical weight crushing my chest. I stared at Dad's planes on the mantel and his portrait on the wall. I wanted to scream, "He died!"

But I said nothing. Still, it was the first hint of an awakening. I went to bed and woke up at 5:00 a.m. with a fear I had never felt before, not while on dangerous assignments with Colombian narco-terrorists or while riding in BMWs with suspected murderers. I stumbled outside and walked through our neighborhood until dawn. I told Mom I had to get away.

We sat in her car at a gas station before I left and I asked her why we never talked about Dad.

"I thought it would be too painful for you," she said. "People told me we should move on and look forward, not back."

I left an hour later. I wandered the country, visiting friends from Chicago to California. I watched the network news extol the bravery of our pilots as footage of their red taillights heading off to Afghanistan played in the background. I changed the channel.

Things between my wife and me deteriorated. When she came back from Pakistan, I met her at Logan in a driver's cap with her name written on a piece of cardboard, but she didn't laugh at all. That's when I knew I was screwed.

Then I got an email from the Navy. I had tried getting on board an aircraft carrier for a magazine story earlier in the year after my wife's urging, but it fell apart after 9/11. But then the Navy changed their mind; this was going to be a long war, and maybe some good publicity in a glossy mag was not a bad thing. I was invited to spend three weeks deployed with a Hornet squadron. When I saw what carrier they were on I lost my breath; it was the *Kitty Hawk*, Dad's last boat.

If this wasn't dealing with his death, nothing short of orchestrating my own plane crash would do. I departed for Hong Kong to meet the carrier two weeks later. We promised not to make any decisions while I was away.

I saw Dad's ready room. I saw where he prayed. On a murky night off Singapore, I wandered onto the deck of the *Kitty Hawk* in an Ambien haze and walked the few hundred feet in the tracks of the catapult that launched him to his death. I stumbled to the edge of the boat, nearly pitching over the side into a sea of darkness. And I wept.

I returned three weeks later, tan and ten pounds heavier from too many midrats corn dogs—and with a new understanding of my father. It didn't pay immediate dividends. That Sunday, in a Gap parking lot, my wife told me she was leaving me.

"It's just not working."

For once in my life, I said nothing. My first thought was, "In a Gap parking lot? Are you fucking kidding?" We rode home in silence. It turned out I was going to be doing the leaving. At the house, I threw some clothes into two giant duffel bags and laughed bitterly at the wallpaper I had been peeling off our bedroom walls—prep work for a renovation that now would never happen. I tossed my CDs into a crate and packed up my Honda for a trip to see the Harrisons in Chicago.

At first, I tried to maintain my dignity, but our goodbye was more Rowlands and Cassavetes than Hepburn and Tracy. I was fine for a while and then flopped on the kitchen floor, bawling uncontrollably. My wife wondered whether she should call the paramedics.

Finally, I gathered myself and drove away. Five minutes later she called me.

"Aha," I smirked. Second thoughts already.

"You forgot your laptop."

That was basically the end. Eventually, I wrote an essay about moving to New York as a newly re-singled man and mentioned our divorce in a setup paragraph. There were no names. She read it and never took another call of mine. In a way, she enacted my most primal fear from childhood: someone I desperately loved walking away and slamming the door shut.

My reaction to the silent treatment was less than manly. I left begging messages. I implored friends to intercede. I made her a mix CD. Then I turned comically thuggish. I read about how the Romans handled the Carthaginians and toyed with driving to Nahant and spreading Morton's salt over her beloved tomato garden. A friend convinced me that might be a felony.

A year or two passed and I avoided Boston at all costs, turning down assignments that brought me anywhere near the so-called Hub of the Universe. But I had an accountant who took profoundly liberal deductions for me. She'd done my taxes over the phone for two years after I moved because of my begging, but then insisted I come and do them in person if I wanted to keep using her. I had to do it. My whole personal financial system was built around her visionary use of the home office deduction. I made plans to stay with friends in Nahant, just two blocks from my former home.

I got drunk with a couple of friends in Manhattan the night before my trip. Around closing time, I proclaimed that maybe it would be a great idea if I toilet-papered my old house the next night. Everyone agreed this was a splendid idea. We all stole rolls of toilet paper from the bathroom at Lucky Strike, a SoHo bar I cherished like an old friend. We crashed back at my place and built a tower of stolen toilet paper on my Danish modern dining room table, the one cool thing I'd claimed in our divorce.

It seemed like a less good idea the next morning. I hit a

baseball game at Shea Stadium for work and then drove up to Nahant that afternoon. I had dinner with my friends and their kids. Still hung over, I turned in early and fell asleep.

I woke at 3:00 a.m., wide-awake. I knew what I had to do. I gathered up two rolls from the guest bathroom and threw on a black jacket. I headed out in my socks—better not to leave shoeprints, I thought. I crossed a cemetery and tripped over a headstone, doing a face plant into some kind of animal feces.

Now covered in shit, I trudged on. A few minutes later, a police car drove by making his nightly rounds. I dove behind a shed into a pile of moldy two-by-fours festooned with rusty nails. Dodging lockjaw, I tiptoed the last block. I saw the old house, an unassuming sky blue Cape Codder. It still made me shiver a little. I looked around and saw that the coast was clear. I tossed a roll into a pear tree that used to carve scratches on my arms when I tried to mow around it. I did it one more time. Then I got the hell out of there. It was such a pathetic job that I'm not sure my ex ever noticed; or she may have just blamed it on neighbor kids. She was much too cool a customer to let on either way.

I was now two years older than Dad when he died. He commanded men and flew off carriers. I was TP-ing my ex's house. The comparison was not flattering.

Chapter Twenty-Four

I FLEW OFF ON THE COD the morning before the Black Ravens so I could get to Whidbey in time for the fly-in. The *Nimitz* had tracked north toward home and the water temperature was below 60 degrees, so all passengers had to wear fluorescent orange cold-weather suits. The suits would keep you alive in the water for three hours, but how you were supposed to survive a crash was another matter. The COD only had a hatch up top; there was no way to bail out. We would all be riding that sucker into the water in case of emergency.

The guys convinced me that wearing civvies under the cold-weather suit would be uncomfortable, so I put my flight suit back on. We shot off the *Nimitz*'s catapult and I thought of Dad being launched from that same catapult when I was a little boy.

We flew two hours to McChord Air Force Base just outside of Tacoma. I meant to change into my civvies right after we landed, but I wanted to share a taxi to Sea-Tac with a Hornet pilot so there was no time. We then sat in I-5 traffic for forty-five minutes. I was bone tired by the time we arrived and just wanted to get on the road before Seattle's nightmare rush hour. I started wandering the frequent-renter row of National Car Rental trying to choose between a Ford Fusion and a Chevy Malibu. I was in full option paralysis when a middle-aged man in a National windbreaker ran up to me. He stuck out his hand.

"We want to give you a free upgrade."

I shook his hand, but I was confused.

"For your service. To welcome you home."

I guess I sort of looked the part. My hair was fairly short and I had a three-week cruise 'stache going. I thanked the man and slid into the leather seat of a maroon Volvo.

I kept driving until I pulled into the parking lot of the Best Western on Whidbey. I didn't have a reservation, but the clerk said they had plenty of rooms. I'd left my wallet in the car and started back for it. The clerk told me not to worry about it.

"You're okay. You're getting the government rate. Your flight suit is your ID."

I just smiled, trudged to my room, and thought, "Well, you took my father when I needed him most, so I might as well save twelve bucks a night and get a comfy car." Sometimes, loss can be glib.

I went to my room and collapsed on the bed, just undoing the laces of my flight boots. I reeked of aviation fuel and desperately needed my first real shower in a month. But I didn't want to take my flight suit off. I knew it might be for the last time. Shedding the suit would make me lose Dad again.

THE NEXT MORNING, I PUT ON the uniform of the marginally employed American man—khakis and a dress shirt. Back on the *Nimitz*, Tupper looked like shit. He sat through the morning brief and tried to listen, but halfway through he excused himself and puked in a garbage can outside the ready room.

The Black Ravens just looked at each other and shrugged.

Getting all the Prowlers airborne was going to suck in the best of circumstances, and now their skipper was barely walking. Doc asked Tupper if he was okay to fly. He lied and said yes. No one said anything. In a way, it was a mirror image of Doogie's fly-off, the one Tupper screamed had been "unsat." Here was Tupper jumping into the cockpit massively dehydrated and with a fever. No one could really blame him, but it was "Do as I say, not as I do."

On the flight deck, mechanics in other squadrons placed bets on whether VAQ-135 could get all their Prowlers airborne. The consensus? No chance. They had watched the Black Ravens struggle all cruise with the Midway fiasco, the Headden accident, and the Crapper screwup. The *Nimitz* senior staff rolled their eyes last week when Tupper gave his bone-tired sailors twenty-four hours off against the recommendation of CAG. Tupper had made a simple deal with his guys: "I'll take care of you, but you need to take care of me and the squadron by getting these jets airborne." The salty old dogs on the *Nimitz* thought it was all so very heartwarming, but that was twenty-four hours to work on ancient planes the squadron wouldn't get back. There was no way they'd all get airborne.

But then Tupper launched first. The rest of the planes followed, even the Hangar Queen getting up without a hitch. It took less than fifteen minutes. The old-timers back on the *Nimitz* admitted maybe they had sold the Black Ravens a little short. The squadron Tupper had preached about, the one he'd always wanted, had come through for their skipper at last.

In the cockpit, Tupper allowed himself an instant of triumph while keeping an eye on his puke bag. He wanted to do a flyover of the *Nimitz* for the sailors of 135 still onboard, but the skies were soupy so the Black Ravens gave it a pass, preventing Tupper from giving the finger to the tower as they passed by at 450 knots. Instead, the Prowlers hit their tanker and then rendezvoused a few miles behind the boat. They were just sixty minutes from home.

I drove over to the base around the same time. I passed by Clover Valley Elementary School, where Timmy Newman had told me about his daddy's crash. I looked at the "Welcome Home Ravens" signs that lined the road to the main gate and thought of Mom and understood better why she had to get out of there. It was thirty years on and I still felt the twinge that everyone else's father was coming home, but not mine.

I walked into the Black Ravens' hangar and watched from a distance. The wind whipped at American flags and the skirts of wives determined to dress sexy no matter how glum the Whidbey weather. I recognized them from the pictures that hung in the ready room. They were all young, beautiful, and nervous.

Their kids whipped around the hangar, nearly toppling a table full of beer. Many of the little boys wore miniature flight suits, their hair slicked back. Chicken's kid came up to me, stopped smartly, and gave me a salute. For a moment, I was a child again. Mom was there too, licking her fingers and trying to tame my cowlick. She's telling me to calm down.

Here, Beth Ware ran the show and did a quick head count. Stonz's wife was running late. Beth knew Tammy Tornga would be ashamed if her husband landed after eight months gone and she was still in the parking lot. Beth called the tower, who relayed the message to Tupper. He understood. So he took the Black Ravens on one more lap around Whidbey.

Fifteen minutes later, the Prowlers came in low over the airfield, their Pratt & Whitney engines screaming. Everyone clapped while a Seattle TV station filmed the scene. The Prowlers then separated and peeled off one by one, landing two minutes apart. The planes then taxied across the runway slowly, a last few minutes of torture for the families.

The engines grew even louder. Moms slapped disposable earplugs into their kids' ears. Then the engines were cut. Canopies popped open, and aviators began climbing down. Decorum vanished. Wives sprinted in high heels across the deck and threw themselves in their husbands' arms. Vinnie gave his wife, Marci, a peck on the cheek and she handed him his boy. He kissed Henry on the cheek tentatively; it was hard to go from carrier deck to a new life so quickly.

Tupper climbed down last. Beth and the girls didn't run at first, but then Brenna sprinted toward him. Caitlin followed. They group-hugged and Tupper wobbled for a moment. But he managed to keep his feet, a boxer staggering back to his corner. Commodore Slais offered a handshake and welcomed him home. Tupper gave the TV station a sound bite about what an honor it was to serve his country and how good it felt to be back in the USA. Then his path crossed with Crapper, his two sons looking smart in their flight suits. There was a momentary pause and then Tupper stuck out his hand.

Twenty minutes later, everyone was gone. Gone to catch up with their kids. Gone to fuck their wives' brains out. I thought about going across the street to the Prowler memorial and putting my hands on Dad's plaque, but it felt like an empty gesture. I watched kids and dads pile into their cars.

I headed back to my motel room, picked up some Chinese takeout, and watched sitcoms for hours.

SHERM WASN'T ON THE FLY-IN. ONE officer had to stay onboard and supervise the load-off of the squadron's gear the next day when the *Nimitz* pulled into Bremerton. Sherm volunteered; he had joined the cruise late, and besides, he reasoned, there was no one waiting for him. He needed a ride home, so I drove down the next morning.

Around 11:00 a.m., the *Nimitz* gracefully slid into its berth. A band played while mothers and fathers, husbands and wives, and sons and daughters cheered and wept. The gangway dropped; and first-time fathers were allowed to disembark first regardless of rank. Tupper was there, still pale in a ski cap and a Carhartt field coat. He shook the hand of each Black Raven as their feet touched back on American soil.

The pier was deserted by 1:00 p.m. Sherm was supposed to be done by two o'clock, but this was the Navy, so the paperwork slid to three and three slid to four. The last papers were finally signed, and we took the ferry across to Seattle and made the long drive north. He called his wife and they talked for a few minutes, but all hope was gone; their marriage was finished. We pulled into his driveway in Anacortes just as last light was fading.

"Let's get this over with," said Sherm in a soft voice.

He took a breath and got out of the car. He turned the key and opened the door. The house was giant and modern, a Pottery Barn showroom after closing time. But there was no sign of life. His kids' closets were bare except for some sad, stray reminders. Trent's Mickey Mouse Halloween costume hung alone in the boys' bedroom. A child's finger-painting had fallen off the refrigerator and was curled up on the kitchen floor.

Sherm didn't say anything. His blue eyes were unreadable. We made a run into town and bought a pizza and some more beer. Back at the house, Sherm wanted to show me something. It was a cruise video from his time flying Prowlers over Iraq during the second Gulf War. He popped the DVD into a giant plasma-screen television downstairs in his living room. Between the television and leather couch was Trent's circular Fisher-Price train tracks complete with a ride-along engine and caboose. It had been too big to pack. Sherm turned up the sound.

"This was one of the greatest moments of my life. I want you to see it."

He fast-forwarded through port calls and onboard pranks. Soon we were over Iraq in the first days of the air war. Sherm was filming it all with a hand-held camera. For the air attack on Iraq, the Prowlers, usually unarmed, were fitted with missiles specifically designed to destroy Iraqi radar stations.

"Watch this. We track on a Iraqi missile site. Then we fire a HARM missile."

On the screen, Sherm's Prowler jumps a bit and a speck of white light fires off from the left wing. Back home, Sherm laughed and pointed at a darker speck on the screen.

"We locked in on an Iraqi radar station. So we fired a missile and we didn't see this B-52. And for a second we thought, 'Oh, shit, we're going to hit the B-52.' But it went way over the B-52's head. And then it went down and it did its job."

Sherm rewound the DVD. We watched it a few more times. Then he told me something I already knew.

"I love what I do for a living. I just love it. It's my life."

He stepped over the train tracks. For a second, I thought he was going to connect the dots between the train tracks and the missiles fired over Iraq, about the cost of the life he had chosen. But he just clicked off the television and got us each another beer.

ABOUT A MILE AWAY, TUPPER HAD company in the master bedroom bathroom. He'd rushed home from Bremerton to hear Caitlin's piano recital, falling asleep as she played "Edelweiss." That night, he and Beth had just gone to sleep when Caitlin barfed in her bed.

Tupper had been home a little more than a day and he'd already given his youngest the flu. They took turns in the bathroom. He'd throw up and then she'd throw up. Tupper told her he was so sorry that he had made her sick. But Caitlin didn't mind. She brushed a stray hair off her face, gave him a weak smile, and held his hand.

"That's okay, Daddy. I'd rather be sick with you here than be better without you."

I LEFT TUPPER AND SHERM IN Anacortes and headed up to Mount Baker two days later. I rented a condo in Snowater, the same complex where my family had come as a boy. The next morning, I drove up the mountain and sat in the same lodge where I waited for Dad to ski his last, icy run of the day. I had not been there in thirty years.

I'd turned the tables, or so I thought. Not long after he died, I happily gave up skiing and devoted my life pursuits to things where I had a baseline of competence. But then a funny thing happened. I missed it. I started skiing a few times a year in my thirties in Park City while covering the Sundance Film Festival and with my sister at Mount Bachelor near her home in Bend, Oregon. I wasn't good, but I'd become proficient, dreamily content to carve down the same blue run off Park City's Thaynes lift for hours and days.

I headed up to Baker with a specific goal. I wanted to ski down a run off the Shuksan lift that I remembered Dad skiing the winter before he died. Back then, we rode the chair up together and Dad tried to talk me into following him. But I was too scared. He went left off the lift and skied through the trees. I took an easier green run. I remember him arriving at the bottom with a big smile creased across the five o'clock shadow he allowed himself on weekends. I remember wishing I had the courage to go with him.

Today I was going to try. It was an idyllic spring afternoon, temperatures in the high forties and the mountain blissfully deserted. After a couple of shakedown runs, I jumped on Shuksan. I went left off the lift in search of a trail whose name I didn't know and a route I was trying to conjure out of memory.

Baker is a tough guy's mountain and prides itself on its lack of signs. I decided to go by feel. This was the first in a series of mistakes. The terrain grew steeper and narrower with every turn of my rental skis. The voice of reason told me to head back or at least ask one of the dwindling numbers of skiers for guidance. I did neither. Instead, I went farther until I found myself surrounded by a glade of trees on my left and an out-of-bounds sign on my right.

I had no idea where I was. All I knew was that the chairlift was to my left. If I found the chair, I could follow it down. So I pushed left, traversing the small sliver of a switchback trail. But I gained too much speed and my arm caught on the branch of an evergreen. My glove and pole were ripped off my left hand. By the time I skidded to a stop, my gear was twenty yards behind me.

Remembering Dad's litter hate, there was no way I was going to abandon my stuff out here in the wilderness. I took off my skis and began hoofing it back toward my gear. No one would tell you this was a smart plan. My ski boots plunged through the spring snow and soon I was chest-deep in slush.

My heart pounded. I could hear my sister Terry calling me an idiot. It was at this moment that I realized I could die here. There was no one around. It was near the end of the day. No one knew I was here. It would be long after dark before someone noticed my car in the parking lot.

I pushed onward toward my glove and pole. At one point, I nearly slid off the trail and down a ravine before grabbing a scraggly pine. If the tree had given way, bad things would have happened. But it held. By the time I got my glove, my clothes were soaked with sweat. I then hiked back to my skis. It took me an hour to complete a fifty-yard round trip.

The morning's brilliant sunshine was gone, replaced by late-afternoon gloom. From what I could see, I still had another seventy-five yards alongside a cliff edge before I made it to the regularly marked trail. A snowboarder stopped on a ledge about a hundred feet above me. He made no offer to help, only a "You stupid tourist" smile. I asked a question.

"Is the trail wider if I keep going straight?"

The snowboarder waited about fifteen seconds before responding.

"Sort of."

He cackled, jumped the cliff, and was gone. I cursed his coordination and sidestepped my way to the trail for another twenty minutes, hoping that salvation waited just ahead.

I was half-right. It wasn't so much a trail as a double black diamond mogul field stretching downward for maybe a quarter mile before leveling off near the chairlift. My sweat had turned into cold water on my skin and I couldn't stop shivering. But at least I could see the bottom. I maneuvered my way down some of the run, falling every other turn, my knees buckling and trembling.

And that's when I gave up. I plopped down in the snow and did a controlled slide down the rest of the trail on my ass.

I turned in my skis and sat in my old spot in the lodge for a half hour before I felt coherent enough to drive down the mountain. Back at the condo I took a hot bath. I then headed over to a cabin not far from where I was staying that was used by the condo association for barbecues, card games, and board meetings. Upstairs was a small room where Mom said Dad used to come and spend hours working on his fitness reports.

The room overlooked a trail and the Nooksack River, water flowing blue and white with the first of the spring's snowmelt. I settled into a chair and looked out the window, my legs still shaking. I sat there and listened to the river run by in the darkness. It was the first moment of stillness I'd felt in months. I thought of my family. Mom, who hadn't been on a date with another man. Terry, forever stoic about Dad.

And Christine, who didn't know him at all. I thought of my condescending attitude toward their denial while I was trying to set the record straight, retracing his steps, poring over his accident reports, and skiing his favorite old trail.

And I knew I was the fool.

Chapter Twenty-Five

I QUICKLY RECOVERED FROM MY MOUNT BAKER debacle and struggled on. Now that I'd bunked on the same aircraft carriers and experienced a flake of his life, I wanted to know more. At the top of the list was Boston College High School, his alma mater. Dad graduated from the Jesuit school in 1960, and that's about all I knew about his four years there. How Dad ended up there was part of his mythology: it was the best Catholic high school in the Boston diocese and he'd aced the admissions test, earning him an academic scholarship. Outside of that, it was a typical Dad black hole. He shared no tales of high school shenanigans with me as a kid, and no high school friends ever dropped in for a visit.

But without B.C. High, there would be no Annapolis, no flight school. I wanted to understand his high-achievement adolescence and contrast it with my own teenage days, where I seemingly ruined Mom's life and put my own future in a deep hole. There would be many great opportunities for self-flagellation.

I hit the B.C. High website and, for once, had perfect timing. The alumni page noted that the class of 1960's fiftieth reunion was in three weeks. I made a couple of calls and was put in touch with the reunion's chairman. The man didn't remember Dad, but he insisted I come as the class's guest. There was only one small problem: the reunion was being held in Boston, a place I still avoided years after the TP Incident. A wedding or work forced me to cross its borders from time to time, but it always left me brooding, self-medicating in a Hampton Inn with a convenience-store Eskimo Pie and a vodka cranberry.

Still, I drove up the Mass Pike on a sluggish Saturday afternoon in May. My breath shortened when I saw the hazy outline of the Prudential Building and then the unlit stadium lights of Fenway Park. I slipped by the Mass Avenue exit to my old South End neighborhood and turned up the Go-Betweens on the stereo, hoping to drown out the shitty memories. My directions told me to take exit 15 off I-93 South and I wound myself through a rotary turning on to Morrissey Boulevard near Dad's alma mater.

That's when it hit me. Christ on a cracker, Boston College High School was located directly across the street from the *Boston Globe*, my ex's employer! I couldn't believe it. I guess I must have known it in my head, but I'd been to the *Globe* only a handful of times and never to B.C. High. I was at the intersection of Dead Parent Avenue and Disappearing Spouse Boulevard.

The *Globe* was her world and I hated the place for that. She had a choice between me and the *Globe*, and the *Globe* won in a rout. Would an impartial observer see it that way? Probably not, but that's why they're called *feelings.* I pulled into the school's parking lot and stopped the car. I sat there for forty-five minutes telling myself not to read too much into it. Meanwhile, the fight-or-flight voice in my head was screaming, "Flight!"

"Just do it for five minutes," I told myself. "You can do anything for five minutes."

That was bullshit. There were a lot of things I couldn't do for five minutes: hammer a nail, hold a yoga position, fake an interest in the Food Network, etc. This seemed like one of them.

Still, I got out of the car, muttered a "Fuck you" in the *Globe*'s general direction and started walking toward B.C. High's glass doors. That's when I remembered I'd neglected to change from my driving outfit of T-shirt and shorts into my suit. I ran back to the car and did a quick change in the backseat, drawing a few sideward glances from elderly arrivals wondering if they should call the cops. Now I was late.

This being Catholic school, there was a Mass scheduled to kick off the reunion. I ran into the school and followed signs toward a theater. I pushed open a door and a hundred sets of eyes fell on me. This wasn't my usual neurosis. I was shaggy-haired and forty-three. All the men in the room were sixty-eight, give or take six months. Outside of a trophy wife, I was the youngest person in the room by a quarter century. I was the thing that was not like the others.

I wobbled up carpeted steps to the top of the theater, sitting a few rows beyond everyone else. I looked at the ruddy faces with their receding hairlines and thought of what Dad would have looked like old. Would he have a belly? Would his hair be gone? Or turned snow white? Would he have become a cranky son of a bitch like his father? Like I was becoming? Would Mom have been at his side in this very room? I wondered why I'd thought so little about this. The idea of Dad growing old rarely occurred to me. He was frozen in that black uniform with the American flag in the background.

Mass started before I could obsess any further. It was presided over by two members of the class of 1960 who had become priests. One of them noticed me sitting in the cheap seats. He urged me to move closer during a pause in the action.

"Come, join the rest of the community."

I moved closer by a single row and cursed the priest under my breath. I had not been to church in many years, but the words came back to me like a 1970s AM radio hit, the rituals, the verses, the refrains.

> Dying you destroyed our death. Rising you restored our life.

This was a modern service, so when it came time to say the Lord's Prayer, everyone held hands. Not my thing. Luckily, I was just out of reach. I recited "Forgive them their trespasses" while staring into space, not making eye contact with anyone. I shook a few hands when it was requested that we show each other the sign of peace, but I remained in my own orbit, separate.

At communion time, I went down and received the Body of Christ. I knew, technically, this was wrong. I was not in a state of grace, since I'd missed the last 1001 days of holy obligation. Then there was all the birth control I'd bankrolled through the years. These were all mortal sins, no-go signs for communion. But I remembered Mom's outcast years in the back pews while the fake pious walked around her. I went up and got my sliver of bread.

The priest held my gaze for an extra second as he placed a wafer on my serrated tongue. I thought somehow he'd used his supernatural powers and was going to out me for being profoundly outside the state of grace. But he said nothing.

Mass came to a close and everyone started to file out. I decided I was leaving. There were some decent Southie bars where I could have a couple of Budweisers before heading home. No one would ever know. And I would be doing everyone a favor. I was a gate-crasher, pure and simple.

I was a step away from escaping when the wafer-dispensing priest cut me off.

"Don't go. Who are you? I know there's a reason why you're here."

I blushed.

"My name is Stephen Rodrick and I'm Pete Rodrick's son. He was a member of the class and . . ."

He cut me off.

"I knew Peter. My name is Paul Kenney. He was in my homeroom. Someone told me you were coming. Come with me, I'll introduce you to people who knew him."

Kenney's right hand attached itself to my forearm. He had the grip of a longshoreman. I was more than a little afraid of him. He told me he was a Jesuit. This put me slightly at ease. The Jesuits are barely even priests, I told myself, the UN peacekeeping soldiers of the cloth. When I was at Loyola, the liquor store delivery van seemed permanently parked in front of the Jesuit residence. That was admirable.

I let him lead me into a large, open hall where cocktails were being served. Everyone was getting soused, and fast. I grabbed a vodka tonic and Kenney handed me off to Bill Flynn, a local surgeon. He was the master of ceremonies for the reunion. You could still see in his face a lady killer with a quick smile and black Irish features. He gave me a handshake and a slap on the back.

"Your dad was a brilliant man. He got 800s on his SATs, perfect scores. Did you know that?"

That I did know—Dad's great grades were part of the family mythology—but I started writing it down in my notebook anyway. Flynn grabbed my hand with delicate care. He spoke softly and it was hard to hear him above the babble of voices.

"You're left-handed too? Pete was left-handed."

"Yes, yes, he was."

The old man's observation left me stuttering to say simple words. His recollection of a small but intimate detail about Dad moved me more than I can say. Somehow, it made Dad seem more alive than any platitude I was told as a kid. I said to myself, "He actually existed."

Flynn kept talking. He told me how Dad liked to sit in the back of the classroom and stare out the window.

"We were in sophomore mathematics class and Father Ruttle was prattling on about some complicated algebraic problem," said Flynn. "Your dad was always half-asleep sitting by the window. Father Ruttle thought he caught him not paying attention and said, "Mr. Rodrick, what is the answer?" Your dad gave this complicated answer and just kept looking at the window. He was a mathematical genius, but the stuff he didn't care about, he didn't give a damn about."

That sounded a lot like me as a child except for the mathematical part and the genius thing. The stuff I gave a shit about—the Raiders, *Sports Illustrated*, Paul Weller—I cared about with a passion bordering on insanity; the stuff I didn't give a shit about, I really didn't give a shit about. I'd always found this to be a fatal character flaw, a sign of laziness and shiftlessness, an assumption that Mom and my teachers were all too happy to confirm. To hear a stranger tell me that Dad shared the same attitude filled me with relief.

I tried to explain this to Flynn. I started to tell how I'd always felt like an alien in my family, with no understanding of where my personality came from. But the words wouldn't come.

Another classmate came over to say hello. He was small with bushy eyebrows and a gentle smile. His name was Richard Ward and he'd just retired after a legal career at a prestigious Boston law firm. He was from Quincy, a town not far from Dad's Brockton.

"Your dad was really good to me, and I'm not sure why," Ward told me. "He had a car senior year and he'd wait after school for me. Not a lot of people had cars, and it made my life so much easier."

Ward told me stories about horsing around with Dad at the Brockton Fair. There was a mildly risqué show that the boys weren't old enough to attend. Dad and another buddy snuck in while Richard waited outside.

"He just had a real joy for life. I can see why men would follow him. He had something, a kindness about him."

Giant tears trickled down his lined face and onto his suit jacket.

"He was my best friend. And he was so good to me. You should know that."

I gave him a hug. Flynn circled back. He was giving the keynote speech after dinner and he wanted to mention Dad. He asked for some details about the accident. I gave him the basics: just made skipper, on his way home, then the *Kitty Hawk* is turned around after the hostages were taken, killed near Diego Garcia during a low-level training flight, nothing found but an oil slick.

He thanked me and walked away. It was dinnertime and I sat next to Father Kenney. He had a neatly trimmed white beard that blended perfectly into the closely cropped ring of hair that circled his bald head. We talked for a while about his various postings around the world and his current project recording the oral histories of elderly Jesuit priests in the United States. I asked him if he was going to record his own story.

"I'm sixty-eight. You have to be seventy. I'll be there soon enough. Time goes by so quickly."

We talked for a while about Dad. Father Kenney remarked that he always seemed so serious. I told him a little about Dad's dad, his long black moods casting a shadow over the family and how Dad had to pick up the slack. Father Kenney nodded slowly.

"That explains a lot. I always got the sense your dad carried some kind of sadness inside him. I can see it in your face too."

I gave a wince of a smile. It wasn't the first time I'd heard this observation from someone about myself, but to hear that Dad was the same tore up my insides. Maybe it was all predestined; maybe I didn't have any say in the matter.

I had another drink. The alcohol lifted my spirits, and I decided to dwell on the good things I'd heard about Dad. I felt understood in a way, surrounded by his fellow travelers from long ago. After the lobster bisque was served, Dr. Flynn stood up and walked to a podium at the front of the room.

"I want to start by having a moment of silence for classmates who gave their life for their country," said Flynn. He adjusted his glasses. "One of them was Pete Rodrick. His son, Stephen, is here tonight and he told me about his accident."

He paused for a moment and looked down at some notes.

"It was during the first Persian Gulf War over Iraq. It was a night flight over the desert and Pete just never returned."

I nearly passed out. Somehow, in the thirty minutes from when I'd told him about Dad's accident Flynn had tarted up the story, moved it up over a decade, shifted from sea to land, and from peacetime to combat. He had totally botched it. I had to set the record straight. I started to stand up, but Father Kenney gave me the death grip again. I told him that wasn't how it had happened.

"I know. I heard what you told him. But some things you just have to let go. Let go."

I slumped back into my chair. After the speech was over, there was more mingling. A line formed of three or four classmates who wanted to meet me. A short, bald man shook my hand, his eyes bugged wide with amazement.

"Your dad must have been almost fifty by the time of the Gulf War! That's really remarkable he was still flying!"

I started telling him it was more complicated than that, but I stopped. Instead, I just smiled and thanked him for his kind words. Maybe Father Kenney was right. Some of it you just had to let go.

I slipped out of the high school a little later. It was dark now, and the glass façade of the *Boston Globe* building was lit up. Green trucks loaded up early editions of the Sunday paper. I thought of childhood days reading the *Globe* with my grandparents on the Cape. The place no longer looked like the Temple of Doom. I turned on the radio and Dad's beloved Celtics were beating the tar out of the Orlando Magic in the Eastern Conference semifinals. For once, I didn't root against a Boston team.

Maybe it was the booze, maybe it was the events of the evening, but I decided to drive the thirty minutes south to Brockton, a place I'd ventured to only once in the seven years I'd lived in Boston. I got off on an exit I faintly remembered from decades ago. I tried to will my car to his old neighborhood in the dark.

But I didn't have a GPS and was blind with exhaustion. I drove around bad neighborhoods for an hour or so until the chances of getting carjacked seemed higher than the chances of finding the house on Herrod Avenue.

I gave up. Usually, this would have meant a drive home full of swearing at myself for not bringing directions, berating myself for not being better organized, for not being more like Dad. But not that night.

Chapter Twenty-Six

Tupper did the math right after his fly-in. He'd been gone for 377 of the previous 500 days. The Navy tried to prepare you for reentry with seminars and brochures, but he was still going from a boat of macho to a house of estrogen. It wasn't easy. His change of command speech about leaving two girls and returning home to young women had been just words, but now the words were true. Some of it would take some getting used to. He looked at Brenna with amazement one morning shortly after returning.

"You've got boobs!"

Brenna turned red, ran to her room, and slammed the door. Beth told him it wasn't his finest moment as a father. He apologized, but he was genuinely dumbstruck. He'd blinked and it had all gone by; one day he was reading Brenna stories before his first cruise, and now she was a young woman, finishing eighth grade and talking about colleges. She wanted to go to law school. Or dance. Or write.

Caitlin's changes were subtler. She was still his tomboy, pestering him to buy her more bottle rockets from the Indian reservation down the road. But she worried too much about life and school—all they seemed to do in school these days was test, test, test. At night, she wondered about death. She believed in God most of the time, but then her hamster would get sick or she'd see a fallen bird and wonder at bedtime whether God had forgotten her. Tupper thought she was just like her old man.

He and Beth tried to get back into a routine. It was harder than he remembered. He started playing guitar in the band at church because he knew it was important to Beth and the girls. They talked about finally building their house on Burrows Bay. Not that he saw Beth a lot—she had gone back to work part-time and he had his job. Between their joint responsibilities and the girls, they hardly had time to talk. It was go, go, go from 6:00 a.m. to 11:00 p.m. and then get up and do it again.

Their time together was largely spent figuring out what they were going to do next. None of the choices were promising. Beth and the girls quickly shot down the idea of Afghanistan, and no one was enthused about a return to Pax River—too many ghosts. The other option was serving as air boss on the USS *Lincoln*. Air boss wouldn't be flying, but it would be close, working up in the carrier's tower supervising the launch and recovery of aircraft. The *Lincoln* was based in Everett, a tolerable one-hour commute away. The girls could stay in Anacortes and in the schools they loved. Of course, the *Lincoln* meant more sea duty, but he wouldn't have to ship out until the following February, an eternity away.

He still had his day job. Every day, there were speeches to give, promotions to sort out, and bullshit to wade through. In May, he flew a Prowler down to NAS Lemoore for his formal fit rep. He listened to CAG list his failings and said less than fifty words. He walked back to the hangar for his flight back in time to notice Socr8tes on the wing checking out a malfunction. He wasn't wearing his helmet, a major violation in the fly-safe Navy. Vinnie reported that Dizzo, another junior officer, had done the same thing on a recent flight.

Back in Whidbey, Tupper called the squadron into their ready room on a Friday afternoon. He waited for silence and then mentioned the helmet violations.

"Socr8tes, Dizzo, your weekend starts right now. Get the fuck out of my command."

There was silence. The two fliers gathered their gear and trudged out. Dizzo sat in his truck, tears in his eyes. The JOs were stunned. They had been taught, "Praise in public, rebuke in private," at the Naval Academy and Officer Candidate School, but they'd just watched two of their colleagues get dressed down before their eyes. Sure, everyone was supposed to wear their helmet up top, but did the violation warrant banishing grown men? After the meeting ended, Wolf asked Tupper for a minute.

"Sir, I think that was wrong."

Tupper thanked him for his opinion, but then told him to shove it up his ass. This was basic safety shit. What if Dizzo had slipped and landed on his head? Didn't the squadron already lose an eye on cruise? He waved Wolf away and went to his office and slammed the door.

Two weeks later, Tupper flew back down to Lemoore with Ralph and Wolf. CAG was moving on to a fleet job, and all the wing COs were mandated to attend the change of command.

He liked the new CAG, a tiny man whose call sign was Satan. He listened as Satan thanked all the other squadron commanders by name and praised their service. He moved on without mentioning Tupper. Tupper did a slow burn. He flew back in silence with neither Ralph nor Wolf mentioning the slight. But the next morning, he was walking down the hangar steps when Linda piped up.

"Skipper, I heard CAG didn't mention you. That must have sucked."

Tupper seethed, but he didn't say anything. He called Satan and told him the snub had undermined his ability to lead. Satan was mortified and told him it was merely an oversight. He promised to call Wolf and Ralph and tell them it was just a mistake. Still, the damage had been done.

The summer was nearly gone. Tupper's change of command was just three months away. Where had the time gone? Had he done any good? Tupper had a new feeling, one he hadn't felt in twenty years. He was done with the Navy.

But the Navy wasn't done with him. Tupper officially passed on the Pax River job and took orders for the air boss job on the *Lincoln*. He would go back to sea and everyone else could stay home. But the decision quickly bit him in the ass. Shortly after he accepted the job, the Navy announced that the *Lincoln* was moving from Everett to Norfolk, Virginia, in the spring of 2012 for repairs. That meant Tupper would have to live in Virginia by himself for the last six months of his tour. There had been rumors of the *Lincoln* relocating that even I'd heard, but Tupper, consumed by command, didn't hear them. Beth was livid.

"How could you not have known? Everyone else knew!"

Tupper didn't know what to say. He was heartbroken. He'd done his best to keep his family in one place, and even that had failed. The head-down laser focus that served him so well as a pilot was screwing him in the real world.

THE BLACK RAVENS HEADED OUT TO sea in August for some pointless exercises off the California coast. The squadron was transitioning to the Growler starting in October, but the Navy insisted the squadron keep current on their carrier qualifications. So Tupper and his men headed out to spin some circles off the coast of San Diego.

That's when his Prowler nearly killed him. He was bringing his jet in for a routine daytime landing, but just as the Prowler was approaching the deck its nose bucked up violently to the left. For a second, Tupper lost sight of the deck. But he yanked the stick forward and kicked the rudder hard to the right. The Prowler corrected and somehow he grabbed the three wire. Even at the end you had to pay attention.

Two days later, Tupper caught his last trap. He jumped down from the plane, and Beav told him that he was needed in the ready room. CAG was waiting for him along with his men. He wondered what the hell had gone wrong this time. But CAG started talking about the special qualities needed to lead a squadron into combat. Tupper didn't immediately understand. Then, CAG pulled something out of his pocket.

"It is with great honor, Commander Ware, that I award you the Bronze Star."

CAG shook his hand and left the room. Tupper's men moved in to shake his hand and give him man-hugs. He looked into the eyes of men he'd yelled at, drunk with, and flown with. He felt love for them. He tried to tell them that it was they who deserved the Bronze Star, not him, and the practice of giving only the skipper a Bronze Star was wrong. But then his eyes welled with tears. He mumbled an excuse and left the room.

He went back to his stateroom and sat down on his bed. He felt hollow. He knew he'd never have to screw up the kind of courage it took to land a Prowler on a carrier. He knew he was losing something at the very core of himself. And he wondered if the rest of his life would be just an epilogue.

BACK HOME, TUPPER AND BETH BATTLED almost daily. It might be about the alarm going off at 4:30 a.m.; it might be over the color of the eaves on the new house they were planning. She had hit the wall on what she was willing to sacrifice for the Navy. Tupper's promises that it wouldn't always be like that rang hollow. Beth had eighteen years of hard time on her side.

"You always say that."

Beth now thought taking orders for the *Lincoln* was a mistake. This kicked Tupper in the gut. He had thought they had made the decision together. Now it was all his fault.

Tupper flew back east to Philadelphia for a friend's wedding. He had a lot of time to think about the decisions he had made, what he might have done differently. For a moment, he rooted for Beth to leave. Things had gotten too hard. It wasn't supposed to be like this. But as he watched his buddy—a confirmed bachelor—make the leap, Tupper's heart melted. He'd fight for Beth. They would make it work. He couldn't lose flying and his true love in the same year.

On his way back through Sea-Tac, Tupper ran into his wife at the airport heading to San Diego for a work conference. He snuck up behind her in the ticket line. She seemed happy to see him. They talked for a few minutes before Tupper had to go. There were no cross words or sarcastic remarks. That was a start. He then made the long drive back to the girls.

Chapter Twenty-Seven

Over time, Sherm became a spirit guide of sorts for me around Whidbey. Without his family, he had plenty of room in his house, and I rented a room for my trips up to see the Black Ravens. Sherm had a falling-out with his parents that he really wouldn't talk about, and the squadron was his life and his family. I became part of his family too. We spent many nights bullshitting about the Navy while drinking down at the Brown Lantern in Anacortes. He was easily the most gung-ho Black Raven and, consequently, also the most easily discouraged.

Like Tupper before him, Sherm was having a hard time making the transition from hell-raising junior officer to his new position as lieutenant commander, the Navy's entry point into middle management. One night, he called me back in New York with a problem.

Before the Navy brass settled on the Growler as the name for the Prowler's successor, it had been known informally in the Whidbey community as the EA-18 Shocker. Someone in the community even informally designed a three-prong lightning bolt with the tag line, "They'll never see it coming." Everyone loved it, including the brass. But then a wise man pointed out to the admirals that the design mirrored a common hand gesture for the simultaneous digital penetration of a woman's vagina and anus.

That wouldn't do. The name "Shocker" was banned, but

the decals lived on and popped up on walls and stop signs at NAS Whidbey. Sherm was outraged by the Shocker shutdown and sometimes wore a nonstandard Shocker patch on his flight jacket that led Vinnie to dress him down on one occasion.

Still, Sherm pushed the issue when he leased a new BMW sports car. He called and told me he wanted to get a vanity plate that read SHOKR. I tried to discourage him.

"Are you sure you want to drive through the gate with that on your car every morning?"

"I think it would be awesome."

"I agree, but less awesome if you want to make command."

Sherm went silent for a second.

"I don't understand. I bust my ass for the Navy. Why do they have to kill all the fun parts?"

I didn't have an answer. In the end, Sherm didn't get the plate. Eventually, he turned his energies to another side project: getting me up on a flight. After my disappointment on the *Nimitz*, I tried not to get my hopes up. But Sherm and Tupper worked the paper and the phones. On a summer afternoon, Sherm called me on my cell phone.

"We did it. You're approved to fly. This is going to be awesome."

I WASN'T AFRAID. THERE WAS NO anxiety about climbing into the same type of plane that killed my father. The songwriter Freedy Johnston has a beautiful song called "Western Sky" about a pilot's son who won't fly after his father is killed in a plane crash. That's not me.

Why? Some of it is a matter of scale. Dad was flying a

twenty-ton coffin at one hundred feet over a glass sea. That can get complicated. A twitch of the stick and the abyss calls. I'm usually a passenger on something called an Airbus. They're called Airbuses for a reason. Plane goes up, plane comes down.

Besides, I was playing the percentages. What were the odds of another Rodrick dying in an aviation disaster? I'm not Job, surviving a tsunami only to get kidnapped by guerrillas or gorillas. I'm a middle-class American with a graduate degree, all of my teeth, and most of my hair. Dad's crash was my one allotted megasad tragedy.

I ARRIVED AT SEA-TAC ON A July Sunday, one of the precious few blue-sky days that trick folks into moving to the Pacific Northwest. Mount Baker was still visible through the gloaming when I reached Sherm's house. We talked about the week ahead. Sherm told me there would be a cursory two-day VIP flight orientation, no big deal—basically telling me what knobs not to pull. My understanding was that the classes were more for my amusement and education than an actual requirement.

This proved incorrect. The next morning, I settled into a conference room with four naval aviators at NAS Whidbey Island. Here's the thing: all of them had passed their swim and survival qualifications back in Pensacola during their flight training. All were under thirty-five and in pretty good shape. They were merely here for their quadrennial requalification. With any luck, they would be drinking beer at the officers' club by 3:00 p.m.

A lieutenant with frizzy hair walked into the room and turned on an overhead projector. The aviators guzzled the last of their coffee and slapped their necks in hopes of staying awake. She spoke about the psychological issues that can screw a pilot up in the cockpit: fights with the wife, mortgage-refinancing issues, a cold Egg McMuffin. It could be anything. There was a discussion of cockpit distractions, with case studies of planes flown straight into mountains because the crew was discussing baseball or checking out a minor cockpit glitch that should have been ignored until they were back on the ground.

The subject rankled me; it got back to the old song and dance: any plane crash was probably the pilot's fault. I thought of my dad managing 150 men, worrying about Mom, plowing through hundreds of pages of fitness reports, and then having to fly 450 knots a hundred feet off the ocean. The instructor focused on a 2006 T-39 Sabreliner crash that killed a Navy instructor, two students, and a civilian pilot in the hills of southern Georgia. The lieutenant theorized that the pilots had been confused by the students' change of seats late in the mission. The pilot had been a friend of Sherm's, and he later told me this was bullshit.

"They just flew straight into the side of mountain. Sometimes, you lock in and it happens."

The lieutenant finished her presentation and it was lunchtime. The Black Ravens' FNG—Fucking New Guy—had been strong-armed into bringing me a Subway sandwich and some chips. Attempts at assigning him a call sign would eventually land on Sling Blade, a reference to his shifty black eyes, buzz cut, and cryptic, guttural utterings. I tried to give him a few bucks for the sandwich. FNG grimaced.

"No, mmm hhh, gotta go."

I unspooled the intricately wrapped sandwich. This took

me more than a minute, a reminder that my motor skills hadn't developed much since third grade. I was about to take my first bite when the lieutenant tapped me on my shoulder. Did I want to knock out my basic swimming qualifications next door in the pool?

Sure.

Maybe it's the memory of Dad tossing me into the waves headfirst on Cape Cod, but entering water has always been like hooking up to a Demerol drip for me—the weightlessness, slipping away from terra firma, my mind switched off. For years, I drove great distances so I could get in one good ocean swim every month. All you have to do is time your duck before the next wave arrives. I started swimming for exercise a decade ago, enjoying the long, languorous turns of my body as I counted down the laps to a mile. (Of course, I skipped the flip turns after a period of experimentation left me with a chipped tooth and a bruised cheek.)

I changed into my trunks and met a civilian instructor in a blue windbreaker. He had grave, sad eyes. We shook hands. I would grow to despise this superficially harmless-looking fellow. He told me to swim 200 meters alternating between the breaststroke, the sidestroke, the backstroke, and the crawl. This would be easy. I climbed to the top of a twenty-five-foot tower, crossed my hands across my chest, and stepped over the edge. The water felt good against my skin. I moved easily through the water, taking about six or seven minutes to swim the distance. I was barely winded as I lifted myself out of the pool.

Mr. Instructor shook his head sorrowfully. He wore an expression frozen between contempt and pity.

"Your crawl was decent, but the rest of the strokes aren't cutting it. You're doing the breaststroke completely wrong. You're giving a frog kick when I want a scissors kick. You'd drown in five minutes trying to do that stroke in full flight gear."

Dread began coursing through my body. Mr. Instructor requisitioned a squat Navy seaman named Nate. For a few minutes, Nate showed me the strokes. The Navy breaststroke was particularly vexing. The leg movement seemed the exact opposite of the breaststroke I'd been apparently doing wrong for my entire life.

"Okay, now give it another try," said Mr. Instructor. He glanced at his watch, pining for a long-past appointment with a cup of noodles.

I jumped in. I started swimming. Mr. Instructor commenced screaming.

'No, no, the stroke is up, in, out, and glide. Up, in, out, and glide."

I sputtered through the water, not drowning. I grabbed the side. Nate swam up next to me.

"Are you nervous?"

"No, why?"

"Both your arms are twitching."

He was right. My forearms were quivering. Sometimes this happens. I do well under pressure until I start thinking about the pressure. It was baseball all over again.

Mr. Instructor sighed dramatically.

"Well, take a break. We can try this again tomorrow at 6:00 a.m., but if you don't pass it, you can't do the rest of the quals."

I slinked out of the pool. What did he mean, the rest of the quals?

I soon found out. I got dressed and headed across the street back to the classroom. The lieutenant took me into a room and showed me a video of how to keep breathing while experiencing five or six Gs, an extreme force that, truth be told, I wasn't likely to encounter unless I was reborn as a Blue Angels pilot. The HICC maneuver involves keeping your core centered and doing a series of short gasping breaths in, followed by short, strangulated breaths out making a HICC, HICC, HICC sound. I kept flashing back to a first-aid film I had seen as a boy where an epileptic made the same exact noises while having a seizure. I tried to get the breathing right, but the instructor told me I was doing it wrong.

"Try and make it sound less like you're choking to death."

I tried it again. This time she stared at my hands. They were still shaking.

"Maybe you should eat your sandwich and go back to the classroom."

I started having the sick feeling that I was not going to get up in a Prowler. I stumbled back into the lecture room. An instructor was already giving tips about ejecting from a plane near the carrier. He chattered on about releasing from your parachute harness and steering your chute away from the carrier deck and the carrier's backwash.

This was, theoretically, good information; Commander Butch Williams suffered a weak catapult launch on the *Kitty Hawk* a month after my father's crash. His A-6 Intruder plunged into the sea. He ejected, floated down, and, legend has it, was seen giving deckhands the finger as the *Kitty*

Hawk's wash pushed him out to sea. But his kneeboard—a small plastic pad strapped to a pilot's leg with maps and other flight information—had slipped down around his ankle and his parachute string became hopelessly entangled around it. The carrier's propeller sucked him under. Divers could see his body but couldn't reach him through the churn. Williams was dead by the time they brought him to the surface twenty minutes later. When the *Kitty Hawk* returned home in April 1980, it did so without the skippers of its two Whidbey squadrons.

But I was too tired to really listen. After yesterday's ten-hour travel day, the current swim disaster, and lack of lunch I was paying attention with perhaps a twelfth of my brain. This was another error. The brief ended. Navy technicians entered the room, and began rigging a parachute to a previously unnoticed contraption hanging from a high ceiling.

A few minutes later, I was told to change into a flight suit. A heavy pack was hoisted onto my back. A too-large helmet was dropped on my head. I was hooked into a harness, and virtual reality goggles were placed over my head. Before I could say "What the hell," I was hoisted up a few feet and then dropped. Through the goggles, I saw my boots and body heading toward a cartoon carrier. Someone started shouting.

"1500 FEET FROM THE DECK, WHAT DO YOU DO. ARE YOU TANGLED? 500 FEET FROM THE DECK. STEER AWAY!"

I did neither. I smashed into the deck. Someone laughed.

"That would have hurt."

Apparently, I missed the part of the lecture about IROC, a helpful acronym for idiots like me:

Inspect your chute.
Release your raft.
Observe your situation.
Control your chute.

By now, I was observing my situation and it sucked. I was given two more tries. I died the second time and was a probable quadriplegic the third. The helmet came off. I noticed sweat pouring from my earlobes, a malady I previously associated with a coke-addled friend.

I was led into another room. I climbed a ladder and was strapped into a mock cockpit. An instructor strapped me in with a canvas seat belt.

"This is going to test your ejection skills."

"What ejection skills?"

My heart thumped through the apparatus. The instructor let out a shout.

"OKAY, RELEASE!"

I tensed. I tensed so hard my back went into spasms typically reserved for bad breakups and IRS audits. Nothing happened.

"Oh, sorry. I was getting a call. My bad."

A few seconds passed.

"OKAY, RELEASE."

This time, my body was thrown backward at 150 mph. The cockpit shuddered before settling.

At this precise moment, I had a thought: the dudes in the squadron are punking me! It wasn't impossible. These are grown men who had been known to wait for hours so they could pour a garbage can of ice water on a friend while he sits on the toilet on the carrier. It was quite possible they had arranged an elaborate practical joke and everyone here was in on it.

I staggered out of the torture chamber. The lieutenant in charge took me aside.

"I understand you had problems with the swim qual, so you're going to have a long day tomorrow. You'll have to do swim quals at 6:00 a.m., have a little rest, and then do the rest of your qualifications around 11:00 a.m."

Crap, this was real, not a prank. I didn't have the energy or the balls to ask what the rest of the qualifications were. I called Sherm over at the squadron.

"Come get me. Things got fucked up."

"What happened?"

"Just come get me."

Sherm arrived a few minutes later. He saw my glazed eyes—bloodshot from chlorine, the right one missing a contact.

"What happened?"

"They're making me pass the same tests that the actual pilots have to pass."

"That wasn't the deal. You're only flying once."

"You tell those fuckers."

My eyes began leaking. Sherm tried not to notice. I followed Sherm back to his place, negotiating Deception Pass Bridge with my one good eye. Sherm told me he would call the skipper. I went to my room, called Alix, and went into full meltdown. I blubbered. In that moment, I was nine years old in the same area code, crying my eyes out because I couldn't hit a baseball or build a catapult, all the things that confer acceptance on a young boy. And there was no one to help. No father, no brother, nobody.

Sherm got off the phone with the swim qual folks. He didn't have good news.

"You have to pass the same test. I don't know what happened, but they said the rules are the rules."

We worked out a small and profoundly humiliating compromise. I wouldn't try to pass the test tomorrow; that was assured failure. Instead, I would work with Seaman Nate for three or four hours a day in the pool, converting my civilian stroke into Navy strokes. Then on Friday, I could try to pass the qualifications under Mr. Instructor's watchful scowl.

My phone rang. It was Tupper. He tried to buck me up with a few "nothing worth having comes easy" bromides. I wasn't in the mood.

I HEADED BACK TO THE BASE that evening. I had thought it would be cool to stay in the Bachelor Officers Quarters while preparing for my flight. The BOQ was where my family spent the first three weeks on Whidbey while we waited for our house to be finished. The building was essentially unchanged from 1974; it had the same squat three-story Warsaw Pact–era design, the only addition being televisions in each of the rooms. The place was designed to depress you so much that you would find your own place pronto.

One night as a seven-year-old, I wandered the same halls in a semi-sleepwalking state. I soon found myself lost, trying random doorknobs until one opened. It was a young aviator, his flight suit draped over a chair. He was wearing nothing but his white T-shirt and briefs. He asked my name and then called down to the front desk. He asked for Peter Rodrick's room number but told the operator not to ring through.

He took me by the hand and led me back home. The pilot opened my family's room and lifted me into my single bed next to my sister. My parents slept a few feet away. He held his finger to his lips in the universal shush signal.

"It will be okay—just go to sleep."

Thirty-six years later, I repeated the pilot's line to myself: It will be okay, just go to sleep. But I couldn't. From my third-floor room, I had an unobstructed view of the chapel where my father's memorial service was held. I lay on my bed for a while, calculating the minutes until I had to be back in the water, an exact replication of how I counted down with dread the minutes until school or baseball practice as a boy.

I couldn't sleep, so I headed over to the base McDonald's and self-medicated with grease. I drove over to the chapel and pulled into the exact parking space in which we had parked our Buick station wagon on the morning of my father's memorial service. It was where my family sat paralyzed afterward. I looked out my window and could see Laddie Coburn standing there, telling my mother she could start a whole new life. And I saw my mother there, just whispering no.

I stared at the taillights of Prowlers circling the base in the midsummer night. And I said over and over again, I am not trying to be my father, I am not trying to be my father. I couldn't tell if I was saying it with pride or shame.

I MET SWIMMER NATE THE NEXT morning. For the next seventy-two hours, he became my best friend and torturer. Nate had done a long stint on a hospital ship after the invasion of Iraq. He had seen some bad things, so trying to get a profoundly uncoordinated fortysomething man to swim laps in the Navy style didn't faze him. I told him I was divorced and he excitedly high-fived me. He was too! This would become our ritual. Every time I swam a stroke right for even five yards he'd high-five me and do a spot-on imitation of the drill sergeant in *Full Metal Jacket.*

I told him I was thinking of heading back east, working on my strokes for a month, and then returning. Nate assured me this wouldn't be necessary.

"You. Are. Not. Going. To. Do. That."

His R. Lee Ermey imitation was top drawer. I felt a little better. The breaststroke was my major malfunction. For hours, we broke the stroke down. First, I used a kickboard and concentrated on the back end of the stroke, bringing my legs to my chest, thrusting them outward, and then snapping them together. This was hard, but not unmanageable. But when I lost the kickboard and tried to coordinate my upper body with my leg kick it all went to shit. Actually, shit became my favorite word. I'd start swimming the stroke, screw up, stop in the water, and scream "Shit!"

The boss watched my progress doubtfully. He gave me an instructional video to watch back in the comfort of my BOQ room. That night, I slipped the DVD into my computer. It was vintage early-1980s, with Village People mustaches on the aviators giving the film a survivor gay porn vibe. But the DVD kept stopping just as a blond man in a khaki uniform started doing the strokes. I handed it back to Mr. Instructor the following morning.

"The DVD is scratched, I couldn't watch it."

He disappeared for a moment into his office.

"It plays fine on my computer; maybe you didn't try hard enough."

I thought of punching him but did a quick cost-benefit analysis and walked away. In the pool, Nate was his smiley self. He kept telling me I was making progress as I swam laps across the short side of the pool. I disagreed but kept my mouth shut. Every minute I hoped Nate would throw his hands up in disgust and ship me back to Brooklyn. Then I prayed that someone might pull the fire alarm. Then I wished for an actual terrorist act. I started holding my breath in hopes of inducing a heart attack. Nothing worked. After three hours, I told Nate I was exhausted.

"Okay, well, let's work on your stretching."

We then spent forty-five minutes trying to strengthen my core. This seemed like a good idea, but not something that was going to pay dividends by Friday. This routine went on for three days. I worked on the stroke for hours, ate a pile of fast food, and went back to my room. There, I watched a new copy of the instructional video and tried to pantomime the strokes on my bed, humping the mattress.

Before I went in on Thursday, Sherm told me a compromise had been brokered. I'd still have to pass the swim test, but some of the other requirements would be waived.

We had a laugh at how inapplicable the swim quals were for a Prowler crew. The Prowler was too heavy: there would be no Captain Sully landing on the Hudson. In a Prowler, you either hit the water and your body disintegrated, as happened to my father, or you ejected, floated down in your automatically opening chute, landed in the water in a self-inflating life vest, and waited the ten or fifteen minutes until the helicopters plucked you from the sea. Mr. Instructor's standards seemed to be based on some vision of Amelia Earhart ditching a single-engine somewhere near the Azores. At the end of Thursday's remedial session, he walked into the pool area. It was time to swim the strokes.

"Okay, let's do this."

He went inside to ask another diver to get into the water in case I drowned in my efforts. I walked laps around the pool, trying to calm myself. It didn't really work. By the time everyone was assembled, I was clutching my hands together behind my back so no one could see them twitching.

Unfortunately, my knees were shaking too. I climbed the tower again. I prepared my hands for the drop as I had been instructed but got too close to the edge. I lost my balance and fell into the water with the grace of a kitten tangled in a burlap bag. I sprang up to the surface, sputtering.

"Sorry, sorry. Let me try that again."

Mr. Instructor just shook his head.

"No, just go. Go!"

I tried to take Nate's advice. Go slow; this wasn't a race. Still, I found my breaststroke breaking down into an imitation of a wheezing accordion. But I didn't hear anyone yell stop, so I kept swimming. I finished my laps and squinted up at Mr. Instructor.

"Well, that wasn't perfect, but it will do."

My elation was fleeting. The boss disappeared for a minute and reemerged with a flight suit, combat boots, and a helmet. I put them on and was thrown in the water. I was told to swim fifty meters in the gear utilizing the Navy breaststroke.

I tried to remember my up, in, out, and glide checklist. It didn't quite work, and soon I was doing an out, out, and dog paddle movement. Still, I made it back and forth.

The next task was to manually inflate my life vest. Mind you, this must be done while wearing thick flying gloves. I would just manage to get one tube out of the vest and start blowing air in before I'd swallow a slug of water.

The boss shouted at me.

"Just put your head down, that helmet floats. You can't drown!"

He had a point, but I had a hard time breathing into a thin tube while I was face down in the drink. Talk about a logistical nightmare! It took ten minutes, but I got the vest inflated. Nate high-fived me. Mr. Instructor almost cracked a smile.

"Okay, well, you got that out of the way. We'll see you tomorrow."

I thought the hell you will, I am done. But I didn't say anything. I got dressed and slipped back over to my room. A few minutes later, I got a text from Sherm:

Come over to the squadron ASAP.

I knew this couldn't be good news. I met him in the parking lot. Sherm did his wince of a smile.

"I've got some good news and bad news. The bad news is, I got bad information yesterday. You have to pass all the quals tomorrow except one."

I slapped my hands on the asphalt and cursed. Sherm cringed.

"The good news is you don't have to do the dunker tomorrow."

The one thing Sherm had gotten me exempted from was

the Dilbert Dunker, a contraption shaped like the inside of a helicopter. It is dropped in the water with four passengers onboard, then spun around; after that, the passengers have to find their way out. If the instructor is feeling particularly sadistic, he makes you do it blindfolded. When I asked what the purpose of this was, Mr. Instructor cheerfully said, "Well, this is in case you're rescued and then your helo crashes." I told him that would be the point where I would just say good night and prepare to meet the baby Jesus.

Skipping the dunker was a good thing, but that left all the other shit.

The next morning I headed over to the swim center. There were four other officers there for their tests. We put on our flight gear and jumped into the water. The first requirements were easy; a line was dropped from a forty-foot tower. All I had to do was hook it to a ring on my flight suit and be pulled up. But from there, things took a bleak turn. I climbed to the top of a platform and was strapped into a parachute harness. I would be dropped and then dragged back and forth across the pool until I extricated myself from my gear. This would require real dexterity since I would be wearing the godforsaken flight gloves.

The four officers got out of their chutes quickly, earning cheers from an elderly tour group that was sitting in the bleachers. Then I was dropped. I was dragged once, twice, three times across the pool before my fingers were able to push up on my metal fasteners and slip out of the harness. The confused old folks went silent, a single out-of-time handclap meeting my accomplishment.

I was led back up to the tower. This time, I'd have to extricate myself from the harness while wearing blackout goggles and using only my "bad" hand. I didn't know what that meant. An instructor filled me in.

"Hold your good hand flat to the side. You're right-handed, right?"

"Uh, yes."

This was a lie. I felt bad about it for about a minute until I remembered the naval aviator's modern mantra: "If you ain't cheatin', you ain't tryin'." This time I was dragged five or six times, but I was past caring. Eventually, I got out of my harness.

I thought the end was in sight. I jumped off the platform again and was told to climb into my tiny life raft, a maneuver harder than it sounds when encumbered by water-soaked boots and helmet. But I did it and let out a yell.

"Fuck, yeah!"

Mr. Instructor looked at me sideways.

"What are you so excited about?"

"I'm done."

"You're not done. Back up the platform, you've got to untangle your parachute."

I climbed back up. This time, I jumped in and a mashed-up parachute was thrown on top of me. I sucked in a half pint of chlorine. For a moment, I nearly cried for help, which would have resulted in a nonpass. Instead, I took a second, gathered myself, and began passing the white mess hand-over-hand until I was in the clear. Mr. Instructor helped me out of the pool.

"Now you're done. Are you sure you don't want to do the dunker?"

"Do I have to?"

"No."

"Then fuck no."

Mr. Instructor cracked a smile. I staggered over to the bleachers. Nate was waiting for me. We exchanged an extremely uncoordinated but heartfelt chest bump. I watched the real guys do the dunker—man, that did not look like fun—and then stumbled into the changing room. I had rarely been happier.

An hour later, Sherm and some of the guys met me over at the officers' club for a celebratory beer. The guys gave me high-fives. Everyone agreed it was insane that I had to go through the paces for a two-hour flight that would be 99 percent over land. Listening in was Socr8tes, the junior officer Tupper was grounding for his bad radio calls. He looked guilty and slowly nosed his way into the conversation.

"Hey, Steve, that was my bad. I did your survival center request form. I guess I wasn't paying attention. I was watching something on YouTube. I think I put in the regular request for us, and not a one-time waiver thing."

The room went quiet. Socr8tes wandered away.

"That makes sense," said Sherm. "When I called over there, they kept saying 'You requested all of this. It's in your request letter.' "

All I could do was laugh. I thought of a long-ago pilot telling a lost seven-year-old boy that it was all going to be okay. For a rare moment, I believed him. I got another beer.

THE FLIGHT WAS SCHEDULED FOR MONDAY; all I had to do was survive the weekend. That wasn't as easy as I thought.

There was Stoli's bachelor party in Vancouver, for one thing, but that wasn't causing much concern. I began thinking about the flight and started to freak out. It wasn't the danger part; it was more practical and gross: I thought I might blow waste from one of my orifices.

Actually, I wasn't so much worried about vomiting—it happens—but shitting myself was a real concern. My bowels are temperamental in climate-controlled circumstances, and that much worse four miles in the air dealing with five Gs. There were apocryphal tales of aviators losing control of their bowels because of a pressure change, bad eggs, and/or tricky maneuvers. They would jump out of their jets on carrier decks, strip off their sullied flight suits, and fling them into the ocean.

That wasn't something you lived down easily. I was certain I didn't want my call sign to be Shitter. I began to plot my strategy. There would be nothing but bananas and soup for the next thirty-six hours, along with lots of clear liquid. I wasn't sure if that was enough.

The morning of the flight, I woke up and slid into my flight suit. The bathroom issue had me in a full-flown panic. I debated going my usual Imodium route but worried that would leave me severely dehydrated, a condition that can lead to passing out in a twisting and turning Prowler. I drove over to the drugstore, paced a bit, and finally went over to the personal-needs section to check out adult diapers. I picked up a four-pack of Depends and carried them weakly to the counter. I removed my sunglasses and tried to grin.

"For my grandfather."

The counter woman said nothing. I quickly threw the

Depends into my backpack, jumped into my car, and headed up to Whidbey. I turned off my iPod as I crossed over Deception Pass Bridge and switched over to the CBC station broadcasting from Victoria, in British Columbia; the drone of the always pleasant, inoffensive Canadian voices usually settled me down. But not today. My heart was pounding. I parked my car across the street from the hangar and next to the Prowler memorial. I stopped and put my hands on my father's etched name.

Then the strangest thing happened. I started laughing. And there was a moment of odd clarity: I was not going to fly in Dad's plane wearing a diaper, no matter the consequences. I tossed the Depends into my trunk and headed in.

On the flight schedule were the names Tupper, Sherm, Shibaz, and Rodrick. The four of us headed into the briefing room where Tupper already sat slouching in a chair poring over a map. He saw me and smiled.

"We're going to take you on the million-dollar ride. The conditions are perfect for it."

Million-dollar ride wasn't an exaggeration. It's VR-1355, an air route that snakes through the canyons and peaks of the Cascades. The route doesn't get flown that often: flying in and out of canyons requires excellent visibility, a rarity in the Northwest. Tupper continued with the brief, noting the different checkpoints and radio frequencies to be monitored.

"We've got someone not that familiar with the aircraft, so let's all keep a lookout for things that could go wrong."

We then all walked down to the equipment room. Behind wire cages hung rows and rows of helmets, parachutes, and flight suits. The equipment was somewhat familiar from my survival training but the helmet, borrowed from the FNG, seemed top-heavy. I slipped on my green pack—containing my parachute and life vest—and nearly tumbled over from the weight. After everyone was suited up, we stomped Munster-like down the steps, out the hangar, and onto the flight line.

Our Prowler awaited with its canopies already opened. The plane was twenty-eight years old, one of the young ones. I gingerly climbed up the jet's steps. This put me next to the backseat cockpit, which meant I had to slide-step another few feet toward the front cockpit. One false step and I'd fall fifteen feet and crack my head on the tarmac. I made it to the front and heaved my body into the front seat. A maintainer scrambled up and strapped me in.

Tupper was already in the pilot's seat and reached over and adjusted some of my straps, making me feel like a special-needs kid settling in on the short bus. He had one question for me.

"You know what not to touch, right?"

This was a relevant question. There was a red handle above my head and another one at my feet. If I pulled either one, I'd be ejected from the plane. This had happened once before on a VIP ride; a surface ship admiral in a Hornet's backseat hadn't been strapped in properly, and he reached down to adjust his seat during a flight. He pulled the wrong handle. The admiral was ejected and the Hornet returned to base minus a passenger. An hour later, the admiral was bragging about his ejection at the officers' club. That's when the pilots threw him out.

I nodded to Tupper. He pulled at my oxygen mask and grabbed a small white bag off my lap.

"Put the puke bag up here. Just know how to get the mask off. You don't want to puke into your mask—that wouldn't be good."

In my obsessing about crapping myself, I'd forgotten the puke possibility. I had been told it was fairly common on a first flight. I'd seen veteran aviators on the *Nimitz* looking green and gray after their flight. Fortunately, someone had forgotten to issue me flight gloves so I had a modicum of dexterity not present during my survivor qualifications. I showed Tupper that I could get the mask off.

"Let's do this."

The canopies closed. The engines were turned on, their grinding whine making it hard to think. A few minutes passed and then Tupper taxied us to the takeoff runway. He waited for clearance and pushed the throttle down. In a moment, we were down the runway and up above the Pacific. Tupper switched the radio over to Seattle air traffic control and we headed south. We moved through the sky to about 21,000 feet. I nodded my head in an ecstatic rhythm. I was a child again. "This is so cool, this is so cool" was all I could say. We headed south passing over Everett, where Shibaz lives with his wife and kids. Tupper squawked over the radio.

"There's Shibaz's house. Hey, Shibaz, whose car's in the driveway? I'd be worried."

I learned later this is the oldest Navy pilot joke, but I'd never heard it before. Maybe it was the altitude, but I let out a giddy laugh.

"That's hilarious."

I was feeling pretty good. Here I was, flying in my dad's plane, no sickness and no nausea. We passed over Boeing Field and Sea-Tac Airport. In the distance was the Tacoma Narrows Bridge. Farther still was a glint at the top of a mountain.

Tupper spoke into the radio.

"Okay, that's Mount Hood in the distance. That's Mount Rainier over there." He paused for a moment. "And this is my ass."

The cockpit filled with flatulence.

"Sorry about that."

We continued south toward the Columbia River on the Washington and Oregon border. Seattle air control had us drop to 10,000 feet. Tupper came back on the radio. "Okay, time for the FOD check."

Tupper put the plane in a slight dive and then pulled the stick back, sending us upward. A screw and some small pieces of metal floated up from the cockpit floor. Tupper grabbed the biggest piece and then leveled off. I began to feel something different, spaciness and queasiness in the belly. Tupper did a G-force warm-up for the flight. He turned the plane 90 degrees to the left and then 90 degrees to the right. This was supposed to increase blood pressure and prep us for more G force to come. I survived the twists and the turns, but bile was creeping up my throat.

Tupper lowered the plane to 5,000 feet and gave a last instrument check. There was one major problem; the radar altimeter—the calculator of air altitude that my father flew without on his final flight—wouldn't turn on, a malfunction that would scrub a low-level flight. For a few minutes, it looked like the flight would be over before it began. But after a series of turn-ons and turn-offs, the radar altimeter light clicked green.

Tupper descended to 500 feet over the Columbia River near the foothills of the Cascades. He gunned the jet up and then sharply to the left. We were soon flying upside down. I stared deep into an ice pond perched on top of an 8,000-foot peak. Tupper came across the radio.

"Get a good look. I bet no man has stood where you're looking."

And then we were right side up. And then we were on our left side. And then we were back on our right side. We bent around a mountaintop close enough that I could count pine-cones on the trees. I focused forward. We swooped down and all of a sudden there were sheer canyon cliffs on three sides. Tupper clicked on.

"If we were in a Cessna, we'd be dead men."

He paused for effect as the canyon wall in front of me moved closer. The radar altimeter started beeping.

"Fortunately, we're in a jet."

Tupper pulled the stick back and the Prowler bucked sky-ward. We cleared the ridge and the beeping stopped. But not for long. Tupper glided us in and out of canyons and cliffs, the beeping altimeter providing a syncopated accompani-ment. At one point, a thought came into my head: is this all completely necessary? VR-1355 has a purpose; all the twist-ing and turning mirrors evasion tactics Prowler pilots use when more nimble and lethal fighters are pursuing them. But Tupper was basically done flying; this was a joy ride, staged for my benefit. I alternately loved every second of it and also wondered whether this kind of flying is what took Dad away from me.

The thought lingered only for a moment. I began to lose consciousness. Well, first came the vomiting. As we skirted the 10,541-foot top of Glacier Peak and then dipped into a valley, the bile burned up through my windpipe. I flipped off my mask and booted a spectacularly bright yellow fluid into my airsickness bag.

It wasn't a lot, but the activity sucked away my life force. I entered an awake coma. Tupper took us into a different canyon and the altimeter began chirping again. But this time, there was no angst, just a vague feeling that if we flew into the side of a mountain at least that would put an end to my misery.

I watched the rest of the flight with a detached third-person feeling. Sweat began dripping down my arms and legs. Tupper gunned the Prowler over the Sauk River low enough that I could see the waves from the floppy-hatted fishermen. We were going 540 miles per hour, at roughly the altitude Dad was at before he crashed. The radar altimeter ticked off again, and in my hazed state I had an obvious thought: "Boy, that radar altimeter would have come in handy for Dad."

We headed for home. Whidbey's Ault Field could be seen in the distance and Tupper put the jet into a shit-hot break. We flew over the runway at about 450 knots—100 knots above the speed limit—and banked to the left at 4.5 Gs and a 90-degree angle. I tried the HICC maneuver, but didn't get much air. Tupper then chopped the throttles and applied the Prowler's speed brakes to bring us below 250 knots so he could lower the landing gear. The gear and flaps were extended and he slowed the Prowler to about 135 knots and brought us toward Earth. We glided down toward the concrete. I let out an exhausted breath of relief. It was over.

But then the nose rose and Tupper went to full power. His mic went back on.

"I need to work on my touch-and-gos."

We circled back around Whidbey. I saw the same things my father would have seen: cows in a pasture, the white caps of the ocean, my elementary school and the peaked roof of the Navy chapel. But the catharsis I was looking for wasn't there, not that I could put my finger on what exactly I was looking for. After four or five touch-and-gos, Tupper set the Prowler down quietly and we taxied back to the hangar. He turned off the engines, and they whined slowly to a stop. He pressed a button and the canopy opened. I immediately began to feel better, gulping in the ocean air. I was helped down the steps and peeled off my helmet. Someone joked about my hippie hair. I threw my arms around Tupper and Sherm and posed for pictures. We headed into the hangar, where I stripped off my sweat-soaked gear. I had not shat myself.

There was a post-flight brief that I remember nothing about. A few minutes later, I walked past the Prowler memorial and got into my car. I wish I could say that I stopped and touched Dad's name again, but I didn't. I drove back to Sherm's, oblivious to everything—the flashing light indicating I was nearly out of gas, the left on red I took near the base. The flight had sucked out all my energy, all my pain, and all my joy.

I slept for the rest of the day, waking once when I thought

I heard the beeping of the plane's radar altimeter. It was just a garbage truck. I spent a lot of time thinking of the line between recklessness and joy, the infinitesimal space between shit-hot flying and mortality. I wondered if the risks Tupper took that day were for my benefit or for his.

Over that summer, we talked for hours about other things—kids, wives, and politics—but never about our flight. But then months later, somewhere at a noisy bar, maybe Jacksonville, maybe Pearl Harbor, Tupper put his glass down.

"When you fly, you're always looking to do something perfect. But usually you fuck something up, miss something, or the plane is broken or your crew isn't there for you. I never had the perfect flight pilots talk about."

He slung a drunken arm around my shoulder. "But that low-level, VR-1355, that was my perfect flight. You saw my perfect flight."

Tupper's face broke into a smile. I wanted to believe him.

Chapter Twenty-Eight

I CALLED MOM A FEW WEEKS after my flight and told her I wanted to drive out to Michigan and sift through Dad's things, maybe sit with her for a formal interview. Her response was chipper, in language cadged from TV commercials.

"Bring it on. Let's do it. "

I was wrong-footed by her happy talk and enthusiasm to discuss our terrible years. I drove to Flint and began questioning my whole narrative. Maybe she had always been the sweet woman whom everyone loved. Maybe I'd just been a bad son, giving her grief and heartache when I needed to lessen her burden. Maybe I was remembering everything exactly wrong.

THINGS THAWED QUICKLY BETWEEN US AFTER I moved out of the house. I'd see her two or three times a year and it would be fine. Mom marveled at my academic success and then my young career. She framed my first articles and hung them in my old bedroom where I used to hide from her. The years passed and I became her first call when she needed some instant courage.

Terry joined the Army as a second lieutenant after college, emulating Dad in a way that I couldn't imagine. She was sent to Kuwait just after the Gulf War started in 1991. Mom was hysterical, weeping on the phone, terrified she was going to lose another loved one.

"I won't survive it, Stephen. I won't survive it."

I took the train from Chicago to Flint to help her ride it out. Thankfully, the war ended quickly. She dropped me at the train station and told me she was lucky to have a son like me. I brushed off her words, telling her that I was glad to help, but on the train back I cracked open a celebratory Budweiser and stared out the window, turning her compliment over in my mind like a new treasure. It was as if all the years of fighting had never happened.

Her own world remained small and contained. Nancy urged her to go back to school—the government would pay for it—but she put it off, claiming that Christine needed her at home. Christine graduated from high school in 1995 and headed to the University of Michigan. I feared Mom would go to pieces living alone. But Mel died and her mother had nowhere to go. Mom took her in, a selfless act that gave her somebody to talk to. Eventually, she regretted the kindness—living with her eighty-year-old neurotic mother aged her before her time—but it eased my mind.

She eventually got a part-time job working in the Ralph Lauren section of a Flint department store, her first job in over thirty years. Sometimes I would pass through the Midwest for work, and I'd drive up to the Genesee Mall and surprise her. Her eyes would fill with tears and she'd clutch me tightly, her nails digging into my ribs like a drowning child grasping a rescue buoy.

But then I hit thirty-six, Dad's age when he crashed. I had dabbled with my grief and loss, mostly on November 28, the anniversary of Dad's death, pushing it away the rest of the year. Denial was less of an option as I aged. Anything could set me off. I was on assignment in a faceless city killing time on its generic boardwalk when I saw a black-haired young man helping his little boy pedal without training wheels. I burst into tears. I started going to Army-Navy games in Philadelphia and the Meadowlands whenever I could. The sight of the academy brigade marching onto the field filled me with pride and then sobs that I'd try and stifle in a press box bathroom stall. Still, I went back year after year. One night in 2003 or 2004, I caught the Denzel Washington submarine flick *Crimson Tide* on cable and was fine until the soundtrack started bleating "Eternal Father," the Navy hymn played at Dad's memorial service. I wept for an hour.

The more I thought about Dad, the less I wanted anything to do with Mom. I replayed my childhood but began looking at it differently, a director sifting through footage shot by the second unit. Now I didn't see our long-ago battles as war between two superpowers. I walked the streets in my Brooklyn neighborhood staring at all the happy moms with their perfect kids in $500 strollers and was struck by a simultaneously banal and profound thought: Wait a second. She was the adult and I was the child. I was a boy with a dead father. Was screaming that I was ruining her life helpful? Did she really think that was right?

So I cut her off. Actually, it was more benign neglect. I stopped returning her calls the same day. Then I waited three days. Sometimes, I didn't call back at all. I lost interest in her squabbles with her mother and sister. I let the burden of Mom pass to Christine and Terry. My relationship with Christine remained close and important to me even if we didn't talk or see each other very often. That childhood bond, me looking out for her and her loving me in return, couldn't be broken.

Things with Terry were more complicated. Being only eleven months apart, we waged a low-intensity conflict with each other for our first eighteen years over everything from *Star Trek* versus football on TV to who was Christine's favorite sibling. By high school, we were exhausted with each other.

We didn't bridge the gap as adults. Our temperaments were always different. She was controlled and quiet. Mom always thought there was a happy carefree part of her that shut down when Dad died and never returned. I was the opposite, a jokey drama queen always playing the fool. We'd go skiing together and the old fault lines would emerge as Terry, a former all-conference skier, tried to goad me down double black diamond runs by questioning my manhood. She'd roll her eyes at my hesitation and call me a wuss. I'd pout, wondering aloud why she was surprised by my lack of coordination after forty years of front-row observation. At the time, she owned a Range Rover, a Miata, and a motorcycle. One day at Mount Bachelor, I muttered under my breath that she was the real man of the family.

"What did you say?"

"Uh, nothing."

We were just wired differently. But we were there for each other when we had to be. In 1993, she stayed with me when she came to Washington, D.C., for a gay rights demonstration, particularly heroic since she was still an officer in the "don't ask, don't tell" Army. We didn't talk about her private life, but we went to the Mall and looked at the AIDS quilt and walked for hours. We didn't say much, but I knew it meant a lot to her that I was by her side.

During my divorce, she flew out to Boston and helped keep me upright when I had no desire to do that. She was the first member of my family to call my ex an asshole. Whether it was true or she meant it didn't matter. I was still grateful.

I often wondered what Dad meant to her, or if she ever thought of him. Maybe she had put him away, the pain too great. But I was wrong. In 2013, Terry and her partner, Bari, prepared for the birth of their son. They arranged to have the Cesarean section on January 6, a Sunday. When the doctor asked why that day, Terry told her it was our father's seventieth birthday. A photo of Dad from flight school was kept in their room during the delivery.

Mom moved to Port St. Lucie, Florida, to escape Michigan's winters. A year later, a hurricane bore down on Florida and an evacuation order was issued. Mom was petrified to drive north with all the fleeing traffic. It was Terry who flew down and drove her to safety, not me.

I wasn't proud of myself. I didn't have the courage to have an actual conversation with her about these things, so she was left to wonder why her son was doing the slow fade. I did the minimum—calling on birthdays and Christmas and visiting once or twice a year—just enough so she had to ask herself if maybe it was all just in her head. Part of me reveled in leaving her alone with her doubts. But, mostly, I was ashamed.

I called her early in 2008 and casually dropped into conversation that I wanted to write something about Dad. There was a momentary pause, and then she squealed with delight.

"Oh, you go, boy! That sounds wonderful! I am so proud of you. I'll go through my phone book and think if I come up with names for you."

I was confused. We had not talked about Dad for more than forty-five minutes in the past thirty years. Now she was fired up that I was going to write about him?

"You write what you want to write. You're owed that much."

The year 2008 slowly rolled by. I watched with everyone else as Barack Obama took over our lives. He was everywhere in my Brooklyn neighborhood. His posters hung in wine bars and his face jumped out from T-shirts on toddlers rushing off to preschool conflict resolution seminars (or so I imagined).

As Obama and John McCain received their parties' nominations, my heart filled with dread. I'd been voting Democrat since I was twenty-two, but this was different. There are few things I knew with certainty that Dad would have done if he had lived. One would have been voting for John McCain, a fellow Annapolis grad and Navy flier. So I would do it for him. That seemed the least I could do.

But it wasn't that simple. I remembered my Chicago years, laboring for black candidates in lost causes, not far from Barack Obama's home. I remembered the tears I shed when they lost. When I worked for Alan Dixon, I had, inexplicably, helped draft the first Senate prayer given by a Muslim, Wallace Mohammed. There was a connection there, too.

I had friends who worked on Obama's staff and swore by him. But I was never a fan of a 2008 Obama candidacy; the Navy brat in me wasn't able to see past him as a line jumper, vaulting from lieutenant to admiral. I was supposed to profile Obama in 2004 for a magazine, but it fell through. I always regretted it—partly out of egotism, but also because I wondered if maybe I would see what others saw if I'd met him.

I followed the campaign without joy. McCain seemed like a lost, tragic hero more than a plausible president. Watching him give his St. Paul acceptance speech, I was struck with sadness—his moment had been 2000 and that seemed long ago.

Still, John McCain felt like kin in some sense. I mentioned to a few friends that I was considering voting for him, and this admission was met with stony silence or the kind of condescending New York chuckle that greeted the revelation that I really liked the film *Love, Actually.*

I bit my lip all fall. I watched the markets fall and McCain's botched response remove the last doubt that he was going to lose, perhaps badly. I avoided political conversations for the most part but found myself at a friend's house watching the last debate with a group of Ivy League policy wonks and literary types. The McCain trashing began early. I left after the seventeenth joke about his strange facial expressions, telling my host that I didn't have a problem with people not supporting him, but the vilification of a man who spent longer in a prison camp than Obama spent in the Senate wasn't how I wanted to spend my evening.

I called Mom on the way home. She could hear the rage in my voice. She let me babble until I ran out of steam.

"I know, son. McCain suffered like we suffered. Other people are never going to understand that. You vote the way you want to vote."

A week or so later, I went to vote in an old, beaten-down Brooklyn school. The line was so long that I was able to concentrate on the excitement on the faces of African Americans as they entered the voting booths with their children. I was envious of their joy. I wondered if the past was really past.

Finally, I entered the booth, closed the curtain, and stared at the names. I stared so long that I could hear folks behind me begin to grumble. I delayed by flipping the switches for all the Democrats in local offices. My finger went to McCain-Palin, but I didn't flip the switch. I moved my hand over the Obama-Biden switch, then flipped it, pulled hard on the main lever, and departed. I could barely breathe. I called Mom to tell her what I had done. She crackled with laughter..

"I did too! Maybe the future will be different. Sugar, it's worth a try."

I didn't know what to make of this new version of Mom. Was that all I needed to do, talk about Dad, and now she was all touchy-feely about our history? Is that how little it took? If so, why did we wait so long?

I ARRIVED IN FLINT ON A low-ceiling, humid summer day that reminded me of my miserable teenage years. The house was not the same. Mom had sold the place in Flushing when she moved to Florida, but once Christine started having kids, she couldn't bear to be so far away and bought a small ranch-style home in Grand Blanc, about twenty minutes from where I lived as a boy. Some things had survived the move; models of Dad's planes still rested above the fireplace next to the flag presented on behalf of a grateful nation.

Mom had adopted the characteristics of an old woman living alone—the too-large television left on for company morning, noon, and night. She hobbled around on an artificial knee, a little uncertain on her feet. Her mind was sharp but her health wasn't great. She had endured an angioplasty a year or two earlier. At the hospital, Christine and I looked on slack-jawed when she told the nutritionist that she would still be cooking with Crisco and it wasn't open for debate. Watching her cook me rigatoni—one of her heart attack specials that I loved—I was struck by the thought that she would die, and not at some abstract point in the future but maybe before the decade was over. Somehow, the thought had never occurred to me before. My battles with her, now mostly in my memory, seemed as necessary to me as oxygen. I couldn't imagine it ending.

I lay awake that night in her spare room like I do most nights before a big interview. I decided what questions I would save for last, an old strategy to get what you can from a source before things turn ugly. In the morning, she made me eggs and bacon with some Pillsbury biscuits—my favorite childhood breakfast—and then she settled onto her sofa with her VAQ-135 mug. Mom's poodle, Ollie—her fourth child—curled up in her lap, sighed, and then slipped off to sleep.

We started with the day they first met. She told the familiar story of meeting at a dance after the 1961 Oyster Bowl game between Navy and Duke. The rest of their courtship went according to legend, except when it didn't. She began making the five-hour drive to Annapolis with other girlfriends dating midshipmen. The girls would stay in "drag houses," local homes chaperoned by widows and matrons. I asked her what she first saw in him.

"He was just extremely smart, but he never made anyone else feel like they were beneath him, as far as intelligence. He was just a very fun, fun person. He liked to pull pranks."

I joked that I'd never heard anyone describe Dad as fun before. Mom cut me off.

"Oh, he was. He loved nature; he loved to go on picnics."

Dad and picnics: now, these were words that didn't go together in my memory. Mom told me they kept courting through the summer of 1962. Dad had six weeks off from the academy and spent them in Norfolk hauling cement bags at the construction company where Mom worked answering phones. Mom's mom had just remarried and moved to Cherry Point with her marine husband, so they had a lot of, let us say, unsupervised time that summer. The following Christmas, Mom was wearing Dad's Naval Academy pin, a pre-engagement move.

"I had to pinch myself. I couldn't believe someone like your father would want to be with someone like me."

We talked about their wedding, but she glossed over it quickly. She wanted to talk about how her fantasy life turned against her, pregnant for eighteen of her first twenty-one months as a bride. This wasn't quite how she'd expected it to go. She wasn't prepared.

"After I had Terry and you, I was on tranquilizers, because I could not sit. I always had to be doing something. My whole personality changed. I was frazzled. I was looking for the fairy-tale marriage; it got to be like, 'Is this what life is all about?' "

Mom broached her unhappiness with my father on only one occasion. It was in 1968, after he told her they would be moving from Rhode Island to NAS Meridian, Mississippi, their third move in three years.

"I said, 'I don't know if I can handle this anymore, two kids and all this stuff.' He said, 'When you married me, you knew I was going to be a Navy pilot; you knew this was my career. If this is making you unhappy, the only thing I can say is either you learn how to live with it or maybe we should just go our separate ways.' That woke me up real fast. I never brought that up ever again."

The thought of perfect Dad bullying Mom threatened to topple their respective roles as the American Hero and the Dragon Lady in the movie of my life. I asked her what she remembered most of Terry and me when we were kids. She gave a sad laugh.

"Terry was my blond-haired, blue-eyed little girl who did all the right things, and then I had my little boy: anything that you did, you did it to irritate me. When you were in the crib, you used to take your head and bang it so hard, I thought you were going to have a concussion. You used to chew holes in your shirt, and then you started chewing the bedspreads."

Now we were back on familiar ground! Apparently, I was a dick even as an infant. Mom told me that the thing that frustrated her most was that Dad would come home, offer a few words of stern instruction, and I'd jump to attention.

"Your father used to say, 'Ignore him,' but he wasn't around you all day."

Mom asked me if I remembered the child psychologist that she took me to in California when I was six or seven. I did, but only vaguely. She sketched in the particulars.

"He tested you and he came out and said he'd never met a boy so little already trying to live up to his father. He felt you were already competing with him."

We sat in silence for a little while. I could feel darkness rising in my heart. If the thought of never measuring up to

Dad was ingrained in me so deeply, so early, what chance did I ever have of winning that war? We kept talking. We talked about Dad's frustration of whiling away the Vietnam War in the A-3 while his peers were flying combat missions.

"I told him he was crazy—did he forget he had two small kids? But he felt he was missing out, not doing his part."

Mom begged Dad to get out after his Mississippi crash and fly for the airlines, but Dad just said no. He didn't want to be a bus driver. That was the end of the conversation.

"I just had to live with always being afraid. That was the deal."

We kept talking for hours, revisiting old battles in Oak Harbor. Even thirty years later, Mom was still baffled.

"I couldn't get through to you. It was in one ear, out the other. I just felt like you couldn't care less, that you were saying, 'There she goes again, the raving mother.' "

It was my turn to laugh. That was exactly what I'd thought. Mom didn't like that. Her jaw jutted out in the old, familiar way.

"I just never thought you were ever telling me the truth. Why was the truth so hard?"

I sat up in my chair and started pulling at hair on my forearm, an old nervous tic. I mentioned one of the last conversations I had with Dad, the one where I admitted to him that I told her whatever she wanted to hear so she would stop yelling. I told her Dad's advice was to "apologize even if you're right." She got angry.

"So you're telling me what you think I want to hear and I'm thinking, 'Why does he keep lying to me?' Great."

We broke for lunch and Mom made me a sandwich. She tossed an observation from the kitchen.

"Your dad was never worried that you wouldn't figure things out. He wasn't panicking. That was me. Maybe he saw something in you of what he was like as a boy. But I had all these people saying how smart you were and you weren't doing anything with it."

I said nothing. There was much more ground to cover, the years after Dad died. I tried to ease into that time, talking about how much I loved taking care of Christine when she was little. Mom said that wasn't surprising.

"She gave you unconditional love. I don't think you really felt that from anyone before, especially not me. She helped fill a void for you."

My eyes welled with tears. She was right, of course. We kept talking, both of our voices cracking. She told me about the last time she saw Dad in Manila.

"He asked me if I could stay a couple more days. I just couldn't see how I could with you kids back here. So I said, 'I just can't do it,' and then he kissed me good-bye. And I went hysterical. I watched him walk away through a window and I just knew that I wouldn't see him again."

I asked why we moved so quickly, only five months after the accident.

"I thought I was going to come home and his car was going to be in the driveway. I thought that since they didn't find anything he'd somehow make it home. I couldn't get that out of my head until we moved."

I'd felt exactly the same way. By now, we'd been talking for four hours. I couldn't really bear to push on, but I feared that if we stopped, Mom would shut down and we'd never speak about Dad again.

We moved on to the Flint years; there were minefields everywhere. She remembered a particularly hairy moment at the dinner table. She was cutting a pizza at the dining room table and I made one of my trademark sarcastic remarks. She flung the pizza slicer in my general direction. According to Mom, this is how it went:

ME: You could have ended in prison on that one.
MOM: I'd love every minute of it.

Somehow, this made us both laugh. What grieving American family doesn't have moments of hurling cutlery? I asked her if that was the lowest moment. She said it wasn't close. Her voiced dropped to a whisper.

"I wrote notes to myself about committing suicide. I'd write, 'I love my family. But I can't see any end to this. I'm so tired.'"

There was silence. All those nights when she locked herself in her room and I sat outside listening to her cry, that was my fear—that she would end it all and leave us with no one. I wasn't wrong. But to hear the actual words tore at my insides. The rational part told me that it wasn't my fault; she needed professional help. But my gut told me something different—I'd let my mother down when she needed me most. I couldn't save her. But I didn't say anything like that.

"Mom, I'm glad you didn't."

She smiled her gap-toothed smile, the one Dad fell in love with, and tears ran down her lined face. I could still see the beautiful woman playing bridge while I watched from the stairs.

"I would have never done it. There was no one left to take care of our kids."

I wondered aloud why she didn't date to ease her loneliness or at least to have some adult conversation.

"I didn't think I had something to offer to anyone. I'm not smart. So why bother? Your dad saw something in me. He could see into my soul and made me feel special. I knew that wasn't going to happen again."

I knew far too well what she meant, sorrow poisoning your blood until you feel like you just don't matter in this world. I told her that she mattered to me and to a lot of people in the world. But I could tell that she didn't believe me.

"I don't know how you turned out as well as you did. I did a terrible job with you. I know it now. I didn't know anything about boys. I didn't have any brothers." She paused and fiddled with her wedding ring. "You were your father's only son. I was so afraid of doing something wrong I overreacted to everything. Stephen, I'm sorry."

And there it was. The apology I'd waited for my entire life. But I didn't feel triumphant. I just ached for my mother sitting right next to me. It wasn't that we had not understood each other for all those years. It was that we were shouting grief and loss and anger at each other so loudly we couldn't hear each other. She had done the best she could. I could finally accept that.

I turned off the tape recorder and casually said that I'd wished we'd had this conversation twenty-five years ago. Mom bolted up on the sofa, sending Ollie sprawling off her lap.

"I was so angry at you and Terry about that! You never mentioned Dad and it made me really sad. That's why his pictures were everywhere. I thought if you saw pictures of him you might talk about him. But you never did."

Her words baffled me.

"Wait a sec, I was furious at *you* because you never talked about him. It made *me* so angry."

It would have been funny if it were not so damn sad. Mom let Ollie out into the backyard and poured herself a Coke.

"Well, that's the Rodrick family. Everyone's so frickin' scared of hurting someone's feelings, nothing really ever gets said."

I didn't say anything. It was too late. The tape recorder was off. Our time was up.

◇◇◇

Chapter Twenty-Nine

MOM WENT TO BED EARLY THAT night and I tried to distract myself with a Tigers game, but I eventually drifted down to the basement and Dad's cruise box. At some point, Mom had combined his Navy stuff with other Dad-related detritus into a treasure chest of things that make up a life. It sat apart from the rest of Mom's old furniture and clothes, a lone box on a cement altar.

I set aside letters sealed in a Tupperware container and dug in. There was his silver sword from the Naval Academy, a black cummerbund from his wedding, and a water-damaged Navy form listing all items shipped back from the *Kitty Hawk* after the accident.

I sorted through Dad's possessions for hours, fingering his rosary beads and trying on the Navy cap he wore at his change of command. Buried underneath a lock box and a newspaper ad of Dwight Eisenhower endorsing someone for Congress was a small, red book with "Daily Diary" embossed on the cover in fading letters. I carefully opened the pages. The words were written in a blurred mixture of print and cursive that mirrored my own handwriting. It was a diary that Dad had kept when he was thirteen, the same age I was when he was killed. I asked Mom about the journal the next day and she didn't bat an eye.

"I didn't know that was in there."

I read the pages. The boy in the diary is more responsible and worldly than I was at the same age. On January 3 and 4, Dad served as an altar boy at four masses ("solemn high funeral, same as yesterday"); took an after-school job in the cafeteria ("emptying barrels and sweeping floors with Joe Barbour"); got screamed at by his mother ("Mom found sexy book & gave me HELL"); figured his brother ratted him out and administered frontier justice ("I slit Dan's shirt with a knife, because he squealed"). In his spare time, he delivered the *Brockton Enterprise* every afternoon.

I sensed an inherent goodness in his heart that I feared I did not inherit. Many of the early entries recount in minute detail the famous used dishwasher Dad bought his mother with his paper route money. Dad was barely thirteen and he was supervising the purchase of a major appliance ("bought second hand dishwasher from one of goody brothers in Randolph, cost $100 paid deposit of $25"). And the follow-through! There are a half-dozen trips to the hardware store ("paid $3.34 for parts").

In March, he crammed for the Boston College High School entrance exam, earning a scholarship, a turning point in his young life. ("Not too bad, Math E A S Y! I think I got close to 100! English a little harder.") He even eased over minor financial issues for his dad. ("Had to lend Dad 85 cents.")

My heart swelled reading about Dad's wonder boy achievements and altruism, but part of it just depressed me. Much of it was genuine sadness that a good soul was taken so early, but some of it was my same old refrain, self-loathing for not measuring up. Sure, I had a paper route at thirteen, but I certainly wasn't buying Mom a damn dishwasher. I was squandering my cash on ice-cream sandwiches and treating Mom like crap. And I'd been the world's worst altar boy.

Fortunately, there were other episodes that made me know that he was my blood. Dad was no angel. He missed a chance at a school trip to New York City because he received Bs in conduct and application. That part sounded like me. His paper route was sliced in half by his boss because he wouldn't stop cutting across his customers' lawns. That after-school job in the cafeteria? He got fired from it a month later. ("Me and joe got fight with a1 salad dressing sauce, joe got wrecked. My hair still stinks.") At least once a week, he was kept after school because of mouthing off. ("Sister said I was 'PUNK' today.")

There was a destructive streak in him that was not limited to carving up his kid brother's shirt. After a spring blizzard, Dad headed downtown to cause trouble.

> After church came home changed and went to store with Woody on way home hit Mr. Smith's car on window with snowball. He chased me, knocked me down in a & p parking lot.

I'm pretty sure there has never been a son more elated to read about his father getting the shit kicked out of him. But that wasn't what really moved me. I didn't need a degree in psychotherapy to see that Dad's home was not a happy place. His whole life—the altar boy gigs, the jobs, wandering in the woods for hours—was devoted to spending as little time as possible in the house on Herrod Avenue. It wasn't open to interpretation. He and his buddies hitchhiked all the time, traveling fifty miles from home and back again in an afternoon.

> Got haircut, thumbed to Providence Rhode Island with Woody arrived at 1:01 and left at 1:54. Got ride to East Providence and waited 1 hr 45min for another ride. Mr. Sankus (287 Oak) went by and didn't stop. . . . Mom saw me thumbing. Caught hell.

And it wasn't just to kill time. That summer, he planned a longer trip with his pal Woody.

> Worked on map for trip leave June 25th with Woody return around July 15 . . . decided to thumb on trip to Washington or Chicago or Pittsburgh.

He never did take that trip, but why did he need to get away? Was it his father, so tragic and distant? I read in his boyish hand the first seeds of restlessness that would take him from Brockton to Annapolis and eventually to a violent death in the Indian Ocean. And in that restlessness I could see myself: my endless need to be somewhere else, doing something else, always moving.

I took the diaries back to New York with me and delicately made copies of the pages. I found myself reading and rereading the passages when I should have been working on other things. I was thirteen years and fifty-nine days old the day he died. One day, I did the math and figured when Dad was the same age. It was March 4, 1956.

> Served 815 mass. Fr Donahue celebrant. Fixed Dots bike. Fooled around in woods with Woody and John Campbell. Got equip back from mike—see Saturday—

went to show—saw Battle Cry. GREAT. Dishwasher all installed.

I rented *Battle Cry* that night. The 1955 film is a Velveeta-laden adaptation of a Leon Uris novel about Marines in World War II. Calling it paint-by-numbers is charitable. The stereotypes burst onto the screen in the first five minutes. There's the damn crazy lumberjack, the bookish kid, the gruff sergeant, and a light-fingered Italian greaser who gives a hot foot—I'm not making this up—to a Navajo who hops around the train going "how, how, how." The boys end up at boot camp where they bond and realize—spoiler alert—that they have much more in common than they think and there's no way they're going to make it out of this cockeyed war without each other.

But once every half hour or so, there was a real moment. Van Heflin plays their leader, Major Sam "High Pockets" Huxley. (We never learn why he's nicknamed High Pockets.) His troops head into a New Zealand town on a day pass, and he's left alone declining another officer's offer of a night of debauchery. Huxley talks of the loneliness of command, a family far away, and I couldn't help but think of Tupper.

But then I watched it again and tried to put myself in a different place. It is a third-run theater on a gray evening in 1956 Brockton. I'm sitting there with Woody. We're eating popcorn and talking at the screen. We watch men from towns just like Brockton fight, drink, chase skirt, and then kill the Japs. We hide our tears when High Pockets buys the farm on Tarawa.

The war ends and the boys come back to their wives and

children and live happily ever after. The credits roll. We cheer. On the way home, we dodge street trolleys, tackle each other, and reenact our favorite scenes, taking turns playing the hero. And maybe, just maybe, we think that's the life we want.

I talked to Dad's sister Dot a little later about when she first remembered Dad talking about joining the military.

"I'd say when he was about thirteen or fourteen. I don't know where it came from or how it started."

Could it have all been put into motion that day at the movies? A boy thirteen years and fifty-nine days old sees a movie and starts down a path that ends with a boy thirteen years and fifty-nine days old losing his father and losing his way.

Is that how it happened?

Chapter Thirty

TUPPER'S FAVORITE FILM IS *This Is Spinal Tap.* The rock mockumentary about arrested men-children trying to be serious about their absurd profession was the perfect corollary for the life of a naval aviator. He prepared for his final flight knowing the angst was about to be turned up to eleven. It wasn't going to be a quick turn around the Northwest and then touchdown and taxi to the Black Ravens hangar. Instead, Tupper was flying a Prowler to NAS Jacksonville, where it would be decommissioned and stripped for parts. The old man and his ride would hit the glue factory simultaneously.

Originally, I was going to be in the backseat with Socr8tes for the flight. I still had my swim and survival quals and there weren't a ton of Black Ravens volunteering for the 6,000-mile round trip. (The crew would fly back commercial.) But at the last minute, Commodore Slais informed Tupper that it would be his honor to take the last seat on his final flight. This was either a touching gesture or the commodore ensuring that Tupper didn't do anything stupid at his last rodeo.

The flight was typical Prowler, aka screwed from the start. Tupper made his way down the stairs from his office on an October morning in full flight gear. He opened the hangar door and found the entire squadron standing on the flight line saluting their skipper. There were pictures and handshakes. He loaded into the Prowler with Stonz next to him and Commodore Slais and Socr8tes in the backseat. He gave his sailors a final wave and taxied down the runway.

That's when the first red light flashed on the cockpit suggesting low pressure in the hydraulics of the landing gear. That should have been a no-go. But the commodore was in the back; he couldn't see Tupper's instruments. Tupper looked at Stonz, and his maintenance officer just shrugged his shoulders. Fuck it, Tupper thought. There was no way he was climbing out of the plane after that dog-and-pony good-bye. He turned back to the runway and gunned the engines.

Flying with the commodore in the backseat made everyone nervous. They had plans to stop for fuel at an Air Force base in Grand Junction, Colorado. But just as they prepared their final approach, Tupper double-checked the field information and realized the base didn't have the equipment needed to restart the Prowler after refueling. If Tupper hadn't noticed, they might have been stranded in Grand Junction with the commodore for days until a starter could be shipped out. That would have sucked. They refueled in Roswell, New Mexico, instead and pushed on, overnighting at Robins Air Force Base outside of Houston.

The Prowler was leaking fluid from its nose gear the next morning. Stonz tightened a few screws with a borrowed wrench and they left right after dawn. Tupper flew along the coast over Mobile, Biloxi, and Pensacola. The men lightened up the closer they got to JAX, sharing hairy stories from flight school. Before Tupper knew it, he was flying his final approach into Jacksonville Naval Air Station. He wanted to bend the sky one last time and bring the Prowler in on a tight break at 4.5 Gs, 450 knots, but he remembered the commodore was in the backseat.

"Hey, Commodore, should we give them a show?"

"Uh, we should stick to 350 and the regs."

So Tupper brought the Prowler in at a mild 350 knots. The Prowler hit the runway, taxied, and Tupper climbed down. His plane was now leaking three kinds of fluid from its nose. It was ready to be put down.

I waited on the flight line at JAX with some of the base's senior command and a giant red fire truck. It's Navy tradition that a naval aviator is hosed down after his final flight. Tupper took off his helmet and waited patiently as the cold water cascaded over him in the brisk October air. Commodore Slais shook his hand and posed for some pictures and then raced off to the airport to catch the last connecting flight back to Seattle.

Someone told me that this Prowler was the oldest in the fleet, dating back to 1977. Had Dad flown it as a Black Raven or at VAQ-129, the training squadron? There was no way of knowing for sure, but I wanted to think he had. Since the plane was bound for the boneyard, the maintainers back in Whidbey had signed their names on the fuselage. Here in Jacksonville, Tupper and the crew did the same. Stonz nudged me on the shoulder and handed me a pen. I signed it "CDR P. T. Rodrick, 1943–1979."

There was nothing else to do except get very, very drunk. But there were obstacles. Canine, an old Prowler guy, ran the boneyard and seemed lonely down here in a forgotten outpost. He offered to give us a quick tour of the base, and we felt like we couldn't say no. We rode over in a van to a faraway hangar and went inside. In front of us were six Prowlers splayed open like the catfish gutted by my grandfather in his

Alabama garage. Some were missing cockpits; some were a pinkish color from being sprayed with preservatives that prevented rusting. Tupper and I exchanged looks. It was hard not to see his career and Dad's life reduced to dissected and discontinued planes withering in the Florida heat. We wanted to be anywhere but there.

But the tour dragged on and on. We were told in excruciating detail how a Prowler is embalmed, catalogued, stripped, and then melted down for scrap. About three hours passed by. We stepped out of the hangar to a fading sun. Socr8tes seriously debated making a break for a nearby exit, climbing a fence, and hitching his way to our hotel.

We thought we had made our escape, but Canine wanted to show us one more thing: the Prowler parts depot that was housed in a nearby warehouse. It was straight out of a hoarders horror show. Rows and rows of Prowler screws, pads, and flaps were stacked to the ceiling. Stonz walked around in stunned silence, picking up random parts and mumbling.

"I tried to get one of these for months. They said they didn't have any."

The depot's manager was a potbellied guy who had flown Prowlers back in the 1970s. I asked him a question.

"Did you know Pete Rodrick?"

The old man paused for a moment.

"Oh, yeah, he was a real asshole."

I told him he was my father. The old man told me he was just joking. No one laughed.

We finally made it to our hotel on Jacksonville Beach around sunset and tried to make up for lost time. There was whiskey, barbecue, and more whiskey. Tupper put up a brave front until the alcohol burned it away. Well past midnight, he asked me a question.

"Can I still call myself a Navy pilot now that I have had my last flight? What if you were told you would never write again? Would you still be a writer?"

I didn't know the answer, so I changed the subject.

"Let's prank-call Sherm."

Tupper thought this was the best idea of the day. We called Sherm, and the skipper cursed him over the fact that the Anacortes Taco Bell closed at 10:00 p.m., an unacceptably early hour.

"Sherm, that is an outrage. I want you to get on this first thing in the morning. This cannot stand."

Sherm's voice was muffled, uncertain if his boss was serious.

"Uh, yessir. I'll get on that first thing."

Tupper gleefully snapped off my phone. We closed down a dive bar and did a final shot of Jack Daniel's. How we got the two blocks back to our hotel I will never know. Tupper hugged me and mumbled something about sharing the last flight with him. I told him I loved him like a brother or some such nonsense. I made it back to my room on the eighth floor. I had to piss. I looked at the toilet and decided that wouldn't do. I headed out onto the balcony. I dropped my jeans and sent a cascading arc eighty feet down into the hotel swimming pool. I zipped up and staggered to my bed. I felt closer to Dad than I had in years.

WE FLEW BACK TO WHIDBEY IN the morning, hungover, barely able to converse for the first leg. Tupper was largely silent; his skipper tour was ending in five days. The following afternoon, I drove up to Whidbey from Anacortes and stopped in to see him in his office. He was buried behind his desk in paperwork like the Robert De Niro character in Terry Gilliam's *Brazil.* He had to write fitness reports on all his officers and sailors in the next five days. He pushed the folders aside and we talked for a little while. He was in a sour mood; the moment his whole life had built to was passing and he couldn't stop time. Tupper flipped through a Navy magazine that had a feature on squadron commanders. He pointed out the ones who would be promoted ahead of him.

"That one was a suck-up." He flipped the page. "That one had a sugar daddy protecting him on CAG's staff." He turned another page and let out a sad laugh. "That one, I have no idea how he got promoted. One of life's great mysteries."

We talked about the squadron for a while. Mongo, the new XO, had arrived, and every time Tupper saw him it was like seeing a ghost. Vinnie was starting to assert himself in staff meetings, which rankled Tupper and made him feel more like a lame duck. But after we talked for a while I realized that wasn't what was bothering Tupper. He talked about Vinnie organizing a bash commemorating the change of command and how excited the junior officers were for the party.

"That was the squadron I was trying to create, but they wouldn't give it to me." He mentioned a long-nursed grudge, his men never showing up on his doorstep for an impromptu bash. "You know, they didn't even green-light me. I've never been in a squadron where the skipper wasn't green-lighted. Did they hate me that much? Was I that awful?"

I reminded him that Doogie hadn't been green-lighted. This just pissed him off more.

"Do they all hate me because of Doogie? You can tell me."

I told him they didn't hate him, but he didn't believe me. That night, there was better evidence. At an Anacortes Italian restaurant, the officers of VAQ-135 gathered with their wives for Tupper's change-of-command dinner. It couldn't have been more different from Doogie's farewell. The couples were dressed casually and the formality of the dining-out was replaced by toasts and drunken skits. Stoli led the JOs in a round of "What I Said, What I Meant."

> What I said: excuse me from the Christmas Party. What I meant: I need to puke. What I said: nothing on a six-hour combat flight. What I meant: you've been in the biz long enough; you realize everyone around you is an idiot.

Everyone laughed. Tupper stood up to cheers. He spoke about how grateful he was for everyone's hard work. He mentioned the Wolf and presented him with a tiny pillow that read "Quiet, the princess is sleeping."

He then singled out his department heads for special praise. Their hard work had so moved Tupper that he bought each of them gifts. He called each of them by name up to the front of the room. He handed each of them a vaguely creepy Hummel-like statue of a German schoolboy in short pants that I'd found at a rummage sale. The wives were skeeved out, but the men loved it.

The following Monday morning, it was all over. A band played for Tupper's change of command. His family was there: Jim and Cindy, Beth and the girls. Tupper had asked me to speak, so I sat up on the podium with Tupper, Vinnie, CAG, and the commodore. The muckety-mucks read rote speeches from binders describing command as a wild roller-coaster ride.

Then it was my turn. I looked out at the squadron and saw Beav and Sherm and Lil Chris and Stoli. And I saw the family I'd always wanted. I talked about how kind they had been to me even if they thought I had hippie hair. Then I recounted what one of Dad's maintainers had said about keeping Prowlers in the air:

> "The normal status was: One plane is close to fully operational. One plane has stuff broken, but works pretty good. One plane can fly, but nothing else works, and one is the hangar queen and sits in the hangar bay all tore apart."
>
> Sound familiar? Now remember, this was when the planes were new. Understandably, the Navy sees all squadrons equal, no matter the age or condition of their aircraft. It doesn't matter if you're flying brand-new, fancy-pants Super Hornets or moaning and groaning middle-aged Prowlers. You must perform.
>
> That's all great in theory, but let me provide some context. Commander Ware took over a bone-tired squadron that had been at sea for much of the past three years. His jets were between twenty-five and thirty-eight years old. And yet the Black Ravens flew an astounding 186 sorties over Afghanistan with a 98 percent completion rate on the last cruise.
>
> This is a tribute to Tupper, the department heads,

> the JOs, and the maintainers, the unsung heroes of the squadron. Tupper took a squadron that could have been counting their days to transition and transformed them—in my humble and biased opinion—into the best damn Prowler squadron in the fleet.

Then Tupper spoke. He thanked CAG and the commodore and then looked at Beth and his girls sitting in the front row. He took a long pause, and when he spoke his voice cracked and wavered. He talked of being in the Black Ravens for thirty months and having been gone from home for seventeen of them.

> Caitlin, I missed your fifth grade. Brenna, I missed your seventh. I came home from eight months at sea and girls had become young women. I was not there to help with homework. I was not there when you needed your dad. I can't get those months back.

> Tupper stopped again, his bottom lip quivering.

> There are more coming before I can come back to you. Just know I think about you every day before every flight, before every move I make.

He then turned to his wife, sitting below him in a black skirt and silver necklace. He thought of the woman who had stood beside him since he was a boy of nineteen. All the sacrifices she had made for him and his dream. He almost couldn't speak.

> Beth, you are the reason I am here today. You made me a better man. And I would never want to be here if you were not by my side. You've sacrificed your career and a lot of other dreams. And you did it for me. I can't thank you enough.

Tupper had written more, but he didn't trust himself to speak again without bawling. He moved on and thanked Vinnie and his men. Soon he was done and sat down. Then he noticed something on a shelf of the lectern. It was one of the creepy figurines he had given out the night before. One of the guys had stashed it there before the ceremony. Tupper's face broke into a wide grin. Maybe his men did love him, just a little.

◇◇◇

Chapter Thirty-One

SHERM WAS ALWAYS COMING UP WITH Navy guys for me to meet when I visited Whidbey. He was particularly insistent about one aviator. His name was Lieutenant Commander Brian "Steamer" Danielson, a flight instructor with VAQ-129, the Prowler training squadron. Sherm didn't know him well, but what he did know filled my heart with dread.

"His dad was shot down over Vietnam when he was a baby. They never found him. You should call him."

Actually, I didn't want anything to do with him. Steamer sounded too much like a fellow traveler. I was barely comfortable with my own grief; commiserating with another lost soul was out of the question. I could drink beers with Sherm and Tupper and shoot the shit with the guys in the ready room. These men were still alive and flying. I could make a separate peace with the present, but the past was always going to be my enemy. I managed to lose Steamer's email multiple times. But Sherm kept prodding and I finally wrote Steamer on a dead gray March morning in Anacortes. He emailed me back immediately.

"I'm actually giving a presentation about my dad to the Navy League at the officers' club today. I can get you in. Not too big of a deal if you can't make it."

His speech started in forty-five minutes. I showered and sped over Deception Pass Bridge, passing cars in the breakdown lane the closer I got to NAS Whidbey, cursing myself for not getting my shit together. It was the same old song.

I stumbled Chevy Chase–style into a banquet room half-filled with civilians eating sandwiches and exchanging business cards. My shaggy hair and dishevelment set me apart as usual. A man in khakis with strawberry blond hair and a slight, sad smile walked up to me. His chest was covered with ribbons.

"Hey, I'm Steamer. You must be Steve."

He spoke slowly and reluctantly, as if he were used to apologizing for things he had not done wrong. He told me he hoped I wouldn't find it too boring. He looked down at his watch and exhaled.

"I guess it's showtime."

He walked to the podium and thanked everyone for coming. He lifted his water glass in a mock toast and patted his stomach.

"Thanks for lunch, but we'll have to call it a rain check," said Steamer. He offered another half-smile. "For those of you who have worn these khaki uniforms, you know they tend to shrink over time."

I chuckled and recognized myself in his preamble. Self-deprecation is an essential tool when trafficking in the tragedy trade. It helps to instruct the audience that your sense of humor remains intact even as you're about to monologue about death.

Danielson flipped on a PowerPoint display and began telling his story. Benjamin Franklin Danielson was born on March 31, 1943—eighty-four days after my father—in Kenyon, Minnesota, a tiny farming community sixty miles south of Minneapolis. He lived in town with his parents and his brother Dennis but longed to be on his uncle Jim's farm a few miles outside of town, milking cows and helping with the corn and soybean harvests.

Benjamin was a star football player who fell in love with Mary Gates, a full-of-beans cheerleader. After graduating, he headed to nearby St. Olaf College on an Air Force ROTC scholarship, and she went to Winona State, a hundred miles away. There were the periodic breakups, but everyone knew they were meant for each other.

They both graduated in 1965 and were married that summer on a blue-sky day at Kenyon's First Evangelical Lutheran Church. Ben wanted to fly jets in the Air Force but he failed the eye test after college. He stayed in the Air Force anyway, training to be a meteorologist in Colorado Springs. He earned his civilian pilot license and began giving lessons to cadets from the nearby Air Force Academy. The cadets put a good word in for him, and he passed the eye exam on the second try.

A few months later, the Danielsons moved to Craig Air Force Base in Selma, Alabama, for flight school. They watched civil rights marches pass not far from the main gate.

Ben earned his wings in March 1968, just a few weeks after Mary gave birth to their son, Brian. Ben then spent the next year learning to fly the F-4 Phantom, a fighter-bomber. The following March, just after Brian's first birthday, Lieutenant Benjamin Danielson shipped over to Cam Ranh Bay Air Base in Vietnam to join the 558th Tactical Fighter Squadron. His wife and baby son moved back to Kenyon and waited out his one-year tour of duty.

It was the year after Tet, and Walter Cronkite had just proclaimed, "We are mired in a stalemate that can only be ended by negotiation, not victory." In Washington, Secretary of Defense Robert McNamara convinced President Lyndon Johnson that the key to victory wasn't destroying the North Vietnamese in the field, but shutting down the Ho Chi Minh Trail, a supply route that wound from North Vietnam through the jungles and ravines of neighboring Laos. Strangle the trail, McNamara argued, and the Vietcong in South Vietnam would starve. A desperate LBJ wanted to believe him, and so did his successor, Richard Nixon.

From 1965 to 1973, the United States dropped more bombs on Laos than it had dropped on all the cities of Europe during World War II. Comparatively, the cost to American aviators was profoundly minor, but the 558th had already lost a handful of pilots to enemy fire during Benjamin Danielson's year in-country. The Phantom was the world's most advanced fighter, renowned for its Mach 2 airspeed—engineers called it the triumph of thrust over aerodynamics—and a nine-ton assortment of bombs, machine guns, and air-to-air missiles. But what the Phantom gained in strength, it lost in finesse. The F-4 could move a mile in six seconds, but it wasn't particularly nimble. When a Phantom entered its bombing run, the jet had to slow down and its trajectory became distressingly predictable, making it easy pickings for surface-to-air missiles and antiaircraft fire. Over 380 Phantoms were lost in Vietnam. Pilots called their plane the Flying Footlocker.

IT'S UNLIKELY THAT BENJAMIN DANIELSON WAS thinking of saturation bombing, power politics, or aircraft mishap rates on the morning of December 5, 1969. Most likely, he thought of getting home. Just twenty-six, he was already a battle-hardened veteran with sixty-seven combat missions under his belt. Like Dad, he was close, just weeks from coming home.

That morning, Danielson and another Phantom—known on the radio as Boxer 21 and Boxer 22—took off from Cam Ranh Bay at around 9:00 a.m. It was the dry season in Laos, and southbound traffic on the Ho Chi Minh Trail had picked up. Every day, Phantoms would hit choke points on the trail, dropping 500-pound MK-36 antipersonnel mines along the road. The MK-36s would hit the endless mud, sink into the ground, and then detonate when a truck or motorcycle crossed over them.

Boxer 21 and Boxer 22 were directed to the Laotian village of Ban Phanop, ten miles below the Mu Gia Pass, a major entry point for the North Vietnamese. The planes descended to about seven thousand feet and let go of their ordnance. Boxer 21 completed its run unscathed, but Boxer 22 was hit by 37-mm antiaircraft fire as it pulled up to 6,000 feet. According to another pilot in the area, Danielson tried to save the plane but it bucked out of control. Danielson and his navigator-bombardier, Woody Bergeron, bailed out at 3,000 feet.

Both men were fired upon during their descent with the wind blowing them to different sides of a small tributary called the Nan Ngo River. Danielson was the unlucky one; he landed in a construction area near a main road, while Bergeron fell to earth in a grove of trees on the less developed side of the river.

The two cleared their chutes and immediately activated their rescue beepers. They both burrowed into the reeds alongside the river and made radio contact with rescue aircraft already gathering above them. Within thirty minutes, a dozen American warplanes were in the area dropping bombs and "hosing down" the area with machine-gun fire in the hopes of setting up a safe zone for helicopters to pluck the airmen to safety.

Danielson was in the more precarious position, so his comrades went after him first. At 12:40 p.m., an Air Force Jolly Green Giant helicopter got within two minutes of picking up Benjamin before ground fire drove the helo away. Another rescue was attempted at sunset. This time, a helicopter got close enough that a pararescuer started firing his machine gun, laying down ground fire so a rope could be dropped to Danielson. But a burst of Laotian machine-gun fire hit the pararescuer and the helicopter skittered away. Airman David M. Davison was dead before the helicopter landed back at base. The sun disappeared around 6:00 p.m., and Danielson and Bergeron were told to sit tight: the Air Force would be back at first light.

Back in Kenyon, it was already morning of the next day. An Air Force officer knocked on the door of Mary Danielson's small apartment. She answered it holding her son, Brian. The officer told her that Benjamin had been shot down, but that he was alive and a rescue mission was under way. She was told to wait by the phone.

The call never came. Through the night, Danielson and Bergeron talked briefly on their radios, never staying on long for fear of being overheard by Laotian soldiers. The Americans were true to their word. At dawn, a dozen helicopters and planes laid more fire on the Laotian strongholds. Around 7:00 a.m., Danielson whispered to Bergeron on the radio that the enemy was drawing closer. Then he went silent. The Air Force tried to raise the two downed airmen on the radio, but only Bergeron responded. Midmorning, Bergeron reported that he'd heard gunfire on the other side of the river followed by the scream of what sounded like an American.

That was the last anyone heard from Benjamin Danielson. Thirty-six hours later, a delirious Bergeron was finally plucked from the shores of the Nan Ngo in the most extensive air rescue operation of the war. Almost five hundred missions were flown in an effort to rescue two men. In Kenyon, Mary Danielson's phone finally rang. She was notified that her husband was officially listed as missing in action. The Air Force only had Bergeron's account of hearing her husband's screams, and he'd become dehydrated and disoriented from the trauma of being hunted for two days. Maybe, just maybe, Bergeron was mistaken.

MARY AND HER SON BRIAN LIVED the next four years in twilight. Information was scarce. When American military involvement ended in 1973, the North Vietnamese repatriated 598 American POWs. The Air Force told Mary to watch her television. It was not impossible, they said, that her husband might just walk off one of the Freedom Birds, flying Americans to Baguio Air Force Base in Subic Bay, Philippines, the place where Mom would last see Dad six years later. Mary watched for days, with her only son playing on the floor in front of her. She didn't see her husband.

By 1976, the Air Force had moved Benjamin Danielson from "missing in action" to "presumed deceased, body not recovered." Mary eventually married a Navy Reserve chaplain and moved to New Hampshire with her eight-year-old son, but it didn't work out. They returned home to Kenyon three years later. Brian spent weekends and summers working the family dairy farm. He went to the same high school as his dad. Everyone told him his father was a great man.

BRIAN DANIELSON DIDN'T SHARE ALL OF this with the audience. He didn't mention the Laotian bombing casualties, and he definitely didn't mention the two Laotian soldiers whom Woody Bergeron saw "disappeared" by an American plane's .50 caliber machine guns. He didn't mention how the failure of his mother's second marriage caused another man to fade out of his life. And he skipped past his teenage years where every Chuck Norris MIA rescue movie pushed his rationality aside and filled his fatherless adolescence with hope that his dad might walk through the front door one day.

Don't get me wrong. I'd have left them out too. When I talk of my father's accident, there's usually no mention that the *Kitty Hawk* was steaming toward the Persian Gulf to rescue fifty-two hostages taken largely because of America's slavish support for the shah of Iran, a cruel despot. You keep the pointlessness of your loss locked away from your friends and yourself.

ABOUT HALFWAY THROUGH, A CRANKY OLD man complained that the pictures being displayed on the overhead projector were not synching up perfectly with Steamer's narration. The old man stepped toward the machine and tried to correct the malfunction. Instead, he crashed the equipment. It took five minutes to reboot and the lunch crowd got impatient and impolitic in the way old people sometimes do.

"So what happened to your dad?" shouted one man. "What did you find out?"

"Well, we're getting to that," said Danielson quietly. "Give me just a minute."

The projector fired back up and Danielson continued. He skimmed over his personal history, skipping over how he attended St. Olaf's and played football for the same coach as his dad. He didn't tell them that he had his heart set on the Air Force after graduating in 1990 but was turned down. He reluctantly accepted a billet as a Prowler ECMO and not a pilot. He knew the crowd was here for his father's story, not his own.

Brian mentioned that in 1991 his father's pistol was found in a North Vietnamese military museum. It was a tantalizing detail that led nowhere. The government reclassified Benjamin Danielson as "last seen alive," a designation that made him a top priority for MIA cases. *Parade* magazine ran Benjamin's handsome face on its cover in 1993, but nothing changed.

But in 2003, Benjamin Danielson's dog tags were found in Laos along with a human shoulder bone not far from his crash site. Ben Danielson's grandmother gave a sample and a DNA analysis began. But it was just a sliver of a bone, less than an ounce. It would take years to figure out whether it was a match.

By now, Steamer was married with three kids of his own. He began personally investigating his father's crash. He contacted his father's squadron mates and spent an afternoon with

Woody Bergeron. He learned the details of the massive rescue mission launched to find his father. He understood how close his dad had come to being saved. In 2005, a joint Laotian-American task force found an eyewitness who had seen exactly where Benjamin Danielson had landed on the banks of the Nan Ngo. An American military task force—known as a Joint POW Accounting Command—mobilized and made plans to sift through the dirt near the river. Danielson petitioned JPAC to be included on the trip.

And that's how, in March 2006, Brian Danielson found himself digging through the Laotian clay looking for his father's remains. Every morning, Danielson and twelve others would leave their Laotian base camp and ride a rickety helicopter fifteen kilometers to a dried-up riverbed where he'd claw and sift with his hands until they bled.

But he didn't find any bones, just pounds and pounds of unexploded American bombs. Because of unexplained Laotian government restrictions, the dig took place almost a kilometer from where Benjamin Danielson actually landed and was likely killed. When Danielson told his superiors they were digging in the wrong place, they politely told him to shut up. It was never explained why they couldn't dig at the exact site.

Finally, on day 26, Brian Danielson, with the help of some smuggled-in whiskey, persuaded the Laotians to fly him the extra kilometer to where his father was murdered. He arrived at the killing spot on his father's sixty-fourth birthday.

At this point, Steamer took a long sip of water and stopped for a moment. The room was quiet. I could hear his breathing through the public address system.

"I was carrying a bag of flowers," said Danielson. "I laid them where we assumed that he was killed."

He paused again and gave the same, sad smile.

"I'm not very happy about admitting this, but I tried to go where I thought he was."

He pointed with his finger at a speck on a map.

"I started walking into the trees, and I got lost. It wasn't what I'd expected."

The room remained silent except for the sound of a woman weeping. Danielson then pivoted to the end of his story. He flew back to Whidbey. Two weeks later, he was on a joint training exercise at Cold Lake Air Force Base in Alberta, with a German squadron that was still flying his Dad's plane, the F-4. Like me, he got a ride and tried to imagine his dad in the same cockpit.

A few weeks later, Steamer deployed with his squadron to Iraq during the busy days of Operation Enduring Freedom. While overseas, he received a message that the sliver of shoulder bone found years earlier in Laos belonged to his father. He had to make a decision for his whole family: accept the fragment of his dad or hold out hope for more significant remains. Brian thought of his aging grandmother and his still grieving mother back in Kenyon. After returning from Iraq, he flew to Hawaii, signed for his father's bones, and brought him home.

The funeral procession on May 8, 2007, made a slow trek toward Kenyon's First Evangelical Lutheran Church, the place where Mary and Benjamin Danielson had been married forty-four years before. The black hearse passed through Kenyon's downtown of two-story storefronts and diners. It didn't look all that different from when Benjamin Danielson last saw it in 1968.

Outside the church, a band played taps as a flag-draped coffin was removed from a hearse. A flag was folded and presented to Mary Gates-Danielson. Another flag was given to Evelyn Danielson, Benjamin Danielson's ninety-year-old mother. A stoic Norwegian, Evelyn rarely spoke of her son. But that day she held an American flag in her wheelchair and wept. Her son had finally come home.

Brian Danielson stood in his dress whites a few feet away, his sword held at attention. He saluted his father as he was carried into the church. Eleven hundred people in a town of fifteen hundred attended Benjamin Danielson's funeral.

Brian Danielson clicked off the overhead. He asked if there were any questions. The cranky old man shouted one.

"What do you think of Jane Fonda?"

Danielson winced.

"Well, I'm not going to be sending her a Christmas card, that's for sure. Eventually, she will have to answer to someone higher than me."

Everyone lined up to shake Steamer's hand. He posed for some pictures. I gazed out the window toward the Navy Chapel and heard some Prowlers rumbling above, unseen in the cloud cover. We then sat down at a table to talk. After a minute or so, Steamer jumped up.

"You know, I'll be a lot more comfortable after I change."

He slipped into the bathroom and returned a minute later in his flight suit—his second skin. Only then did the lines on his face ease.

We talked warily if sympathetically at first, two men trying to feel their way around each other's pain. We talked about Prowlers and his career. He mentioned that he had gotten out of the Navy in 2002 for two years. I assumed it was because of money issues or he was sick of being away from his wife and kids, but it wasn't that at all.

"I was at a weapons school in Nevada and I decided to see my dad's Vietnam roommate," said Danielson. "Hearing all the stories made me feel like being a navigator wasn't enough. I had to be a pilot like my dad."

Danielson left the Navy against the advice of his mentors and began applying for pilot billets with air national guard programs in three states. But then 9/11 happened right as he was being processed out. Guard pilots felt the call to serve and few retired. There were never any open slots for Danielson.

"It was a gamble and it blew up in my face," said Danielson. He exhaled and took in a deep breath. "I got really low. I never felt like I was owed anything because of what happened to my dad, but I thought, Christ, can't something good come from it?"

Steamer rejoined the Navy in 2004, but the career interruption means he won't ever command his own squadron. He spoke of missed opportunities to measure up to his father.

"I did my first cruise in 1996 after the first Gulf War and then missed things in 2002 when I got out. A friend once said I couldn't get in a fight if I hit somebody in the face with a baseball bat."

But the more we talked, the more it became clear Danielson had been in combat, first flying missions enforcing no-fly zones in the late 1990s, during Operation Enduring Freedom, and then on the ground in Iraq in 2008, coordinating Prowler use in-country. He just shrugged as he dolefully ticked off his duty stations.

"You hear stories about Vietnam and combat and it makes me not even want to wear my air medal. It's like, 'big whoop.'"

I tried to tell him he'd done more than enough, but I knew that whatever I said would not salve a man trying to please a ghost. We talked about our differences—me knowing my father, him having no memories. His dad's favorite uncle helped out, but Steamer refused to bring him to father-son gatherings.

"I was always, 'Look, I don't have a father—there's no sense pretending here.' Everyone knew my father and said I was just like him, but I never felt I matched up. He was a star. I barely passed algebra."

He told me about driving a tractor on his uncle's farm when he was twelve or thirteen. He busted a chain hot-dogging the tractor over a pile of mud. His uncle was pissed, but his aunt just laughed.

"She said, 'Times like this you remind me so much of your father. He'd do dumb things like that all the time.'" Steamer broke into a big smile. "That's the story I told at the funeral because that's real and specific. The rest isn't."

But just as quickly, his face went somber. "I did the whole funeral for other people's closure. That's a word my mother always used, closure, closure, closure. It doesn't change that I still don't have a father and I never will."

Feeling he'd just let his guard down too much, Danielson

corrected himself. "Well, I came to grips with it a long time ago."

I didn't have the heart to tell him he clearly hasn't, never will, and that's okay. Instead, I mumbled something, urging him not to be so hard on himself. It was advice I easily give but never take.

STEAMER INVITED ME OVER FOR DINNER that night. He and his wife, Pam, lived about a mile from where I grew up in Oak Harbor. Their neighborhood was more reminiscent of my childhood than the faux Craftsman houses and brew pubs of Anacortes. Navy friends lived down and up the street and they all watched each other's kids and drank wine when the spouses were deployed.

When I arrived, Steamer was making quesadillas for his daughter with his left hand while throwing crab cakes in the oven for the grown-ups with his right. His oldest son, Benjamin, barreled into the room. "Ben, you've got to do your homework," implored his father. Ben nodded like teenagers do, but his father wasn't convinced of his intentions.

"I don't know what I was expecting, but, boy, being a father with a son isn't what I thought," said Danielson. "It's not like a mother and a daughter. There's so much I want to teach him, but he's intent on learning everything the hard way. Now I just pray that he passes algebra."

It wasn't clear whether he was referencing his own algebra issues or not. I didn't get a chance to ask because Pam, a tall, angular Mississippian, ambled into the kitchen. She was charismatic and bubbly, the perfect companion to her husband's solemnity.

"I'm so glad you could come over. Brian doesn't get enough male bonding. He's usually just here with me and the other wives. This is the real Navy, not all the stuck-up folk in Anacortes."

We made small talk about the Navy and Oak Harbor's sprawl since my childhood. Pam poured me another glass of wine and said a friend was coming over. "I wanted her to meet the famous writer," she teased. "Her husband's on the *Lincoln*. That's the one problem with all our friends making command: we're not on the same schedule anymore."

Steamer sighed and Pam quickly changed the subject. A few minutes later, the crab cakes were ready and we sat down for dinner. Sure enough, her friend Tiffany came over trailing a kid or two. Then another wife magically appeared. There were tales of sick babies, sick parents, and a Huck Finn book report that was due in a matter of hours. One husband was back in two weeks; another husband was shipping out over the summer. They all seemed to be hanging on by their fingernails but somehow thriving. The happy chaos made me long for my childhood.

When it was time to go, Steamer said he had something for me. He went upstairs and gave me a copy of *A Pilot's Life*, the diary of a Vietnam pilot kept from the day he shipped out on the USS *Oriskany* until the day he was shot down and killed over South Vietnam. I told him it was a rare book; there was no way I could take it. He insisted.

"Give it back when you can."

We walked out into the spring night and talked about mothers and widows.

"My mother still says, 'You're just like your father,'" said

Danielson. "But how does she know? He's been gone for forty years."

We shook hands, both of us holding it for an extra beat. He wanted to tell me one more thing,

"Look, I don't want you to have the wrong impression. Some of this has been tough, but I have a great, great life."

I wanted to believe him. A month or two later, I got an email from Steamer. He was down at Pensacola Naval Air Station on a cross-country flight, training a young pilot. He wrote: "Click on the attachment. I think you'll appreciate it. This is hanging behind the bar at the officers' club here."

I clicked and squinted at the cell phone photo. It was a cruise plaque. I looked closer. It read "VAQ-135 May 1979–April 1980." In a small box at the bottom I could just barely make out the writing: "In Memoriam of Prowler 626-158541." There were four names. At the top was Commander Peter T. Rodrick.

Chapter Thirty-Two

Shortly after Steamer's speech, I learned that Dad was a shitty pilot.

It took all of twenty minutes. My best friend, Mark, and I were banging out the fourteenth draft of the screenplay *Long in the Tooth*, a puckish vampire comedy set in a Philly nursing home. We thought it was hilarious, a viewpoint shared by exactly zero people in Hollywood. We were tweaking a cheery line for Reggie the old boxer: "I used to wear silk trunks, now I wear Depends. I want this to end"—when my phone rang.

It was Tim Radel, an officer who'd served with Dad on his department head tour at VAQ-130. I'd tracked him to Florida through an acquaintance and sent him three emails. He ignored the first two but finally left me a message.

"Here's my number. But I think it's best if I don't say anything."

The reporter in me pricked up his ears. The guy who says it's best if he doesn't say anything is always the guy you want to talk to. I left him a voice mail saying I was a big boy and prepared to hear whatever he had to say. Radel called me the next day. We bullshitted for a few minutes before he asked me a question.

"Do you really want to hear this?"

"I do."

Radel proceeded to rip Dad a new one. In 1976, Dad's

squadron, VAQ-130, was flying back to Whidbey from work-ups on the East Coast. Radel was assigned the backseat behind Dad. The flight was uneventful until the Prowler hit the Cascade Mountains east of Whidbey. The sky grew thick with clouds, usually a sign for the pilot to take his jet high above the mountains. But Dad didn't do that. Instead, Radel looked out the window and saw peaks appearing between the clouds on both sides of the plane. Dad was cloud-surfing in the mountains, a sphincter-puckering move. Radel was scared shitless.

"We landed and I asked the guy up front what the hell that was all about, and he just said, 'Ah, that's just the way Pete flies.'"

Radel told me that wasn't a one-time deal. He was in the front seat with Dad on another flight, a low-level exercise. The Prowler had to hit certain air coordinates, and Dad had the map on his left knee. He kept glancing down at it as the earth passed a few hundred feet below. Radel offered to help.

"Pete, let me take a look."

"No, damn it, I've got it."

Radel did his best not to fly with Dad after that.

"He was flat-hatting it, and he wouldn't let me help him. I didn't want any part of that."

Radel survived a cancer scare and two years later was an instructor in VAQ-129, the Prowler training squadron. Dad had screened for command and was returning for a refresher course in the Prowler after six months at Armed Forces Staff College. Radel told the scheduler that he didn't want to be in the same cockpit with my father.

"Rodrick scares the shit out of me."

This being the Navy, the scheduler quickly put Radel on the schedule with Dad. It was a routine training mission where the instructor has the pilot turn off his navigational system and then the pilot must find his way home with just compass, radar, and some dead reckoning. Dad took off and maneuvered the plane over the Pacific. Radel started the test. Dad got his bearings and started heading for Vancouver. Unfortunately, that would be Vancouver, Washington, 250 miles south of Whidbey. He thought he was flying north when he was heading south. Radel lost it.

"Jesus, Pete, look at the radar. Do you have any idea where you're going?"

"Shut up, give me a minute."

Dad finally got his bearings after a series of wrong turns and flew the Prowler back to Whidbey. Radel gave Dad a "down," meaning he'd have to repeat the flight. Dad smirked at him.

"You're kidding me, right?"

Radel wasn't. But Dad pulled rank and told the squadron CO that Radel had it in for him. The CO overrode the down. Radel was furious.

"This guy is going to kill someone."

Radel finally took a breath.

"When I heard about the accident, I wasn't surprised it was your dad's plane. I thought it was just a matter of time."

We talked for a few more minutes. In some ways, it was thrilling to talk with someone who didn't idolize Dad. The more I listened, the less Radel maintained any pretense that he liked Dad on any level.

"He'd sit in the ready room reading old papers until 3:00

a.m. We'd tell him, 'Pete, go to sleep,' but he'd just keep reading. He was a hard-ass. I heard that he used to correct your mom's letters with a red pen. Is that true?"

I told him I didn't know. I filed away the assholic anecdote about editing Mom's letters—no one else I talked to copped to seeing him do it—and centered in on Dad reading the newspaper until 3:00 a.m. Somehow, that seemed as important as Radel telling me Dad sucked in the cockpit. It opened a door for me. I'd wait up for my *Seattle Times* to be dropped off at 3:00 a.m. on Sunday. I'd read every page until 4:30 a.m. and then deliver my papers before dawn, not sleeping until I was done. Did I somehow pick that up from him?

Radel was a musician, and we found some common ground talking about bands we liked. We wrapped things up and Radel had a last question.

"So are you glad I called you back?"

I told him I was. It wasn't even a lie. I hung up the phone and Mark tried to read my face.

"Are you okay?"

I made a bad joke.

"Hey, it's not every day that someone tells you that your dad sucked at his job and his death was only a matter of time. Good times."

We laughed and went back to writing jokes for Reggie.

NOT EVERYONE BOUGHT TIM RADEL'S VERSION. Mom and a couple of Dad's buddies said he was a subpar junior officer and Dad let him know it. They said he was just settling an old score.

Maybe so, but I found other evidence of Dad's flying acumen, or lack thereof, jammed at the bottom of his cruise box. It was a U.S. Navy computer printout of Dad's official pilot history report, a dry accounting of mishaps that occurred while he was a pilot. The first one begins: 30 APRIL 68: LAND SHORT OF RWY.

It's exactly as it sounds. Dad, just learning jets, brought his T-2 in too fast and landed in the Meridian, Mississippi, clay 208 feet short of the runway. The jet bounced and stumbled its way onto the runway. Dad and his instructor got out without a problem. Still, it reflected poorly on him.

The next page read 06 FEB 69 and was an accounting of his crash.

> CLB MADE TO 18000 FT, 2 MORE ACCEL CKS MADE. ON 2ND CHK ENG MADE EXPLODING NOISE, PLT ATTEMPTED TO SET UP GLIDE FOR FLD, HOWEVER HE EJT AT APPROX 900 FT, WHEN REACHING FIELD WAS IMPROBABLE.

The rest of the report made it clear it wasn't his fault.

> IN CONTROL PILOT FACTOR NOT ASSIGNED TO THIS INDIVIDUAL.

I anxiously flipped through the next six or seven mishaps. They were all minor mechanical issues, no screwups on Dad's behalf. But I still wondered. Another friend of Dad's told me that Dad liked to fly low and fast.

"Everyone knew that. He liked to bend the airplane around, but a lot of guys did back then."

But didn't he know the danger? Back in flight school, instructors told aviators to take a look around the room: "In ten years, one in four of you will be dead." It wasn't bullshit. In the 1960s and 1970s, the fatality rate for a Navy pilot hovered around 20 percent for a twenty-year career. In 1978, the year before Dad's crash, 128 naval aviators were killed in 102 crashes. That was in peacetime.

Dad was a smart man; he must have known the risk. If he didn't, Mom was sure to remind him. When he started flight school, she wrote of her fear.

> *I know you must think it is silly me worrying about planes going down. I want you to fly because that's what you want and will be happy doing. I'll just have to have faith that someone greater will watch over you and bring you back to me safe and sound.*
>
> *I love you forever, Barb.*

By chance, Dad's sister, Dorothy, and her husband, Sonny, visited us at NAS Meridian two days after his 1969 crash. We stayed home with Mom while Dad gave them a tour of the base. Dad came around a corner where workers were loading a pile of burnt, twisted metal onto a flatbed truck. Dad drove around the truck and then provided a little background.

"That was my jet."

He didn't slow down. He didn't say anything else. He just kept driving.

Chapter Thirty-Three

TUPPER WAS BACK AT SEA FIFTY days after his change of command. It wasn't supposed to go down like that, but the guy he was replacing on the *Lincoln* was busted for alcohol in his stateroom and bounced off the boat three months early. Tupper was told he'd have to report to the *Lincoln* before Christmas, obliterating the promise the Navy gave him that he could spend the holidays with his family.

One morning, Tupper ran into the guy he was replacing while filling out paperwork at Naval Station Everett. The man didn't seem to care that he had lost his job, and why should he? He was back home and still on track to retire with the same pay and benefits as Tupper, his sober replacement. Only Tupper's family would suffer for his fuckup.

Tupper spent his last month at home traversing the country for air boss training. He'd join the *Lincoln* as the mini boss, the number two man controlling air traffic on and off the carrier, and there was a lot to learn in a compressed time. On his flights back and forth he'd dwell on what he'd miss in the girls' lives, and it filled him with darkness. He'd become familiar with the rising tide of depression—by now it was an old adversary—and tried to push it out of his head. He repeated an old Sufi saying he'd once read: "Too much internal reflection when not bounded by limits and direction leads to despair." He was there.

He dreaded leaving, but he and Beth needed a break. The

pre-Christmas departure had frayed her last threads of patience. All they seemed to do was fight. It was different from their usual pulling apart before parting. Something seemed permanently broken.

This time, the family rose at 6:00 a.m. and drove him to Sea-Tac for the twenty-hour flight to Bahrain where he'd catch a COD out to the *Lincoln*. He couldn't hold back the tears. His girls told him it was going to be okay, but he wasn't sure if he believed them. He changed planes in Amsterdam, rolling his eyes at the Euro men in their pointed leather shoes and skinny jeans. He wondered why it was Americans who had to keep the peace while these guys got to sashay around with their man purses. But then he laughed to himself. Clearly, the Euros were the smart ones and he was the dumb ass.

There was six hours in Bahrain and then a three-hour COD flight out to the boat. That first night, he wandered into the wardroom, jet-lagged and disoriented. He filled his plate and stabbed at wilted lettuce and fruit cocktail. It felt like home. The thought depressed him beyond words.

Every morning he climbed six flights of stairs from his stateroom to the *Lincoln*'s tower where he stood for twelve hours at a time helping Commander Brad "Flats" Jensen supervise the launching and recovery of airplanes. He wrote me an email one day describing his life: "I am now literally in a tower of isolation filled with loneliness."

Tupper was grateful that the job was challenging and exhausting because he knew he was slipping into depression. He could joke about it to himself—he knew he was listening to Cat Stevens' "Sad Lisa" far too many times on his iPod. All he could tell himself was it was not forever. But it seemed that way at times. The ship pulled into Dubai for Christmas, and between the calls for prayer and the wind and the heat, it didn't seem like Christmas at all. He had built his life around making the Navy think he was a great man who could lead men and fly jets into harm's way. The Navy had responded by telling him they thought he was a slightly above average man perfect for middle management on a ship at sea.

He spent Christmas Eve in a hotel bar and marveled that so many people of so many races and backgrounds could be so vacuous, burning away the hours of their lives. And he knew he was part of that world. He went to the movies on Christmas and had a club sandwich from room service for dinner. He counted the hours until it was 7:00 a.m. back in Anacortes. He Skyped the girls, but they were still too sleepy to really talk. He wanted to tell them he needed them, but he didn't want to ruin their day. They talked awkwardly for a few minutes and then he was alone again.

UP IN THE TOWER, HE THRIVED on the chaos. One moment, jets were launching and recovering with no problems and then a Hornet was in distress and Tupper was supervising the flight deck for a possible emergency landing. Or some knucklehead kid would dart in front of a catapult about to launch a jet and Tupper would scream, "Suspend!"

Almost every day there was some VIP or admiral visiting the *Lincoln* who wanted to watch flight ops from the tower. Tupper smiled at the sultan of Brunei's entourage while privately wondering why the whole crew was doing somersaults for a dictator no better than the guys in Tunisia and Egypt.

He wondered how he and the rest of the Navy had become yes men to autocrats who would desert America at the first sign of trouble.

Finally, in February, the *Lincoln* began to make its way home. Beth was supposed to meet him in Singapore, but she canceled at the last minute, citing the girls' schedule. It was just as well; Tupper caught a virus and spent three days in a hotel, hallucinating and delirious, his weight dropping from 180 to 165. As he recovered, he surfed the Internet and came across a marital survey where couples ranked their spouses in a number of areas, with 1 being the lowest and 10 being perfect. He sent it to Beth, saying she didn't need to respond but maybe it was something they could talk about when he got home. The next morning, he woke up to an email from Beth entitled "You Asked for It." He didn't know if he was more hurt that she gave him a 2 for family contributions or a 9 on the physical attraction scale. He wondered who her 10 was.

A COUPLE OF WEEKS LATER, I flew to the *Lincoln* out of Hawaii. I was there to watch Tupper orchestrate flight operations for the Tiger Cruise kids who were boarding at Pearl Harbor and riding the carrier back to San Diego with their dads. But in classic Navy fashion, the *Lincoln* ordered Tupper to attend all-day seminars on the Pentagon's recently updated don't ask, don't tell policy, and had to pass his duty on to a subordinate. Tupper tried to explain that I'd flown 6,000 miles to watch him work and maybe, just maybe, he could do the DADT seminar on a different day. The boss said no.

So we were both in a foul mood as the *Lincoln* made its way into Pearl Harbor a couple of days later. I watched the boat being prepared for Tigers and I obsessed about the Tiger Cruise I never spent with Dad. The *Lincoln*'s deck was lined the next morning with sailors in dress whites as the carrier silently slipped into the harbor, gliding past the USS *Arizona* Memorial with the *Lincoln*'s sailors saluting the watery grave of 1,500 men. It moved me more than I could say, but it also made me angry. It was just one more thing I almost shared with my father.

We disembarked a few hours later and took a cab to a Waikiki hotel, checking into a room on the second floor. We went out for steak sandwiches, and Tupper hungrily downed his first decent meal in a month. We tried to make each other laugh, topping each other's dark thoughts. That night, we ate more red meat at the hotel restaurant before retiring to the bar. Tupper got the first round.

"Well, my career sucks and my family's going on without me. Might as well get drunk."

I completely agreed. But just as the night threatened to become irrevocably maudlin, Jitters, a tall, lanky *Lincoln* operations officer, walked into the bar with a beautiful blonde on his arm. He shook Tupper's hand and then pronounced in a loud voice that he and his girl had decided to get married the next day. They had been a couple for two years, but Jitters had been at sea for over half of their time together. I bought a bottle of champagne and toasted to hope triumphing over experience.

Jitters told us that he was getting out of the Navy and moving to Florida so he could be with his wife. We raised our glasses to his sacrifice, a sacrifice that neither Tupper, my father, nor I had made in our marriages. Past midnight, we stumbled back to our room. I flipped on the television and there was some newsflash about a tsunami or something, but we didn't really pay much attention.

Someone pounding on our door awakened us about ninety minutes later.

"Anyone in there? You must evacuate to a higher floor."

Tupper said he wasn't moving.

"This is my first night in a real bed in a month. I'm not leaving."

I agreed and we fell back asleep. Wind and waves lashed the beach about a hundred feet away. An hour later, there was more pounding, and, finally, the door was forced open. A large Hawaiian man shone a flashlight in our eyes.

"There's a tsunami warning. I could have you arrested for not complying with the evacuation."

One or both of us mumbled "Go ahead." The Hawaiian ignored us and asked a question.

"Is there anyone else in here?"

I swore and muttered louder than I meant.

"Yeah, there are six little people in the bathroom."

The Hawaiian opened the door and shone a flashlight.

"There's no one in there."

We couldn't stop laughing. The Hawaiian was not amused.

"You think this is the time for sarcasm?"

Tupper beat me to the punch.

"Yes, considering everything we've been through, this is the perfect time for sarcasm."

The Hawaiian stared at us, contemplating calling the police. But his walkie-talkie crackled something about winds picking up and he just waved us out of the room.

We took the back stairs up three flights and entered a hallway filled with sunburned yuppie refugees and their spawn. Tupper utilized his decades of sleeping on a carrier experience and propped himself up with his backpack. He pulled his USS *Lincoln* cap down over his eyes.

"If it wasn't for the Navy screwing up our lives we never would have survived a tsunami together."

He giggled and fell asleep. I was wide awake, staring at tiles on the hotel ceiling trying to not let my mind go to a dark place, a place where a boy meets his father returning from the sea and goes for a swim on the very same beach with his daddy.

◇◇◇

Chapter Thirty-Four

NOT LONG AFTER MY TRIP TO Michigan, my uncle Danny invited me to his Virginia Beach home for a reunion of the remaining sons and daughters of Dorothy and Tom Rodrick. (Dad's older sister Lyn died in a car accident fifteen years after Dad's crash.) I wasn't particularly close to Dad's sisters and brothers; geography and our joint loss kept us at a distance. I'd blown off reunions in the past, but my recent trips into Dad's life made me curious. I drove down from New York and met Mom there.

Danny was the middle of the three Rodrick boys, the quiet one. He had morphed into a Fox News enthusiast who talked about the right to bear arms as if he had been raised shooting bison in Wyoming and not on the streets of Brockton. But he had a good heart, never pushing his beliefs on the rest of us. His wife, Toom, cooked all weekend long and said very little, her sweetness hidden behind Thai shyness. Dad's sisters, Dorothy and Marie, were there too, with their husbands, Mark and Sonny, but I latched on to my uncle Paul, my dad's youngest brother.

Paul was only thirteen years older than me and I used to watch with awe as he snuck in and out of the Herrod Avenue house, his curly hair piled high in a white man's 'fro. He spent much of his twenties hitchhiking across the country, showing up on our doorstep every once in a while, his T-shirt and jeans covered in dust. He moved to Whidbey with his wife shortly after we did, doing odd jobs and some painting. His house was full of comic books and science fiction paperbacks. It was Paul, not my parents, who took Terry and me to see *Star Wars* for the first time.

Mom always eyed him suspiciously, worried that his long hair and weird clothes would reflect badly on Dad. I remember all of us going out for dinner at the officers' club one night and Mom suggesting to Dad that Paul wasn't dressed appropriately. Dad exploded.

"I don't give a damn. He's my brother."

Paul had always been a lost soul, drifting from job to job, surviving minor scrapes with the law. When I was a teenager, he sent me a copy of the lyrics to the Police's "Synchronicity," suggesting we were the same man, just a generation apart. ("If we share this nightmare / Then we can dream / Spiritus mundi.") He now lived in Hawaii in a house without electricity near his two boys whose mother disappeared on them when they were young. From time to time, I thought of how easy it would have been to follow Paul's wayward path after Dad died, just drifting along.

We were at the liquor store when he said how much he still missed Dad. He used to listen to Buddy Holly on the radio and watch my dad do his homework until he fell asleep. But it wasn't all good memories. Paul told me that the Rodrick kids had a slightly sadistic streak. They liked to pile on top of the youngest, Paul or Marie, and tickle them until they screamed. Paul hated it.

"They'd do it until I peed my pants. But your father would come in and start pulling off everybody. He was my protector. But then he left for the academy and I was just lost."

We brought the booze back to Danny's, and those who still drank started pounding beers and downing burgers. We talked about the old house on Herrod Avenue; some of their memories broke my heart. The inkling I had that my grandfather had been a difficult man was largely confirmed. Dinners were eaten in silence. All the kids knew they'd catch hell if they disturbed their dad in his den. So they went over to other friends' houses to play, trying to be ghosts in their own home. Dessert was served and Uncle Danny started telling a story by prefacing it with "This was right after Pete got arrested."

"Whaat?"

Danny looked at me over his glasses.

"You don't know the story?"

I looked at Mom. She just shrugged.

Danny explained. Like Tupper, Dad had a weakness for fast cars behind his perfect son persona. He spent his weekends tuning up jalopies that his friends raced in demolition derbies. Back then, everyone left their keys in their cars. Dad wasn't above "borrowing" one for a few hours and returning it to its original resting place.

Dad snuck out of the house one night shortly after receiving his academy appointment and slowly backed his mother's Chevy out of the driveway. He pushed the car half a block down the street before starting it. A few hours later, Dad's parents were awakened by a call from the police. Dad had wrapped the family car around a pole and there was a case of beer in the backseat. He was booked for drunk driving. His father was livid.

"Let him rot. I'm not bailing him out."

Luckily, his mother played the long game. She knew all of Dad's plans could come crashing down with a conviction. She scraped together the bail, rushed down to the station, and dragged him home. She then called her father, a onetime Massachusetts state representative. He made a few calls. Dad went to court the next day in a jacket and tie. The charges were dropped and Dad headed off to the academy a few months later. The Navy never knew.

I laughed along, but I wondered to myself what else I didn't know. Is this what happens when a man dies? Are all the things about a man that do not burnish the myth swept away? Or was the information always there, waiting for me? Maybe all I needed to do was ask.

I STARTED DIGGING WHEN I GOT HOME. Among the papers in Dad's belongings I found a letter written on Naval Academy stationery dated April 22, 1963, sent by my father to his mother. (How it ended back with him I don't know.) The letter talked about minor matters and the upcoming June Week at the academy. But at the bottom of the page there was a line that read, "You will probably be getting a letter from the Commandant's office about my conduct. It's sort of a long story. It's not a big deal but I will have to do some marching."

I asked Mom what that was about.

"Oh, that was a shoeshine business he'd started with his roommate, Art."

That rang a bell. Mom had put condolence notes in Dad's box at her house, and I'd come across a letter from Art Holz, one of his Annapolis roommates. I dug it out after the reunion. The letter was a Byronic ode to Dad:

Dear Barbara and children,

I knew, just the instant before you told me this morning that Pete was gone. . . . My heart sank, a part of me gone and I'm now realizing that empty space can't be filled again. . . .

Pete knew more than I did then about some things. I don't know how. When he set a goal, he was disciplined and determined. I remember his unorthodox study habits, rising at 2:00 a.m. His determination is still a model for me, an ideal to strive for. But more, he taught me about friendship and love, just by being my friend and loving me a love I could not comprehend but only wonder at and return as best I could. He never asked, only gave, and even sacrificed for me.

He took the rap for me with a stiff upper lip when he got caught selling Shoe-Glo at the Naval Academy. All the evidence was in his room and he protected me from the demerits that might have sunk me. I felt guilty and he grumbled about it, but he laughed too, and told me not to worry. I wanted to write to him just last week; an Amway salesman tried to sell me some Shoe-Glo and he would have laughed again about that. . . .

Some lessons Pete gave me that never dawned on me until years later. We would talk for hours about work and play, life and God, and the things in store for us. Looking back more in what Pete did than what he said; that his faith in God was something he carried into every part of his life. He didn't keep it in a box as I was inclined to do, or judge his daily actions by any lesser standard. He lived what he believed and what he believed was love. I remember that he loved and was loved.

There were times when I felt spiritually as close to Pete as two men can be, two boys who became men together. I feel close to him now, realizing how much I owe for his gifts to me. All that I owed to Pete, I owe you now and I hope that in some way you will let me make some payment on that debt.

Art

There was so much in his words that I fantasized Art Holz might be Dad's Rosebud, someone who could explain it all to me. Art was practicing law in San Diego when he wrote the letter and Mom said she never heard from him again. I made a couple of calls. An academy classmate told me that Holz had died of a heart attack in Mexico a decade ago. Another window slammed shut.

There was a third roommate, but I was told he was a long shot. John Frazier was one of the lost boys of the class of 1964. He never returned for reunions and kept in touch with almost no one. But one of Dad's classmates had an old email address. I gave it a shot. Frazier emailed back from Kauai. He confirmed the shoe polish episode and had some other stories.

Dad and John had been academic stars, and their room was filled with grinders looking for an edge, including, according to Frazier, Roger Staubach, a member of the class of 1965. They explained calculus problems until lights out.

After graduating, Dad headed off to flight school, and Frazier went to submarine school in New London, Connecticut. By 1966, Dad wasn't too far away, flying the P-2 Neptune, a bulky prop sub chaser out of Quonset Point, Rhode Island, where I was born. On February 27, Dad checked out a Neptune and took Frazier down to Florida for the Daytona 500. They landed at Sanford Air Force Base, about thirty miles from the raceway, and parked the plane on a grass airfield. They hitched a ride to the track and watched Richard Petty take the lead late in the race. A heavy rain began to fall. The race was ended two laps short of completion with Petty declared the winner.

By the time Dad and Frazier made it back to Sanford it was almost dark and there was a big problem: the Neptune had sunk a foot into the Florida mud.

They were screwed. If they didn't get back to Rhode Island in twelve hours, they'd both be AWOL. Dad thought quickly. He called the local fire department and paid them fifty bucks to pull the plane out of the mud. It took a half hour, but they got the plane onto the runway.

Dad finally took off, but the weather was still shitty, so they had to head south and then west before they could loop back north. It took them nearly ten hours to make it home.

Or at least that's how Frazier told me the story via email. By chance, I found myself vacationing on Kauai a few months later, and we met for lunch at Dukes, a beachside bar. Frazier was a rail-thin sixty-eight-year-old man who still surfed, built low-income housing, and made occasional trips to Brazil to see faith healers. He talked about Dad and his Navy days with an incredulous chuckle, hardly believing that was him in the stories that he told. The duality of my father, the churchgoer and the adrenaline junkie, fascinated John.

After their second year at the academy, they'd driven cross-country so they could visit the Seattle World's Fair and then head down to Los Angeles to see a girl that Frazier was sweet on. They made the drive in two and a half days, pulling over to sleep under their car when they were exhausted. They had a nerdy contest to see who could get the best gas mileage, and Frazier could still see Dad's calculations in his memory.

"He beat me. His mind was so precise he figured exactly fifty-seven miles per hour would give him the best mileage and he wouldn't go faster."

The conversation swung back to the Daytona flight and Frazier gave a little shiver at the memory. He told me that when they approached Quonset Point on the return trip, visibility was so bad that the tower suggested they divert to a different airfield. But Dad didn't want to be late for duty. Frazier looked out the window and saw nothing but thick, angry clouds.

"Pete, maybe we should land somewhere else."

"No, we're fine."

"You sure?"

"I've got this."

A few seconds later, there was a deafening noise. It took Frazier a second to place it: the Neptune had hit the runway hard and fast.

"I thought for sure the plane was breaking in half. But it didn't."

Frazier told the story with a smile on his face, clearly hoping to amuse me with a tale of madcap Dad and how he wasn't the straight arrow everyone made him out to be. All that was true, but that wasn't what popped into my head. Instead, I heard Tim Radel saying, "Your dad was an accident waiting to happen."

I HEADED TO ANNAPOLIS TO SEE what else I could find. I made arrangements to have lunch with the journalist Robert Timberg, a fellow class of 1964 graduate. Timberg had chosen the Marine Corps as his vocation. In 1967, his face and body were badly burned by a land mine while he was leading troops in Vietnam. He spent two years in the hospital enduring dozens of skin grafts, his face barely recognizable to the one I saw in Dad's 1964 *Lucky Bag*, the Naval Academy yearbook.

Timberg became a journalist and through pure chance found himself at the *Annapolis Capital* and then the nearby *Baltimore Sun*. His Annapolis years were never far away, and he eventually spent more than five years writing *The Nightingale's Song*, a brilliant account of the academy's five most famous, or notorious, 1950s and 1960s graduates—John McCain, Oliver North, James Webb, Bud McFarlane, and John Poindexter—following their lives from Annapolis to Vietnam and then on to Washington. The book helped me understand my father's time, and it was a privilege to get a tour of Bancroft Hall by a man who'd sacrificed so much. But there was one omission in Timberg's book that I didn't quite understand. He never described the horrors he personally survived.

We had lunch before our walk, and I mentioned that my mother had not gone through my father's cruise box since the accident. I told him I couldn't understand why she wouldn't want to look in there again. Timberg put his fork down and sighed.

"I've got a box of my own from my Vietnam tour. It's filled with pictures and letters. I've never looked in there. I'm not sure I could handle knowing what I was like before that."

I think I understood what he meant. Timberg and I walked around Bancroft Hall, putting our fingers on a statue listing all the Annapolis grads who died in Vietnam. He told me stories about some of them.

Then he dropped me back downtown and there was Laddie Coburn waiting for me, the man who told me that Dad was gone. Thirty years on, Laddie didn't look all that different from the day at the Roller Barn when he told me that Dad had been in an accident. There was a little bit of paunch on his tall frame and his mustache had gone steel gray, but otherwise he looked the same. We caught up quickly. Laddie had divorced his first wife, Ulla, a decade ago and had lived the life of an aging playboy nerd, working in Prowler-related defense fields outside of D.C. He told me those days were behind him, and he was moving out to Colorado and getting married again. I congratulated him and we walked across town to a seaside restaurant for dinner.

We made small talk, and Laddie casually mentioned that he'd become interested in astrology after the breakup of his first marriage. I bit my lip to stop myself from breaking into howls of laughter. This was like Colonel Sanders confessing he had become a vegan. But Laddie was way into the occult.

"Pete was a Capricorn and I'm an Aquarius. Guess what? My ex-wife was a Capricorn and I'm an Aquarius. A lot of Capricorns are CEOs, strong people, and good leaders. But the downside of Capricorns is that they're assholes."

I did a cartoon double-take. Was Dad's best friend saying he was actually an asshole? Yes, he was.

"There's no bullshit here. Pete was a strong male Capricorn. He had his own frustrations, he couldn't get people to do what he wanted to do, and he would carry all that turmoil inside of him."

We were now at the restaurant. Sailboats carrying happy, drunken revelers slipped by our dockside table. When I started the journey this was exactly what I was looking for, but right now I was filled with "careful what you wish for." I let Laddie keep talking. He debunked some other long-held myths. I'd always been told Dad and Laddie were best friends, rooming together on early cruises. Laddie let me know that it wasn't exactly a great experience.

"A lot of women accuse me of being very uptight. Pete was much more uptight than I am. Your father was truly a workaholic. I'd want to go to bed; he would be up until two o'clock in the morning with the lights on, doing paperwork. I had a strong sense of duty, but not like your Dad."

Our food arrived. Laddie kept babbling. He told me everyone thought Dad was a hard worker but he had a tendency to get "snarly" with people under his command.

"Your dad was not the greatest communicator. A lot of times he'd just choke up and he wouldn't say anything."

It wasn't the first I was hearing of Dad's temper. Dad was once so frustrated by a junior ECMO's bad radio calls that he slammed his fist against the rearview mirror of his Prowler and shattered it. But Laddie's depictions of my dad's impatience could have been ripped out of my own life: the days I couldn't hit the goddamned baseball. The days spent with my fists clenched as I wrestled with some Cub Scout project that required unobtainable dexterity. The days I needed someone to tell me that it didn't matter . . . but that man was never there.

Laddie ordered another drink and then piled on Dad some more.

"Your dad wanted us to be best friends. But I had other friends I'd rather spend time with."

It was at this point I debated letting Laddie know how

much as a boy I'd enjoyed his porn stash that I'd found in his bedroom at the condo we shared. But I didn't say anything. Instead, I asked why they had bought property together if they weren't really good friends. Laddie said that a couple of other guys fell through.

"I knew your dad would be good for it. And he was. Every month, he was there with the mortgage check."

Well, if I'd been searching and searching for someone to puncture Dad's hallowed image in my head, I'd found the guy! Perhaps thinking he'd said too much, Laddie tried to backtrack. It wasn't exactly true, he said, that Dad always had a stick up his ass. Sometimes, when they were in port Dad would split from the guys and head out on his own. Laddie didn't know where he went. All he knew was the next day Dad was back in the confessional.

"Your father was one of these ninety-ten guys. Ninety percent of the time, he was totally straight arrow and did everything by the books, but every once in a while, he would just wander off and nobody knew where he went. The 10 percent was totally irrational and unaccounted for, and you couldn't quite figure out what happened. Only Pete knew."

I decided that was a good place to leave it. I picked up the check. Laddie and I wandered out into the Annapolis night. I thought of Mom and Dad on these same streets, young and vital and not knowing what would come next. I shook Laddie's hand and we headed our separate ways. But then I stopped and turned back. I watched my messenger of death vanish into the summer crowd. Still, I waited, making sure he was completely gone. Only then did I head for home.

Chapter Thirty-Five

ONE OF THE THINGS I FOUND buried in Dad's cruise box was a faded patch from the 1970s trips to Tailhook, the annual drunkfest-reunion of naval aviators.

All you need to know about Tailhook is that the first one was held in 1956 at a hotel in Rosarito Beach in Baja, Mexico. In other words, the decadence was so high that naval aviators thought it best to take their party to another country. Maybe it should have stayed there. Tailhook moved to Las Vegas while Dad was at the academy. He never talked about the trips, but I remember him coming back from one and going to sleep for a very long time.

Tailhook remained an underground bacchanal until 1991, when eighty-three female officers and civilians were groped in a hallway of the Las Vegas Hilton packed with intoxicated aviators. Some of the victims threatened to sue, so the Naval Investigation Service launched a tepid investigation under the less than vigilant command of Rear Admiral Duvall Williams. Williams professed to have found no evidence of less than gentlemanly behavior and quipped that "a lot of female Navy pilots are go-go dancers, topless dancers or hookers."

This didn't instill a ton of confidence in his investigation, so the Department of Defense launched its own probe. The DOD determined that groping wasn't an isolated incident and had been witnessed by senior officers who did nothing to stop it. After the second investigation, Secretary of the Navy H. Lawrence Garrett resigned and fourteen admirals lost their jobs. The careers of another two to three hundred naval aviators were either ended or permanently crippled merely for being on the floor.

Depending on where you stood, it was either a comeuppance for decades of asshole behavior or a witch hunt that killed the careers of good men who did nothing wrong except laugh along and not rat out their friends. Tupper was in flight school during Tailhook '91, but he saw that Vegas night as the end for the old Navy. He wasn't for sexual assault or criminal behavior, but he believed that all the drinking, all the jackass behavior, had an actual point: a happy few building camaraderie that could come in handy for aviators feeling their way back to a bobbing speck of light in a dark gulf.

Tailhook moved from Vegas to Reno after the scandal, and I had planned to go in 2010, during Tupper's CO tour, but I woke up the morning of my trip with a searing pain in my stomach that ended with first my appendix and then my gallbladder leaving my body. Going the next year didn't look much more promising.

Alix and I were moving out to Los Angeles, and we detoured to Whidbey for a few days. Getting to Reno seemed a logistical impossibility. But we stayed with Sherm in Anacortes and he talked up Tailhook. "It's the hundredth anniversary of naval aviation, you should go," Sherm told me.

It was easy for him to say. He would be flying down on a chartered plane the Navy provides every naval air station. There was no way I could swing it; we had to be in LA in two days to meet our movers. But then I looked up directions.

Reno would only add a few hours to our trip. I'd drop off Alix and the dog and head over to the hotel for a cameo. She sighed but agreed.

Twenty-four hours later, we arrived at Reno near dinnertime. I took a shower and headed over to the Nugget Hotel, expecting a lame evening of bad jokes and warm beer. Sure, guys like Tupper still let their freak flag fly from time to time, prancing around Japanese bases in a kimono. And yes, guys like Sherm complained about not being able to wear an electronic warfare patch on their flight jackets that resembled the anal, digital penetration of a woman. But those were retreating, final-guard actions. Most of the aviators I'd met were more Jimmy Neutron than Maverick. (Of course, every last one of them thought of himself as the last Maverick while everyone else was the Neutron sellout.) The old days weren't coming back.

Or maybe they were. I parked my car and took an escalator upstairs to the Nugget's ballroom. I was deposited in an ocean of flight suits clutching beer mugs. There were thousands of them, most in standard green, but peppered with old timers in optic orange—a brief 1970s infatuation of the Navy—and Iraqi vets in suits the color of desert sand.

I quickly spotted the jet black hair and sleepy smile of Brandon "Dozer" Sellers. Dozer had been a pilot in VFA-195, the Hornet squadron I'd followed onboard the *Kitty Hawk* back in 2002. The Georgian had steered me through Navy bureaucracy and dim *Kitty Hawk* passages. I repaid him by serving as his wingman on a long, slow night in Singapore that ended at an after-party held in the circular drive of an abandoned hotel. Dozer earned his call sign when he got drunk as a young pilot, found the keys in a bulldozer, and crashed it into a fence. He loved telling women that he worked in military construction as a civilian contractor. We drank warm beer that night and listened to an American expat woman rip on the Navy until the sun came up. It was only when we stumbled into a cab at 6:00 a.m. that Dozer flashed his Navy ID at the woman. He happily gave her the finger as we drove away.

We caught up and he told me not to expect much from Tailhook.

"A few years back, there would be two girls making out at a squadron party. I don't think that's gonna happen tonight."

The last time I'd seen Dozer was in New York two years ago for a boys' weekend. He had just been grounded for repeated dizzy spells while exercising. He ran marathons to prove he was fit, but he never got back his wings. Now he worked for Senator John McCain as his Navy liaison—a not-bad job, but it was a long way from doing barrel rolls in his Hornet over Iraq. Being back here among his kin was bittersweet. We drank beers for a while as we ogled a Boeing exhibit on the hundredth anniversary of naval aviation and maybe the hot girl in the next booth over selling $5,000 Rolex aviator watches.

Dozer then elbowed me in the ribs.

"Hey, you got to meet this guy."

He introduced me to another Hornet pilot and former squadron mate. The pilot was still active, but he wore a golf shirt and shorts. I could tell he thought the old men in flight suits were foolish. We swapped Dozer stories for a few minutes, and then the pilot shook my hand and vanished into the crowd. Dozer whispered in my ear.

"That's Gordo Cross, the guy who married OJ's widow."

The name OJ transported me back to my time on the *Kitty Hawk*. Dozer's squadron was nicknamed the Chippies and was a storied fighter squadron. Unlike the Prowlers, where the testosterone is spread between one pilot and three ECMOs, everyone in the Chippies flew one-seaters and ran his own show. They exuded swagger wherever they went, whether it was pulling shit-hot breaks on carrier approaches or doing shots in a Hong Kong dive.

With his movie star jaw and blond hair, Lieutenant Nathan "OJ" White looked the part of a fighter pilot. But he was different, beginning with his call sign, given to him because he was a Mormon and drank nothing stronger than juice when everyone else was getting wasted. I remembered a late-night poker game in a junior officer's room on the *Kitty Hawk*. OJ's religion didn't allow him to play, but he watched intently, talking strategy between hands.

He was the son of a Vietnam-era Air Force pilot, the seventh of eight children who interrupted his studies at Brigham Young to serve a two-year mission in Japan. That's where he met his wife, Akiko. From there, he went to OCS and on to flight school. OJ didn't lord his religion over anyone, but people knew it mattered to him. He spotted me wandering around the *Kitty Hawk* one afternoon and helped me find the chapel where my father prayed every day. It was a kindness I never forgot.

The air war in Iraq began less than a year after I left the *Kitty Hawk*. The Chippies were right in the middle of it. One morning, I saw on the CNN crawl news that a Hornet had been shot down over the Iraqi desert. My heart filled with dread. There were a half dozen Hornet squadrons in the zone, but my bones told me it was a Chippie guy. It was reported two days later that it was Lieutenant Nathan White.

Initially, the Prowler squadron aboard the *Kitty Hawk* was scapegoated. Hornet pilots grumbled the Prowler had only one job in the fight: jam Iraqi missile sites so they couldn't track and kill American pilots. Clearly, the Prowlers had failed, and it was their fault a young man was dead.

But then a few days later it was announced that White had been killed by friendly fire; a Patriot missile mistook him for an Iraqi aircraft. It was just the latest indignity for the Prowler community; everyone joked about their ugly planes, no one knew exactly what they did, but everyone was ready to crucify them if someone got killed. In a way, it didn't matter. Dead is dead. White left behind Akiko, two sons, and a daughter. After the end of the Iraqi air war, White was laid to rest in Arlington. Dozer invited me to come, and I agonized about it for days, but I didn't make it, choosing to honor an earlier commitment to profile a musician who was recording at Abbey Road in London. It's a decision I still regret.

Akiko remained in Japan where the Chippies were based so her boys could stay in the schools they loved and she could be around her family. By then, Dozer had moved on to another squadron based in Japan, this one commanded by Gordo Cross. One afternoon, his commander took him aside.

"He asked me if I thought it was okay for him to go out with Akiko," Dozer told me, shouting to be heard. "He wanted to get approval from someone in the Chippies. I told him, 'Those boys have been too long without a father. If you're up to it, you should do it.'"

They were married last year. I felt myself getting angry at what should have been happy news. Hearing about another pilot's son getting a second father made me profoundly jealous. I waited until Dozer was talking with another pilot and slipped away. I stumbled down to the hotel lobby. I slumped into a chair and checked my email on my phone. There was one from Tupper. It included a link to an article written by former Navy secretary John Lehman entitled "Is Naval Aviation Culture Dead?" Tupper could have written it. Lehman lamented the death of everything from happy hours in officers' clubs and raunchy call signs to the mandate that naval aviators spend four years out of the cockpit doing soul-crushing staff duty before they can screen for command. I read the story and nodded along, sharing Tupper's outrage about something having been lost, another connection to Dad vanishing in a haze of bureaucracy.

But then a young woman with a ponytail walked through the hotel lobby, pushing a toddler in a stroller. Mother and daughter were wearing matching green flight suits. It made me think of Terry and her difficult Army years. There were more women leading platoons and squadrons, and "don't ask, don't tell" was coming to an end. Yes, something had been lost, but something else had been gained.

Not everyone saw it that way. I texted Tupper that I was in Reno, and he wrote back, "Ah, Tailhook. Dead to me like so many other things. Couldn't stomach running into so many people I no longer respect."

By chance, I received another email while I sat in the lobby. It was from James McGaughey, an officer who had served under my father in the Black Ravens. I took a breath and read his attached letter.

What he said both soothed me and reignited my fear that Dad's accident had been his own fault. McGaughey wrote of Dad taking forty minutes to do a flight brief that usually took ten just so everyone was sure of his responsibility. But then he paid Dad a compliment that kicked hard in my stomach: "Your father was clearly one of the best pilots I have ever flown with. He would spend hours in the manual looking up the edges of the flight envelope of the aircraft."

And there it was again, the idea that Dad pushed his plane beyond its capability. I know McGaughey meant it as a compliment—he ended his letter with "I have no idea what happened on that day in the Indian Ocean, but I can tell you this, it had NOTHING to do with pilot error"—but I fixated on the "edges of the flight envelope" part. Who pushes the edges of the flight envelope in a deathtrap like the Prowler? He knew it was a beast to maneuver. How dare he do that to us.

I then read McGaughey's email again. He had Bill Coffey in the front seat, which I knew was flat-out wrong. Maybe what he had to say wasn't reliable. Maybe nothing anyone had to say about my father was reliable. Not the words of his wife, not the words of his fellow pilots, and not the words of his only son.

I headed back upstairs looking for a friendly face. The cocktail party had split into smaller "admin" rooms hosted by each squadron. In the Prowler room, junior officers were getting their fleet wings, signifying the completion of flight training. Their fellow aviators chanted, "go, go, go" as they chugged thirty-two-ounce glasses filled with grenadine, vodka, cranberry juice, and beer. Their eyes bulged as they choked back their own retch. The new kids were then given Velcro squadron badges for their flight suits. Their superiors attached the badges by punching their chests so hard I could hear muscles snapping. The old culture wasn't completely dead.

The tiny room was filled with mirrors on the ceiling. I looked up and could see a hundred faces in flight suits, all looking familiar and strange at the same time. I finally found Sherm. He'd been fixed up on a blind date with Beav's sister-in-law. I laughed to myself. That dude could fall off the back of a carrier and land with a date. I gave him a hug, one that he refused to relinquish for a moment. His eyes were running more red than blue.

"You're like a brother to me."

I smiled back at him. We were from different worlds but both desperate for another family, something, anything, to fill the space in our hearts. I told him I felt the same way. I turned to leave, not wanting to cramp his style, but he grabbed my arm. He pointed to another aviator with coal black eyes nursing a glass of bourbon. His call sign badge read Joe Dirt.

"Talk to Joe Dirt before you go. We were JOs together. He's a good guy, little weird, but good guy. He's writing a book. Mean a lot to me."

Before I could say no, Sherm pushed his friend toward me and vanished with his girl, swallowed up by the horde of green. I shook his friend's hand, and we headed toward a quieter part of the hotel.

THEN AIR FORCE CAPTAIN CHRISTOPHER "Joe Dirt" Lucas told me about his life, a story that made my own narrative seem like a rejected afterschool special. Nothing had come easy for him. He was raised on the Louisiana bayou and still spoke with a deep drawl. That's how he got his call sign, named after the white-trash janitor played by David Spade in a 2001 comedy. His father was drafted into the Army in 1968 and could have gotten out of it because his new wife was pregnant, but if he didn't go, someone else in his small town would have to go instead. So he went to Vietnam right before his son was born in 1969.

He returned home a year later. His legs had been blown away by a Vietcong grenade. Something else was missing too.

"He became a high school counselor, but he was so compartmentalized," said Lucas softly. "He could talk about other people's problems, but he couldn't talk to me or my mom."

I listened quietly. I let him take his time. Lucas had done everything the hard way. He enlisted in the Navy at seventeen, working his way up from sailor to Officer Candidate School. He then went back for his degree and became a naval flight officer, flying Prowlers with Sherm over Iraq. Passed over for promotion, he transferred to the Air Force, serving as an electronic warfare officer flying B-52s over Afghanistan. I asked him where he was stationed.

"A place called Diego Garcia. Just a speck of land in the middle of nowhere. Have you ever heard of it?"

"Yes."

Not content with having flown two planes into combat, Lucas then volunteered to serve as a forward air controller attached to the Army outside Kandahar, coordinating Air Force and Navy air support for ground troops. He was the ground guy that pilots like Tupper talked to from five miles above. For weeks, he pleaded with his battalion commander to let him go on night patrol with the soldiers. He told him it was just so he could understand their needs better. In reality, he wanted to know what his father knew but never shared.

The sky filled with tracer bullets his first night out. His patrol had walked into a firefight.

"It didn't last that long, maybe fifteen minutes," Lucas said with a shrug. He swirled whiskey around in his plastic glass. "But when the sun comes up and you can see the bullets lodged in the walls a few inches from where your head was, well, it makes you think."

Lucas told me that a few years back he tried to reconnect with his father when he was home on leave. His first son was about to be born, and he wanted him to know his granddad. He stopped by his dad's school and went to his office. He spoke calmly about how his dad's neglect had made him feel unwanted as a kid. His father sat impassively in his wheelchair. He offered no apology and told his son to get over himself. Lucas got up and walked out of the office; he hasn't spoken to his father since.

We sat in silence for a minute. I didn't know what to say. A cheesy video of 1980s-era Blue Angels blasted behind us on a massive television. It was all there: a distant and disfigured father, a son trying to understand him through combat. I finally spoke.

"That sounds like a hell of a book."

Joe Dirt just laughed.

"No, my book isn't about that at all. It's called *Killing Jane Fonda*."

For the next twenty minutes, he laid out the plot of the novel he'd been working on for seven years. It involved Fonda, the Weathermen, the son of a Vietnam vet, and a murder that may or not be in the protagonist's head. The story was dizzyingly intricate, and I soon lost track of the characters. Lucas talked excitedly about drafts and redrafts until he snapped his own head back.

"Oh, man, sorry to go on like that. Shit. That's the bourbon talking."

I told him it was fine, but I had a question.

"Why don't you write about your dad? That seems really interesting."

He looked at me with benign confusion.

"Why? In this story I can move things around. My dad? I can't change any of that. It happened and it's never going to change. He's never going to change. Why waste my time on things I can't change?"

I didn't know what to say. I just stared at the video of long-ago Blue Angels pilots shaking hands with a wide-eyed kid. The boy beamed back at the pilot. There was no context, just awe and joy. Then I shook Chris's hand, wished him luck, and pushed my way past shitfaced aviators playing grab-ass with their brothers. Their laughter sounded like it would never die.

Chapter Thirty-Six

I'M NOT AN ORGANIZED MAN. PLANE tickets get tossed with the takeout. If I only have to request two copies of my 1099s in a tax year I declare victory. I left Dad's academy watch in an office desk drawer until it was stolen. I swear things will be different every six months or so. Receipts are filed, piles of crap are dismantled, and then two weeks later I'm hunting for my birth certificate amid the Chipotle wrappers.

I've made an uneasy peace with the remnants of my childhood ADD. I still curse and kick the filing cabinets, but I let it go. I have to. It's a part of me that is not going away.

Merging the precious and the worthless is just my way. For almost a year, three flyers advertising 1979 Thanksgiving dinner at the Cubi Point Naval Air Station's Bachelor Officers Quarters fought for space on my desk with magazines and desiccated bento boxes. Dinner came in two options, waiter-served for $4.75 and buffet-style from 5:00 to 7:00 p.m. for $3. Kids were $2.75.

But decades-old buffet information wasn't the lure for me. Dad had used the back of the flyers to write his second-to-last letter to Mom. ("I'm out of money and can't afford to buy any stationery. Seriously—I'm at the Cubi BOQ and don't have anything else to write on.") The letter isn't one of Dad's best—he had to hand it off by 7:00 a.m. to a squadron mate heading back to Whidbey—but it's a relic of sorts. It's written on November 19, 1979, the last moment when Dad thought he was almost home. He wrote of homecoming parties and vacations and my trip out to Hawaii for the Tiger Cruise. ("I know Steve is probably getting excited and driving you crazy but 10 December will be here soon and you'll have some peace and quiet.") He even mentioned a rumor that the Black Ravens would be home for all of 1980, meaning Dad would not have to go to sea again before his change of command.

I stapled the flyers to another found document of last hope. It's an invitation from Mom to the VAQ-135 wives for an end-of-cruise party. The front page features a drawing of an old-timey pilot coming in for a landing with a headline reading "Here Come Those Black Ravens Again." The second page invites the wives over for wine and ends with a note from Mom:

Dear VAQ 135 Wives,

I would like to take this time and opportunity to thank you for your support during this cruise. Thank heavens, it's finally coming to an end. As wives we are supposed to play both roles as mother and dad, besides keep dad happy with letters. You have handled it beautifully. Happy Homecoming!

Mrs. Barbara Rodrick.

After a few months on my desk, Mom's words had soy sauce smeared across her signature and Dad's letter was faded from the summer sun coming through my office window. I knew I was ruining them, but I didn't care. I thought treating them like bills and junk mail would demystify them.

That didn't happen. Instead, I read them repeatedly and was reminded of *before.* A prior life of Mom and Dad chattering about Christmas parties and whose marriages in the squadron were on the rocks. Normal conversation, not the obscene silence of death that was waiting for all of us.

I decided to piece together Dad's last days, hoping to better understand our family's final moments as a real family. Was it masochism? Perhaps, but I thought that if I knew what Dad's life was like right before the crash I could recapture the better part of him, the better part of us.

MOM LEFT THE PHILIPPINES IN TEARS on July 9, 1979. Dad and the *Kitty Hawk* spent the next four months maneuvering up and down the Asian coast making port calls in Hong Kong, Japan, and Thailand. A crisis in North Korea appeared and vanished.

The flying was good. In October, the *Kitty Hawk* participated in Operation Cope Thunder, a series of elaborate war games with the Air Force. Dad and the Black Ravens took off and set up their jammers and then watched with glee as Air Force F-15s drifted below them, unable to pick them up on their jammed radar. He took pride in that. After a career in the backwater of A-3s, he was flying a plane that mattered.

Dad's landing grades were above average, suffering only one wave-off when he broke too close to the carrier at 450 knots and came in too fast and high. Still, according to a fellow pilot, he berated himself in the post-flight brief.

"Why do I do that? Why didn't I give myself enough time to get set up? What's wrong with me?"

But that was a minor thing. It was peacetime and he was a skipper of a squadron at sea. He was still sending paperwork back to the JOs covered in red, but he let other things slide. The Prowlers had high-frequency radios capable of reaching Japan from 500 miles away. There, calls could be bounced home to wives and Navy personnel officers with news of next assignments. Soon, other squadrons were scrambling for backseat rides in the Prowler so they could call home. Dad let it go as long as mission accomplishments were still being met. He was a hard-ass, but not an asshole.

The menu letter was dated November 19, nine days and 1,500 miles from Diego Garcia. Everyone was just running out the clock. Ordnance was loaded off and empty ammunition stores were filled with recently purchased stereo equipment, wooden plates for the wives, and black market Adidas for the kids.

But then President Carter ordered the *Kitty Hawk* to head for the Strait of Hormuz and the Persian Gulf. The *Midway* was already there, but Carter and the Joint Chiefs thought two carriers camped off the Iranian coast might persuade the ayatollah to let the hostages go, or at least educate him that there would be a lethal price to pay if they came to harm. So stereo equipment was dumped overboard and bombs were reloaded. The decision came so quickly that some pilots learned the *Kitty Hawk* was pulling out when they watched the ship leave the harbor from their hotel rooms. That's the night Dad called me from the Cubi Point BOQ bar and said he was sorry.

Dad and the Black Ravens flew their Prowlers onto the boat on November 21. They wouldn't fly again until November 28. The reason for the no-fly days was simple: the *Kitty Hawk* was trucking toward the Gulf at maximum speed, and there was no time for turning into the wind and all the other things the carrier needed to do to facilitate landing and takeoffs.

The *Kitty Hawk* then made a clandestine detour that would determine the location of Dad's last flight. Once the *Kitty Hawk* battle group—consisting of the carrier, a cruiser, two destroyers, and a supply frigate—passed through the Strait of Malacca south of Singapore they didn't head directly west toward the Strait of Hormuz, the gateway to the Gulf. Instead, the *Kitty Hawk* dipped 700 miles south toward Diego Garcia, a spit of an island in the Indian Ocean that served as a British air base. The reason was simple: the *Kitty Hawk* needed to pick up six RH-53D Sea Stallion helicopters for use in a possible rescue mission.

President Carter wanted to get the helos onboard without word funneling back to Tehran via the Soviet spy trawlers that habitually shadowed American carriers during the cold war. Naval Command ordered the *Kitty Hawk* to go "dark," cutting off radio communications and most of its radar capabilities, anything that might help the Soviets track the ships.

The *Kitty Hawk*'s CAG added an extra wrinkle: launched jets wouldn't use their radios except in absolute emergencies. More important, pilots would fly with their radar altimeters turned off. All Navy planes had two devices that read their altitude. There was the barometer altimeter, the hoary old instrument used since before World War II to judge altitude by tracking barometric pressure. But the radar altimeter was far more precise: a "ping" sent from the plane's belly would bounce off land or sea and give an accurate altitude reading. Of course, if you were an A-4 Skyhawk escorting bombers at 12,000 feet, a precise reading of your altitude wasn't all that important. But if you were flying at low levels, a faulty altimeter reading could mean the difference between death and life.

November 28 was set as the day the *Kitty Hawk* would restart air operations. (The helos from Diego Garcia would be flown aboard in the afternoon.) The only aircraft scheduled to fly low and fast that day was an EA-6B Prowler flown by my father.

THE LAST THIRTY-SIX HOURS OF DAD'S life were typical Navy, serious, idiotic, and lonely. The *Kitty Hawk* crossed the equator in the small hours of November 27. This meant there would be a Wog Day, a shellback initiation in the morning for first-time crossers. The tradition dates back to the seventeenth-century British Navy and has mellowed in the modern Navy. But in the 1970s, it was still fairly brutal, a rite of passage where bones might be broken. Dad met with the squadron at 5:00 a.m. in Ready Room 5 for the festivities. He watched as first-time crossers—pollywogs—were clad in shorts with underwear on the outside. First, they were blindfolded and then covered in Crisco, gravy, and whatever else viscous was on hand. Then they were run up and down ladders and passageways and whipped with fire hoses and screamed at until they bled from their knees and elbows and ears.

The wogs reached the flight deck only to meet another gauntlet of punches and paddling from shellback vets. They finally reached the throne of Neptune, a crusty thirty-year chief petty officer with the most equatorial crossings. The wogs kissed his belly and it was over.

Dad watched from the flight deck and laughed as his young men stripped off their stained clothes, tossed them into the ocean, and got a fire hose shower.

He did paperwork in the afternoon and had an early dinner. Around 8:00 p.m., he briefed with his XO, Zeke Zardeskas, and his electronic warfare officer, Lieutenant Commander Bill Coffey, about the next day's flight.

The *Kitty Hawk*'s air wing was operating under the assumption that there was a strong possibility of an air strike against Iran, particularly if any of the hostages were executed. The fact that Iran had been an American ally just a year earlier created some problems. The Iranians had American-made Hawk antiaircraft missiles, the precursor to the Patriot missile, and mobile launch sites with sophisticated tracking equipment. The Navy had piles of tactics and battle plans for destroying Soviet-made SAMs, but no one had come up with a plan for defeating an American missile.

The Prowler's pods were set to jam the frequencies used by Soviet radar stations and SAMs, but Hawks were at a completely different bandwidth. Zeke took the pods off and recalibrated them so the Black Ravens would be covered. Dad and Zeke both agreed the best way to defend against the Hawk was to fly in low and fast below enemy radar. When they arrived in-country, they would pop up to 20,000 feet, above Hawk missile range, and begin jamming. A-6 Intruder bombers would follow as soon as Iranian radars were reading a blizzard of snow. Zeke and the technicians made adjustments to the jamming pods, but that didn't make them battle ready.

The pods were temperamental and susceptible to falling offline when set at unfamiliar frequencies.

That meant the Prowlers had to be taken out for a rigorous test drive. Dad decided that as skipper he should take the first Prowler out with the new specs. There was an added wrinkle: The *Kitty Hawk* had intelligence that Soviet trawlers were just north of the carrier. So Dad filed a flight plan that would take his Prowler south of the *Kitty Hawk*. He planned to keep his plane low and close to the ocean, minimizing chances that Soviet radar could pick up his movements.

Bill Coffey, the squadron's top electronic warfare officer, requested to be subbed in for Lieutenant Steve Underriter. Dad agreed that was a good idea. That night, the squadron gathered in the ready room and watched *The Champ* with Jon Voight and Ricky Schroder. The projector jittered and jumped, a sign that the *Kitty Hawk* was hauling at its maximum of 28 knots. Dad headed back to his stateroom around midnight. At 1:15 a.m., he wrote a letter to Mom.

> *Nobody is more disappointed than me that we're not on our way home—but it's part of the reason we were out here in the first place . . .*

The letter closed, as always, with a message of devotion:

> *I love you Barbara, and want to be with you always. I will be with you sometime soon and we will make up for all the days*

and nights we missed. I am thinking of you constantly and am waiting to hold you in my arms and kiss your wonderful lips and feel your body around me. Just knowing you love me and are waiting for me makes it all worthwhile. Take good care of yourself and we'll all be together soon.

All my love forever, Pete.

By the time he finished the letter it was almost 2:00 a.m. He woke six hours later and made his way to the flight deck for the Black Ravens cruise picture, scheduled long ago when they thought they were almost home. The photographer positioned them in front of Prowler 626, the plane Dad would fly later in the day. The sky above was an endless blue and the water was glassy and clear. Dad stood to the left, a step separated from his men. He looked gaunt and exhausted.

The men returned to the ready room and shot the shit for a while. Dad had early chow with Zeke and then briefed his flight. Coffey would be in the back monitoring the pods with Lieutenant James Bradley Brown, the husband of Cathy Brown, who lived behind us in Crosswoods.

In the front seat, Dad put Lieutenant John Chorey, a soft-spoken redhead who had become an ECMO after washing out of the pilot program after some hairy moments around the boat in an A-4. He was a quiet guy with a beautiful blond wife and a baby boy at home. He had just 300 hours in the Prowler, by far the fewest in the crew. Chorey had received an earful from Dad after he misspelled his name on a flight schedule, so he tried to keep out of Dad's way. Placing him in the front seat was counterintuitive but standard Navy: the only way a rookie gets experience is to play the game.

The crew briefed the flight. The plan was to take off, head south of the *Kitty Hawk*, and practice low-level tactics. Dad would fly low and then pop the Prowler up to 10,000 feet and dive back to the ocean. Coffey would run scans on the pods and see which ones stayed online during the maneuvers. Dad would repeat the maneuvers for about an hour until it was time for the afternoon recovery on the *Kitty Hawk*.

Zeke ran into Dad as he left Ready Room 5. Dad had a smile on his tired face.

"I'm gonna throw her around."

The crew walked to their plane around 12:15 p.m. Dad kicked the tires and then shoved his fingers into the plane's nooks and crannies checking for pins in the right positions. He dropped on all fours and checked the screws on the landing gear. He looked for hydraulic leaks on the tacky tarmac below his Prowler. He walked around back and checked the tailhook and its cable.

Then he climbed up. He strapped himself in and did a cockpit check, making sure all his gauges were up and in the go position. He connected his communication cord and flipped on the radio and waited for the rest of his crew to settle in. He checked the landing lights. And then he waited while the plane captain fired up his engines.

On the flight deck, Aviation Technician Mark Hagood plugged his headphones into the pilot's side of the jet. He listened as Dad ran through his checks. He recognized his voice because Dad did the preflight checklist by the book every time. Everything was set.

The Prowler was scheduled to launch from catapult two, and it was Hagood's job to keep an eye on the plane as it was taxied to the catapult: checking tires, brakes, hydraulic systems, wings, slats, flaps, nose trim, rudder, and anything else that was visible from outside the plane. He was only twenty-two, but he knew Dad could change his life with a grunt or a signature. He paid attention.

As Dad's Prowler was hooked up to the catapult, Hagood noticed some white steam or smoke coming from the nose wheel area of 626. He called over Chief Petty Officer Jack Pimley, part of Dad's Goat Locker.

"I see smoke coming out of the nose wheel."

But just as quickly as it appeared, the smoke was gone. Pimley motioned for the launch to continue. Hagood gave the thumbs up to the plane captain. Another sailor held up a sign reading 45,500, the weight of his Prowler. Dad did his usual final check, moving the stick in a 360-degree motion to check the flaps and slats. He kicked the two pedals at his feet and moved the rudder from side to side. He moved the Prowler to 85 percent power and waited for launch.

But then Hagood saw the white smoke again. He threw his arms up and made an X, the sign for downing an airplane.

Dad powered down the Prowler, and Pimley headed toward Hagood. Planes were backing up behind 626. The tower started crackling through headphones.

"Is 626 a go or a no-go?"

Pimley asked Hagood what was wrong.

"Smoke from the nose wheel."

Pimley shook his head.

"It's air-conditioning vapor, it's not smoke. Let it go."

Hagood conceded to his boss. He dropped his hands and gave 626 the thumbs up and moved out of the way.

A voice from the catapult cockpit at deck level crackled through Dad's headphones.

"Ready to go? Tension."

"Roger that."

It was 1324.

The catapult fired and Prowler 626 with Commander Peter Thomas Rodrick at the controls was launched cleanly. Hagood watched the plane until it faded over the horizon. He would wonder for the rest of his life how close he came to saving the lives of four men.

AN A-6 INTRUDER LAUNCHED FROM THE *Kitty Hawk* a minute after Dad. The Intruder climbed to 500 feet in preparation for a bombing exercise. The pilot looked out the window and saw a Prowler at his three o'clock moving at over 450 knots per hour and less than a hundred feet off the sea. He clicked on his mic and talked to his navigator.

"Shit, he's moving fast and low."

He watched the Prowler move aft of the fantail of the USS *Jouett*, the *Kitty Hawk*'s cruiser. The Prowler then began a 90-degree nose-up climb, the beginning of an Immelmann maneuver, an aerial loop where a pilot rolls his wings level at the top of the vertical circle before plunging downward. The pilot watched the plane reach an altitude of between 7,000 and 9,000 feet and then begin its descent back toward the sea.

That was the last the Intruder saw of him. He went off on his own mission. And that was the last sighting of Dad's plane.

Around 1445, the planes launched at 1324 returned to the sky above the *Kitty Hawk* for recovery. Dad's Prowler was missing. In the *Kitty Hawk*'s pri-fli, the carrier's flight headquarters, CAG turned to Ensign Tim Sparks, one of Dad's junior officers.

"Ensign, do you have any information on your Prowler?"

"No, sir. Boss, maybe they diverted to Diego Garcia."

It was possible. Everyone had their radios off, so the Prowler could have headed to Diego Garcia without anyone knowing. A call was made to the island. There was no Prowler. A terse message was sent back to NAS Whidbey Island.

"626 is missing."

There were no names. Dad had fuel for two and a half hours. There was another recovery of aircraft at 1545 and the *Kitty Hawk* air ops thought maybe Dad would turn up for that. But he didn't. The two-and-a-half-hour mark passed at 1554. Another message was sent to Whidbey, this time with four names. An officer came down to the ready room and secured the flying records for Dad and his crew.

At 1653, Diego Garcia launched a P-3, while the *Kitty Hawk* sent out four search-and-rescue helicopters. Back at 2125 Conifer Drive in Oak Harbor, it was almost 4:00 a.m. and I'd just sneaked downstairs and scored my nightly six Chips Ahoy! cookies. I slipped back upstairs, looked in on Christine, and flipped on Larry King's overnight radio show on 710 KIRO. I fell back asleep.

Around the same time, the P-3 spotted an oil slick sixty-three miles southeast of Diego Garcia. Soon, helos arrived on the scene. There were no signs of life. The sun was setting by the time the USS *Jouett* arrived at the crash site. There wasn't much to salvage: some oxygen bottles, a seat cushion, and a map. Then a crewman spotted the cracked visor of a helmet. A long pole with a net was dropped over the side to fish it out. But the piece of helmet disintegrated as it was picked up. It dissolved into pieces and drifted to the bottom of the ocean. At midnight, the search was called off and the flight surgeon on the *Kitty Hawk* began writing up four death certificates.

BECAUSE OF THE RADIO BLACKOUT, IT took hours for that information to reach Whidbey. Early in the morning, Laddie Coburn got a call at home and was told to report immediately to the commodore's office. He was briefed that 626 was missing and Pete Rodrick was the pilot. The Coburns lived just three houses away, so he called his wife, Ulla, and told her to watch our house. Mom didn't know anything. Chrissie had an ear infection, and she wondered whether she should take her to the base emergency room. She called Ulla for advice. Should she go?

"Barb, just stay at home for a while."

Lieutenant Greg Elcock was a VAQ-135 pilot who had just returned home early to prepare the squadron's homecoming. But the commodore had a harder job for him. He had to find the four wives and tell them their husbands were officially missing at sea. A chaplain's car would trail behind if things went badly. He started at our home. Mom answered the door carrying Christine.

"Barb, Pete's plane is missing. They're looking for him. It was Brown, Coffey, and Chorey with him."

Mom let the news set in for a second.

"Was it his fault? Did he do something wrong?"

"Barb, we don't know. Don't worry about that."

"I should call the other wives. I'll call them."

Elcock made Mom sit down.

"Barb, you just stay here. I'll handle it."

Elcock left to notify the other wives. About an hour later, he got another call. There were no survivors. Laddie was dispatched to pick me up at the Roller Barn. By the time we arrived home, the chaplain was pulling out of our drive. It was all over.

A MEMORIAL SERVICE WAS HELD THE next morning on the *Kitty Hawk*. There were four caps—one with the oak leaves signifying command on the bill—placed on a white altar. The men sang "Eternal Father" and taps were played. The ship's MPs fired a sixteen-gun salute. The *Kitty Hawk*'s staff then began an investigation.

I made a Freedom of Information request a few years ago and was sent a declassified version of the mishap report. It confirmed some of my worst fears. The investigation started with a few basic assumptions. The wreckage showed no signs that any member of the crew had tried to eject, suggesting there had not been a fire or an ongoing mechanical failure. Based on what the Intruder pilot and navigator saw, the investigators surmised that Dad was flying low and fast when he began pulling the plane skyward. The jerk of the plane can result in a momentary ten- or twenty-foot dip of the wings. If you're flying very low, that dip can mean a wing hits the water and the plane disintegrates.

The report doesn't explicitly say Dad was flying recklessly, but it is there if you read between the lines.

> (1) It had been seven days since the pilot had flown. The fact that the aircraft was flying at approximately 100 feet and 450 knots followed by a max gross weight overhead maneuver is indicative of one overtaxing his "rusty" capabilities by unnecessarily flying the aircraft at the very edge of its envelope.

The report also theorized that a junior ECMO like John Chorey "had neither the experience nor the personality which would lend itself to 'calling down' a senior pilot in command."

That rang true as well. But from Tim Radel's stories, it doesn't seem likely that Dad would have listened even to a senior ECMO. He was going to fly the way he wanted to fly.

But it was all an educated guess. No one knew for sure. The investigators left open the door for doubt. It could have been something banal:

> The pilot could have been incapacitated by a bird strike. Sea birds were noted in the operating area.

I wanted to conclude that it was some factor beyond Dad's control, but I didn't really believe it. For years, that's where I left it. Dad was flying too low and too fast for the situation and it cost four lives. But as I started tracking people down, I got an email from Steve Underriter, the officer in Dad's squadron who was replaced on his last flight by Bill Coffey at the last minute. He pointed me back toward the radar altimeter being turned off on Dad's flight.

> It was later determined that in high-speed, low-altitude

> flying over the water there is a disparity between the radar altimeter and the pressure altimeter. The radar altimeter reads lower than the pressure altimeter. The high-speed, low-altitude would cause the pressure altimeter to read higher than the actual aircraft as a result in air pressure changes from low-altitude, high-speed flight.

I went back to the accident report. And there it was in the fine print:

> The barometric altimeter position error for the acft would have been negative thirty eight feet for 45,500 lb gross weight aircraft at 300 kts and negative 115 feet at 400 kts.

The report also notes: "squadron did not have barometric altimeter adjustment knowledge."

That snapped my head back. Dad was going 450 knots, according to the Intruder pilot. The sea was glassy smooth; there were no waves to offer a reference point. His altimeter could have read 150 feet, plenty of clearance to begin a turn and climb. But maybe it was off by 115 feet and he was just 35 feet above the sea. At 450 knots, Dad wouldn't have known the difference.

Steve Underriter is now sixty-three and works at the Pentagon on parts procurement for the Prowler and the Growler. I met him there late on a summer afternoon and we had a beer back at his desk.

The Prowler world is small, and some of the guys knew

Tupper. We told some old stories; a few of them might even have been true. Underriter was passing around the *Kitty Hawk*'s cruise picture and a photo of my dad when another officer walked by.

"That guy doesn't have any ribbons. Look at that."

Underriter explained it was my dad, and the guy went red and apologized. I told him it wasn't necessary. Dad felt as guilty about his lack of Vietnam combat as anyone. He hadn't earned any combat ribbons. Still, he was just as dead as if he'd been shot down over Laos or Hanoi.

After a while, Underriter and I drifted out of the building past the stained-glass windows of the Pentagon 9/11 memorial and headed to Crystal City in Arlington for dinner. I asked Steve if he thought that the faulty barometric altimeter reading was the cause of Dad's accident.

"I think so. Your dad was too careful. He wouldn't have risked it if he thought he was that low. That's the thing about flying; we always learn the lesson the hard way. They teach about barometric altimeter problems at flight school because of your Dad's flight."

I excused myself and hit the bathroom. I wiped bitter tears of relief from my eyes, the weight of carrying Dad's sin for all those years ebbing away. Maybe it wasn't his fault. Maybe I didn't need to carry that anymore. I splashed water on my face and went back to the table.

We ordered another beer and talked about that last *Kitty Hawk* cruise. In the end, there was no air strike. The helos were transferred to the relieving *Nimitz* in March and launched from their deck on April 25, 1980. They ended up as burnt-out rubble in the Iranian desert. Underriter let out a sad chuckle.

"We found out later that the Soviets couldn't track us by radar altimeters. We had them off for no reason."

We got the check and shook hands and headed our separate ways. I was left in my car trying to recalibrate my father in my head. Dad's death had moved from being his fault to being maybe not his fault but absolutely, completely pointless. I didn't know if that was any better.

I had some more interviews the next day and checked into a hotel not far from Arlington National Cemetery. I'd meant to visit my Dad's marker before the sun went down. But really, what was the point? His remains weren't even there. They weren't anywhere. It was just his birth and death date written on a thirty-inch-tall piece of marble.

That night, Hurricane Irene started to work its way up the East Coast. The windows began to rattle and shake in my room. I slumped on the bed and flipped open my laptop and looked for some music to match my mood. I settled on Peggy Lee's "Is That All There Is?" I put the song on repeat and turned out the lights.

If that's all there is my friends, then let's keep dancing
Let's break out the booze and have a ball

I fell asleep and dreamed of my father. He was young and I was little. He buckled me into his MG, rubbing his bristly whiskers across my neck until I giggled. We drove off—to where I didn't know. It didn't matter. We were heading off for a great adventure. Just Dad and me.

I woke up to rain falling sideways. I met Cathy Brown the next day for brunch at the house of Phil Heisey, another

VAQ-135 pilot. Cathy's hair was now long and streaked with gray. I asked her if she blamed Dad for taking away her husband. She told me she didn't. Matter of fact, she said with a smile, she had screamed at a local Seattle TV reporter who had shown up on her doorstep the day it was announced the crash's probable cause was pilot error.

"I know Brad trusted your dad. There's no one else I'd rather he had been flying with."

Cathy then told me another story. She had been laying flowers at my father's marker the previous Memorial Day when a man walked over to thank her. It was my uncle Danny. In typical Rodrick family tradition, he didn't tell anyone; he just went every year.

By now, Irene was lashing at the windows. My hosts suggested I stay and ride out the storm with them, but I insisted on driving back to New York. A few minutes later, I was on a deserted I-95 bombing north at seventy-five miles per hour. The wind shook and rocked my car and I fishtailed a time or two. Even the rest areas were abandoned, but still I drove on. Then, out of nowhere, there was wood and garbage in the road in front of me. I swerved around the debris, crossing into the breakdown lane, barely missing the concrete barrier separating north and south traffic.

I slowed down, half to catch my breath and half to check and see if I had pissed myself. I started to laugh, a happy one this time. I was driving like an idiot. I was driving just like Dad.

◇◇

Chapter Thirty-Seven

DAD NEVER MADE IT TO THE Persian Gulf, so I went for him. Little had changed: Americans and Iranians were still at each other's throats. It was early 2012, and Iran was rumored to be on the cusp of nuclear capabilities. This didn't sit well with the Americans and Israelis; both were contemplating a preemptive strike on Iran's nuclear labs.

The possibility whipped the Iranians into a nationalistic furor rarely seen since November 1979. President Mahmoud Ahmadinejad huffed and puffed about closing off the Strait of Hormuz and choking U.S. access to Middle East oil. It was bullshit—the Iranians didn't have the muscle to pull it off—but everyone was getting itchy.

I walked onto the USS *Lincoln* in Bahrain and joined Tupper up in the tower. He was now an air boss and ran the show. We had the best seat in the house as the *Lincoln* sauntered down toward the Strait and another two months on station in the Arabian Sea. We watched through binoculars as Iranian trawlers with a nest of antennas bobbed in the Gulf maybe a kilometer away. The *Lincoln* was impregnable and vulnerable at the same time. There was no way a trawler could sink the boat, but we were in international waters and there was nothing to stop a boat from moving within 200 meters and launching a couple of Stinger missiles onto the *Lincoln*'s deck, killing hundreds.

In another time, Tupper and I might have chattered with

adrenaline about the situation, Tupper talking about Plan Bs and me babbling about finally getting aboard a carrier that was sailing into harm's way. But we were both exhausted; we had no distance left to run.

I had spent much of the summer of 2011 up in Anacortes watching Tupper try to figure out the rest of his life. It was hard to keep up. One day Tupper was loading boxes from their home and moving them into storage in preparation for selling their home and building their dream house on Burrows Bay. That afternoon, he was definitely getting out and hoping to get a job at Boeing in Seattle. A few weeks later, Tupper and Beth had talked some more, and he was staying in for another five years so he could retire with the higher pay of a captain. Or maybe he would open a vineyard in Walla Walla.

The Fourth of July found us standing on Commercial Street in downtown Anacortes playfully mocking the town parade as cheerleaders in convertibles and fire trucks rolled by. The reality of staying in the Navy and moving his family to a new town—or worse, leaving them here and commuting on the weekends—was giving Tupper second and third thoughts.

"I really don't know what I'm going to do with the rest of my life. Any ideas?"

I wasn't helping. In August, the *Lincoln* headed down the coast and pulled into San Pedro Harbor for LA Fleet Week. As a senior officer, Tupper was assigned to give a few wave-the-flag speeches, but the rest of his days were free. I flew in to keep him company.

We checked into a hotel and went over his command tour. Tupper brought out his journal to refresh his memory.

Sometimes, just reading the entries unleashed lashes of self-recrimination:

> January 2009, this year I promise to put my family before the Navy. That is my solemn goal.

Tupper read the lines and threw his journal on the table, his face red with fury. He paced for a minute before slumping into his chair, a look of utter defeat on his face.

"That's another fucking promise that I didn't keep. God, what have I done to my family?"

I was torturing him by making him relive the past. But I was torturing myself as well. Tupper was having his come-to-Jesus moment about the Navy screwing his family. It took almost twenty years to realize it, but at least he was having it. Did Dad ever have it? Sure, he wrote about missing us in his letters and he was always promising Mom that he'd be around in the always distant future, but did he really feel that? His words about us being together after his command tour now rang false. Most likely he'd have been sent back out to sea just like Tupper. Maybe they were just words Dad used to buy time with Mom. I would never know.

It took an eighty-five-year-old man to cheer us up. One of Tupper's speeches was before the Hollywood/Los Feliz Kiwanis Club luncheon in a hipster neighborhood. It seemed an unlikely place for an officer and a gentleman to speak platitudes about duty and honor. But it wasn't going to be all hipsters. We did some Googling and found out about an octogenarian named Jimmy Weldon who ran the club. Weldon used to have a morning show in Dallas that he hosted with his puppet Webster Webfoot. He moved to LA and did some voice-overs for Hanna-Barbera cartoons but never quite made the big time. Jimmy Weldon now spent his free time putting together highly entertaining YouTube summaries of Kiwanis Club activities. We cracked up at his videos, and tomorrow's speech seemed like less of a drag.

The next day, a distinguished officer in his dress whites and a writer desperately in need of a haircut walked into a cut-rate Mexican restaurant. Tupper gave his usual ripping speech about sacrifice and duty and country before a spellbound crowd of seventeen. The mostly geriatric types came up to Tupper afterward to shake his hand. As the room cleared, an elderly man with a walker made his way across the room and stuck out a shaky hand.

"I want to thank you for your service."

Tupper shook the old man's hand and looked him straight in the eye.

"No, I want to thank you, Mr. Weldon. I've been a fan for a long time."

Jimmy Weldon's blue eyes popped open, his aching back straightening for a moment.

"How did you know that?"

Tupper smiled.

"Everyone knows Jimmy Weldon. You did the voice of Solomon Grundy on *The SuperFriends*. I love that show."

Weldon smiled and shook his head in wonder.

"Thank you for remembering."

Tupper told him it was an honor to meet him. Jimmy Weldon teetered away with a smile on his face.

Tupper's face looked happier than it had in a long time.

"Let's go have a beer. Our work here is done."

THAT NOVEMBER, I GAVE TUPPER A ride to his last speech. It was Veterans Day, and he was speaking before the student body at Anacortes High School, a particularly daunting endeavor since Brenna was now a freshman. Tupper didn't tell her he was speaking until the night before.

"She's at that age where Dad coming to school is completely mortifying," Tupper told me. "She may hate me afterward."

She didn't. I sat with Beth as Tupper spoke about the usual stuff, the thrill of flying off a carrier and the privilege of defending American freedom across the globe. Then he glanced down and made eye contact with his daughter in the third row.

> What I didn't understand when I started were the sacrifices to be made by my family—birthdays missed, anniversaries absent, Christmases spent floating in some God-forsaken corner of a very unfriendly part of the world.

Tupper paused for a moment. The kids were silent.

> Those days and months, that now add up to years in the lives of my family, are ones I'll never get back. But as I spent those months at sea away from those that I loved, I came to realize what I really believed in life. It was ironic that I surrendered, willfully, personal freedoms to achieve what I saw as the greater good—to defend our Constitution, to keep our families safe, and to protect

> those people from *all* nations not strong enough to protect themselves from the tyranny of evil men.
>
> Fifteen years ago, when someone asked me, "What do you do?" I would have said, "I'm a Navy pilot," with all the ego and bravado I could muster. But if someone asked me of what I am most proud, I say, "I'm a dad."

Tupper stopped there. The kids gave him a standing ovation. Brenna came over and gave him a giant hug. She didn't care who saw.

Tupper changed back into civvies at home and we headed downtown in his pickup for a sandwich. I told him the crowd loved his speech. He winced a little.

"That's the last one. I'm getting out."

I asked him if he was sure this time. He said absolutely. I asked him what made him finally decide to give up the only life he'd known since he was a boy.

"You know that stuff about defending freedom for everyone and all that stuff? I don't think I believe it anymore."

We pulled into a parking space and stepped out into the weak afternoon sun. Tupper locked the car and smiled.

"The only part I know I believe in is being a dad."

A FEW WEEKS LATER, TUPPER SHIPPED out for the last time. He just had to make it through one last cruise, one that almost immediately was extended from six months to nine months. The only good news was the cruise was now so long he wouldn't have to spend the last few months of his tour in Norfolk, he could just get out when they pulled back into port.

Meanwhile, the buffoonery reached new, untold heights. In December, the USS *Stennis* rescued an Iranian crew whose boat had been seized by Somali pirates. The Iranians were returned home, but the Navy decided that handing the pirates over to the Iranians, where they would meet certain death, would be a bad PR move. But no one knew what to do with them. So the pirates were CODed from the *Stennis* to the *Vinson* and finally to the *Lincoln* as they sat in legal limbo.

Tupper had to shut down the flight deck and a hangar bay to facilitate the pirate transfer. It was an extra shift of work for everyone. That night, Tupper got on the intercom and thanked his sailors for their hard work.

"We're the only country that would so freely spend our resources on those so undeserving of our grace. This is what makes the United States great."

But then Tupper learned that the pirates were feasting on Klondike bars and Navy-supplied cigarettes, perks none of his sailors were entitled to. Five times a day, a call came up to the tower for the ship's exact coordinates so the pirates would know exactly where to place their prayer mats to face Mecca. And then Tupper thought to himself, "This is what makes the United States the idiots of the world."

He was now more certain than ever that retiring was the right call. I met him in Bahrain in February and he was in emotional shutdown mode. There was a five-hour alcohol brunch, but it didn't lighten his mood. Bahrain was a tin-pot kingdom that brutally oppressed its own people, while the United States looked the other way because the Navy needed Bahrain's ports. Tupper was sick of it all, sick of Americans being led around by a bunch of criminals.

We headed to Bahrain's Naval Support Activity Base the next day so he could get a haircut and buy Beth a Valentine's Day card. The base was designated an American safe space in the troubled kingdom and was overrun with hundreds of *Lincoln* sailors drunk off their asses, building pyramids out of empty beer cans. Afterward, we rode a bus reeking of vomit back to the *Lincoln*. Where he once would have dived headlong into the depravity, now it just made Tupper depressed.

"I can't be around this anymore."

Two days later, back in the tower, the light returned to Tupper's eyes little by little. We watched flames shoot up from oil rigs at sunset, the sky a golden storm, while the Iranian trawlers bobbed and weaved off the *Lincoln*'s bow. The phones chattered with intel about the boats' intentions. The sun receded and Tupper began supervising the afternoon launches, jumping on the ship's intercom.

"Clear the catwalk and catapults; we're launching aircraft."

Two dozen planes took off without a hitch. Running the tower wasn't that different from flying: minutes of terror followed by hours of nothing. We waited on the recovery and bullshitted the afternoon away. Tupper was just hoping Beth could make it through his final cruise. I'd watched them struggle through three years of good-byes and misunderstandings. I knew they still loved each other with a devotion that was real and substantial. It was now sixteen years since he had placed his bride and their wedding day ahead of getting his wings of gold. Now, finally, Hunter Ware had once again chosen Beth over the Navy. He just prayed it wasn't too late.

"I'm not sure she's ever going to forgive me for what I took away from her," Tupper told me as he scanned the sea with binoculars. "But now that I've filed my papers, she can see the end. It's no more bullshit; it's the actual end. That gives her hope."

He put down the binoculars and slipped his sunglasses back on.

"It gives *us* hope."

An hour later, the recovery started smoothly, with three Hornets catching the two wire. But up next was a Prowler being flown by a junior pilot. Trouble began when the plane entered the landing pattern. Tupper watched the Prowler begin to imperceptibly drop from 800 to 500 feet.

"Jesus Christ."

Tupper jumped on his radio.

"501 Prowler, altitude."

The plane didn't respond. Tupper spoke louder this time.

"PROWLER ALTITUDE."

"Roger that."

The Prowler popped up in the sky and made his turn for home. Tupper kept an eye on him. Everything seemed to be fine. But on final approach the Prowler dipped below the *Lincoln*'s deck for an instant. Tupper noticed it first. The LSOs barked at the pilot to pull up. The Prowler surged in the sky, rising above the deck and passing us at eye level. The ECMO in the front seat seemed to be looking right at us. Tupper shook his head.

"What the hell was that? I can see the pilot losing track of his altitude, but what the hell is his ECMO doing?"

Tupper got on the radio with the pilot, but his tone was soothing, not harsh, more like the voice he used with his daughters than the one he used with the Black Ravens. He wanted to buck up the guy, not tear him down. The Prowler landed safely on its next pass.

"Sometimes, I can't believe I used to do that," said Tupper, his voice barely a whisper. "It already seems so long ago."

I WAS SCHEDULED TO FLY OFF the *Lincoln* a couple days later. At the last minute, I tried to extend my stay. I wanted to keep Tupper company, but I also knew this was going to be my last trip on an aircraft carrier. I mourned a connection to Dad that was about to end forever. But I only had a seven-day visa to travel in and out of Bahrain, and the Navy refused to pick up the phone and ask for an extension. I packed my bags with a better understanding of American subservience to an oil conglomerate. Tupper walked me down to the COD office the next afternoon. He'd done 840 days at sea in the last five years and talked like a prisoner doing short time.

"I can do six months, no problem. Piece of cake. Sometimes, I feel like I could stay out here forever; this is the life I know." He smiled a little. "But I'll see you down the road."

We said good-bye quickly, before either one of us could go weepy. He headed back up to the tower. About a half hour later, I was led out onto the flight deck toward the COD. I looked up and gave Tupper a final wave. But Tupper wasn't looking. I waited a second longer, I wanted him to see me saying good-bye. But then deck personnel politely pushed me into the COD. I strapped myself into my seat and thought of a boy waving good-bye to his father. He didn't look back either.

MOM CALLED ME WHILE TUPPER WAS at sea. She wanted to come out to Whidbey for her first visit in over thirty years. She asked me to be her guide. I told her I'd be honored.

She brought along her old friend Ulla. We met at Sea-Tac and drove up I-5. We crossed over the Deception Pass Bridge, which was shrouded in fog, just as it had been on August 10, 1974. The next day, we hit all the old places. We drove over to Crosswoods, and she and Ulla snapped pictures of their old homes, tsk-tsking at cars now parked on their once pristine lawns. We headed over to NAS Whidbey past signs welcoming squadrons home. Mom happily chattered through it all. Sherm gave us a tour of the VAQ-135 hangar, and Mom grinned that old forgotten smile, excited at the planes and the men and women running through a building that was once presided over by her one true love.

We crossed the street and she put her hands on Dad's name at the Prowler memorial. We stopped at the chapel where the memorial service was held and lit a candle for my father. I waited, but her eyes never filled with tears. She conquered all the stops that even now, after many visits, could bring me low.

That night, Steamer and Pam Danielson had us over for dinner. It was typical Whidbey craziness; kids coming and going, wine flowing, Steamer still in his flight suit. Everyone talked happily about all that had changed and all that had remained the same in the town we used to call home.

But then Ulla's face went white. She grabbed Mom's hand.

"Barb, I don't feel right. Something isn't . . ."

Ulla's eyes rolled back in her head and she fell to the floor. There was momentary silence before the room erupted in noise. Steamer called 911 and Mom dropped to her knees and held up Ulla's head.

"Ulla! Ulla!"

I couldn't believe it. Was Mom's best friend going to die just a mile from the house where Mom was told her husband was dead? It seemed cosmically unfair. Mom kept talking to Ulla and stroked her face. Ulla opened her eyes after a minute or two and Mom helped her sit up. Mom held her hand.

"Ulla, everything is going to be fine. You passed out but you're okay now. Paramedics should be here any minute."

Ulla was more embarrassed than ill by the time the paramedics arrived. They took her blood pressure, pronounced her okay, and blamed her fainting on low blood sugar and jet lag. All the old feelings of loss and pain came back and made my legs wobble. I sat down for a minute in the back bedroom of Benjamin, Steamer's oldest son.

There were Lego towers and *Star Wars* gear, all the signs of a teenage boy not quite ready to surrender his childhood. Then I spotted a framed picture sitting on the desk. It was Steamer in his flight suit—just back from cruise—tossing his boy skyward. The picture catches Benji at his highest point, arms and leg splayed, a giant smile on his little-boy face.

For a moment, I concentrated on the sadness of what was missing. I thought of Steamer not ever being tossed in the air by his own dad. I thought of my father never knowing how much his only son missed him, how much he wanted him to be proud of him, how much he wanted to be worthy of being called Peter Rodrick's son.

But then I thought of what was there: the son Steamer was raising, Benjamin Danielson IV, proudly carrying his grandfather's name. I thought of the son I hoped to have some day, the one I would name after my father. We had become good men, worthy of our fathers' names, and that was no small thing. We had survived. We had not been lost. There were mothers to thank for that. Mothers we battled. Mothers we sometimes hated. Mothers who had done the best they could when their bright worlds fell black. We were their only sons too.

I took a breath, stood up, and went back into the kitchen. I had to make sure Mom was okay.

Afterword

On the morning of March 11, 2013, a Whidbey-based EA-6B Prowler on a low-level training mission crashed in a field about fifty miles west of Spokane. There were no survivors.

The crew members were Lieutenant Commander Alan Patterson, thirty-four; Lieutenant Junior Grade Valerie Delaney, twenty-six; and Lieutenant Junior Grade William McIlvaine, twenty-four.

I hope that this book, in some small way, honors their memory and the sacrifice of all who loved them.

Acknowledgments

THIS BOOK WOULD NOT BE POSSIBLE without my family. My uncles, aunts, and cousins endured their private lives going public, gave me endless encouragement, shared old photos and painful memories all with good cheer and grace. I cannot thank them enough. My sisters, Terry and Christine—and their partners, Bari Liebowitz and Kevin Bessert—gave me love, forgiveness, and understanding when I needed it the most. I cherish them.

And then there's my mother, Barbara Ann Rodrick. She could have stopped this book with one phone call or one shake of the head, but she didn't, allowing me to tell our story in hopes of others understanding what happens to a military family after "Eternal Father" is sung and the wives go home. Left alone with three young children, she never faltered in making sure Pete Rodrick's kids were taken care of and loved. Her achievement can be seen in our successes. She is the strongest, bravest woman I know. Her friend Ulla Coburn has been with her—with us, really—through it all. Thank you, Ulla.

On the Navy side, this book would not have happened without the enthusiasm, kindness, and wry sense of humor of Commander James Hunter "Tupper" Ware. His endless generosity and patience in answering my idiotic questions should earn him another Bronze Star. His friendship is one of the great blessings of my life, and his dedication to his children will serve as a guidepost for me if I am fortunate to have children of my own. A man my father never met taught me more about what it means to be a naval officer, a pilot, and a daddy than the rest of the world combined. I will be forever grateful to Beth Ware for sharing her husband with me on his rare times at home. She and my mother have never met, but they share a selflessness that is at the heart and soul of what makes the Navy great. To Beth and Hunter's daughters, Brenna and Caitlin, I hope your father hasn't embarrassed you too much and I look forward to learning about the great things you do with your lives.

Lieutenant Commander Scott "Sherm" Oliver gave me a home when I needed one, enduring my late-night arrivals and post-midnight raiding of his refrigerator. We shared long talks, late-night Taco Bell runs, vodka cranberries, and several escapades that could have ended with either of us in the morgue or Leavenworth. I regret nothing!

Then there's Commander Brian "Steamer" Danielson; all he did was help me understand my own life in a way I couldn't quite grasp until I met him. Somewhere high above the blue sky, Benjamin Danielson and Peter Rodrick are sharing a cold one and thinking, "Hell, they turned out okay." I never had a brother, but in Tupper, Sherm, and Steamer I now have three.

There are too many officers in VAQ-135 to thank by name, but special shout-outs to Commander Vincent "Vinnie" Johnson; Lieutenant Commander Todd "Beav" Zenter; Commander Blake "Stonz" Tornga; and my three roomies; Lieutenant Jeff "Stoli" Stodola; Lieutenant Chris "Lil Chris" Sutherland, and Lieutenant Devon "the Wolf" Benbow. To the rest of the World Famous Black Ravens: anywhere, anytime, the first seven beers are on me.

Back in the civilian world, thank-yous to Hugo Lindgren,

Sheila Glaser, Jason Fine, and Mark Healy for being patient with me, as I seemed adrift on permanent book leave. My ace agent, David McCormick, navigated me through unfamiliar waters and led me to HarperCollins and Tim Duggan, whose enthusiasm for the book never waned, even when mine did. Emily Cunningham artfully steered me through the editing process with patience and good humor.

Elyse Moody, Eileen Finkelstein, Alex Star, Evan Hughes, David Dyas, Alison Buckholtz, Dan Halpern, Scott DeSimon, Gordon Young, Eliot Kaplan, Bill Gifford, Bob Kolker, Joe Hagan, and Molly Knight all read drafts and/or provided hope when all hope seemed lost. Chris Steffen, my transcriber, became a trusted friend and confidant and fellow hater of the St. Louis Cardinals. Tom Scocca, Jason Gay, and Michael Crowley provided much-needed laughs through email and the stray dinner at Dan Tanas. The Harrison family gave me a second home and more love than this stray Gentile deserved. Then there is my best friend, Mark Aznavourian; he was with me every step of this journey, always willing to listen, plot, and conspire. He is the best man I know.

Finally, my wife, Alix Ohlin. She is as sweet and private as I am loud and melodramatic. She has never ever let me down. This book would not exist without her love and kindness. I am a lucky man.

This is for my father. I wish you all could have met him.

About the Author

STEPHEN RODRICK IS A CONTRIBUTING WRITER at *The New York Times Magazine* and also a contributing editor at *Men's Journal.* His writing has been anthologized in *The Best American Sports Writing, The Best American Crime Reporting,* and *The Best American Political Writing.* He lives in Los Angeles.